LYRICAL BALLADS

Lyrical Ballads

WORDSWORTH
AND COLERIDGE

The text of the 1798 edition
with the additional 1800 poems
and the Prefaces
edited with
introduction, notes and appendices by

R. L. BRETT

and

A. R. JONES

METHUEN

LONDON and NEW YORK

First published 1963
New and revised impression, 1965
Reprinted 1968
Reprinted 1971

First published as a University Paperback 1968
Reprinted four times
Reprinted 1981

Published in the USA by
Methuen & Co.
in association with Methuen, Inc.
733 Third Avenue, New York, NY 10017

ISBN 0 416 29720 X

Introduction and Notes © 1963
R. L. Brett & A. R. Jones

Printed in Great Britain at the
University Press, Cambridge

Contents

Foreword

For many years now the student of *Lyrical Ballads* has had to rely either upon the edition of H. Littledale, first published in 1911, or upon that of G. Sampson, first published in 1903.[1] However, Littledale reproduces the 1798 poems only, while Sampson's edition is an exact reprint of the 1805 text, though it gives the readings of earlier versions. In any case both appeared too early to draw upon the great amount of scholarly work on Wordsworth and Coleridge completed since that date. The letters of Wordsworth and his sister, and those of Coleridge, have since appeared in the admirable editions prepared respectively by Professor de Selincourt and Professor E. L. Griggs; and Professor de Selincourt has also given us the Journals of Dorothy Wordsworth. E. K. Chambers and Mrs. Mary Moorman have provided excellent biographies of the two poets; Miss Kathleen Coburn has made available a wealth of hitherto unpublished material in Coleridge's Notebooks; and there has been a stream of critical studies. A new edition not only profits from this scholarship but makes it possible to provide the student with an up-to-date bibliography of this work.

The present edition owes much to the work of Miss Helen Darbishire and Professor E. de Selincourt, the editors of the Oxford English Texts edition of Wordsworth's Poetical Works and to the work of E. H. Coleridge, the editor of the Oxford edition of Coleridge's Poems. Their editions stand as monuments of scholarship which cannot be rivalled or superseded, but, nevertheless, they do not conveniently provide the student

[1] Cf. also *Lyrical Ballads, with a few other poems*, N. Douglas, London, 1926 (Facsimile of 1798 ed.).

with *Lyrical Ballads* as it first appeared to the public. The Oxford *Wordsworth*, rightly for its purpose, uses the grouping of the poems and the text chosen by Wordsworth himself for the 1850 edition. Similarly, the Oxford *Coleridge* uses the 1834 text. Only by a certain editorial labour can the reader achieve from these the text and grouping of the poems as they were originally published.

The aim of the present volume is to make available to the reader the text of *Lyrical Ballads* as it appeared in print in 1798 and 1800, together with the variant readings of the 1802 and 1805 editions. We have incorporated in the text the *Errata* which were issued with the first two editions, but otherwise we have reproduced the poems exactly as they were first published. We have endeavoured in the text and by means of notes to provide a history of the poems from 1798 to 1805, after which Wordsworth's poems were merged in the 1815 and subsequent editions of his collected works and Coleridge's contributions were transferred to his *Sybilline Leaves* of 1817 and to later collections of his poetry.

Lyrical Ballads was originally published in September, 1798.[1] The title-page bore the Bristol imprint and the book was printed by Biggs and Cottle of Bristol for T. N. Longman of Paternoster Row, London. While the 1798 volume was in the press it occurred to the authors that one of the poems, *Lewti; or, the Circassian Love-Chant*, might disclose the secret of the authorship, for it had been published in *The Morning Post* for April 13th, 1798, and was known to be by Coleridge. The sheets containing this poem were, therefore, cancelled and *The Nightingale* substituted. A few copies of the volume with *Lewti* found their way on to the market, but most copies contain *The Nightingale*. We have given the text of *The Nightingale* where it appeared in the majority of copies and reprinted

---

[1] Cf. ' The Publication of the "Lyrical Ballads" ', R. W. Daniels, *Modern Language Review*, vol. xxxiii, 1938, pp. 406-410, and 'The Printing of *Lyrical Ballads*, 1798', D. F. Foxon, *The Library*, 5th Series, vol. ix, 1954, pp. 221-241.

Lewti in Appendix A. Soon after publication Cottle sold the whole of the remaining copies of the first edition, which had numbered five hundred copies, to Messrs. J. and A. Arch of Gracechurch Street, London. This firm issued the book with a new title-page which bore a London imprint.

The second edition of the poems was published in two volumes which bore the date 1800, though they were not issued until January 1801. Only the first volume bore the words Second Edition on the title-page, for the second volume had entirely new contents and was regarded as à first edition. The poems in the first volume were the same as those of the 1798 edition which contained *The Nightingale*, except that *The Convict* was omitted, Coleridge's poem *Love* was added, and *Lines Written near Richmond* was divided into two separate poems. The order of the poems was changed in this first volume, the titles of some poems altered, and substantial changes made in the text. We have given details of these changes in footnotes to the 1798 text.

In addition to the poems, we have also reprinted the *Advertisement* with which Wordsworth prefaced the 1798 poems, and the *Preface* which took its place in the 1800 edition. The alterations and additions which Wordsworth made to this *Preface* in the 1802 edition of the poems are given in footnotes to the 1800 text. We have also reproduced in Appendix B the text of Wordsworth's Appendix on Poetic Diction which first appeared in the 1802 edition.

It is curious that despite the industry of scholars there is still no *practical* edition of *Lyrical Ballads* to which students may refer. In the attempt to fill this gap, we have thought it unnecessary to produce a variorum edition of the poems; the history of individual poems is well enough documented in the collected works of Wordsworth and Coleridge. Our main concern has been to make the poems readily available as a unique *body* of poetry – in all its freshness and naïvety – relying on the original texts of 1798 and 1800 to make their own impact. For this reason we have indicated only what we consider to be the significant variants between the texts and tried to keep the text as clear and unencumbered as possible. We have, for the most part, ignored the various *trivia* such as changes in capitalisation and punctuation as being likely to obscure the text so far as the average reader is concerned. In noting variants we have recorded only the text in which the change first appeared so that the reader may assume that if no subsequent emendation is recorded the variant stands in the subsequent texts also. We are convinced that it is as a *body* of poetry that *Lyrical Ballads* first influenced the course of English poetry and that it is as a body of poetry that it should be studied. This edition enables the reader to study the poems in their original context as they appeared to Coleridge's and Wordsworth's contemporaries.

We would like to express our indebtedness to Mr. Patrick Yarker of King's College, University of London, who read the typescript and made many valuable suggestions, and to Mrs. Mary Moorman and the Clarendon Press for permission to quote from *William Wordsworth: A Biography*.

We should also like to express our thanks to Miss Janet Pope and Miss Kay Holmes who have undertaken the typing of this edition.

We have taken the opportunity provided by the reprinting of this volume to make a number of minor alterations and improvements in the lay-out of the poems. We would like to express our gratitude to those whose advice has guided us in making certain of these changes.

University of Hull   1965

A Selected Bibliography
and List of Abbreviations

A] TEXTS BY WORDSWORTH AND COLERIDGE

Abbreviations

1798.
Lyrical Ballads, With a Few Other Poems. Bristol, 1798; Second issue, London, 1798.
Lyrical Ballads, reprinted from the first edn. of 1798, ed. E. Dowden, London, 1890; second edn. 1891.
Lyrical Ballads, ed. with certain poems of 1798, T. Hutchinson, London, 1898.
Lyrical Ballads, reprinted from the first edn. of 1798, ed. H. Littledale, Oxford, 1911.
Lyrical Ballads, With a Few Other Poems, N. Douglas, London, 1926.

1800.
Lyrical Ballads, With Other Poems. In two volumes, London, 1800.

1802.
Lyrical Ballads, With Pastoral and Other Poems. In two volumes, London, 1802.

1805.
Lyrical Ballads, With Pastoral and Other Poems. In two volumes, London, 1805.
Lyrical Ballads, 1798-1805, ed. G. Sampson, London, 1903.

P.W.
The Poetical Works of William Wordsworth, ed. E. de Selincourt and H. Darbishire, 5 volumes, Oxford, 1940-49.

I.F.
Notes dictated to Isabella Fenwick by William Wordsworth in 1843, and published in *The Poetical Works of Wordsworth*, ed. Moxon, 6 volumes, 1857.

Abbreviations

Prelude.   *The Prelude or Growth of a Poet's Mind by William Wordsworth*, ed. E. de Selincourt, Oxford, 1926.

E.L.   *The Early Letters of William and Dorothy Wordsworth*, ed. E. de Selincourt, Oxford, 1935.

M.Y.   *The Letters of William and Dorothy Wordsworth, The Middle Years*, ed. E. de Selincourt, 2 volumes, Oxford, 1937.

L.Y.   *The Letters of William and Dorothy Wordsworth, The Later Years*, ed. E. de Selincourt, 3 volumes, Oxford, 1939.

D.W.   *Journals of Dorothy Wordsworth*, ed. E. de Selincourt, 2 volumes, London, 1952.

P. of C.   *The Poetical Works of S. T. Coleridge*, ed. E. H. Coleridge, 2 volumes, Oxford, 1912.

C. Letters.   *Letters of S. T. Coleridge, 1785-1819*, ed. E. L. Griggs, 4 volumes, Oxford, 1956-59.
Letters of S. T. Coleridge, ed. E. H. Coleridge, 2 volumes, London, 1895.
Unpublished Letters of S. T. Coleridge, ed. E. L. Griggs, 2 volumes, Oxford, 1932.

C. Notebooks. *The Notebooks of S. T. Coleridge*, ed. Kathleen Coburn, 5 volumes, London, 1957-   (each of the volumes is to be in two parts, text and notes. Only the first two volumes, which cover the years 1799-1808, have been published).

Biog. Lit.   *Biographia Literaria, by S. T. Coleridge* (first published 1817), ed. J. Shawcross, 2 volumes, Oxford, 1907.

T.T.   *The Table Talk and Omniana of Samuel Taylor Coleridge*, Oxford, 1917.

B] SOME CRITICAL, BIOGRAPHICAL AND
BIBLIOGRAPHICAL STUDIES

Abbreviations

ABERCROMBIE, Lascelles, *The Art of Wordsworth*, London, 1952.

BALD, R. C., 'Coleridge and "The Ancient Mariner"', *Nineteenth Century Studies*, collected and edited by Herbert Davis, W. C. De Vane, R. C. Bald, Cornell University Press, Ithaca, 1940.

BARSTOW, Marjorie L., *Wordsworth's Theory of Poetic Diction*, New Haven, 1917.

BATESON, F. W., *Wordsworth, A Reinterpretation*, London, 1954.

BATHO, Edith C., *The Later Wordsworth*, London, 1933.

BEATTY, Arthur, *William Wordsworth: His Doctrine and Art in Their Historical Relations*, Univ. of Wisconsin Studies, Madison, 1927.

BEER, J. B., *Coleridge The Visionary*, London, 1959.

CHAMBERS, E. K., *Samuel Taylor Coleridge*, London, 1938.

DANBY, J. F., *The Simple Wordsworth*, London, 1960.

DANIEL, R. N., 'The Publication of the "Lyrical Ballads"', *Modern Language Review*, Vol. XXXIII, 1938, pp. 406-410.

H.D.   DARBISHIRE, Helen, *The Poet Wordsworth*, London, 1950.

FERRY, D., *The Limits of Mortality*, Middletown, Conn., 1959.

FINK, Z. S., *The Early Wordsworthian Milieu*, Oxford, 1958.

Abbreviations

FOXON, D. F., 'The Printing of *Lyrical Ballads*, 1798', *The Library*, Fifth Series, Vol. IX, 1954, pp. 221-241.

GARROD, H. W., *Wordsworth*, London, 1923.

GRIGGS, E. L., *Wordsworth and Coleridge, Studies in Honor of George McLean Harper*, ed. E. L. Griggs, Princeton, 1939.

HANSON, L., *The Life of S. T. Coleridge: The Early Years*, London, 1938.

G.M.H.   HARPER, G. M., *William Wordsworth: His Life, Works, and Influence*, London, 1916. Revised edition 1929.

HAZLITT, William, *Lectures on the English Poets*, London, 1818. *The Spirit of the Age*, London, 1825.

HOUSE, Humphry, *Coleridge: The Clark Lectures 1951-2*, London, 1953.

JONES, H. J. F., *The Egotistical Sublime: A History of Wordsworth's Imagination*, London, 1954.

Lamb   *The Letters of Charles and Mary Lamb*, ed. E. V. Lucas, London, 1935.

LEGOUIS, Emile, *The Early Life of William Wordsworth*, London, 1897. *William Wordsworth and Annette Vallon*, London, 1922.

LOWES, J. L., *The Road to Xanadu*, London, 1927.

MARGOLIOUTH, H. M., *Wordsworth and Coleridge 1795-1834*, Oxford, 1953.

K.M.   MACLEAN, Kenneth, *Agrarian Age: A Background for Wordsworth*, Yale Studies in English, vol. 115, 1950.

MEYER, G. W., *Wordsworth, Formative Years*, Michigan, 1943.

Abbreviations

M.M.   MOORMAN, Mary, *William Wordsworth: A Biography*, vol. I. *The Early Years, 1770-1803*, Oxford, 1957.

OWEN, W. J. B., *Wordsworth's Preface to Lyrical Ballads*, ed. W. J. B. Owen with an Introduction and Commentary, Copenhagen, 1957.

READ, Herbert, *Wordsworth*, London, 1930. Revised edn. 1948.

SCHNEIDER, B. R., *Wordsworth's Cambridge Education*, Cambridge, 1957.

SCHNEIDER, E., *Coleridge, Opium and Kubla Khan*, Chicago, 1953.

SELINCOURT, E. de, *Dorothy Wordsworth: A Biography*, London, 1933.

SMITH, Elsie, *An Estimate of William Wordsworth by his Contemporaries*, Oxford, 1932.

SMITH, J. C., *A Study of Wordsworth*, London, 1944.

STALLKNECHT, N. P., *Strange Seas of Thought: Studies in Wordsworth's Philosophy of Man and Nature*, Duke University Press, 1945.

WAIN, J. (ed.), *Contemporary Reviews of Romantic Poetry*, London, 1953.

WHALLEY, G., *Poetic Process*, London, 1953. *Coleridge and Sara Hutchinson and the Asra Poems*, London, 1955.

WISE, T. J., *A Bibliography of the Writings in Prose and Verse of William Wordsworth*, London, 1916. *Two Lake Poets. A Catalogue of Printed Books, Manuscripts, Etc., by W. Wordsworth and S. T. Coleridge*, London, 1927.

Introduction

THE idea of *Lyrical Ballads* was conceived when Wordsworth and Coleridge were living as neighbours in the Quantocks; Wordsworth at Alfoxden and Coleridge at Nether Stowey. Wordsworth and Coleridge, accompanied by Dorothy Wordsworth, left Alfoxden on the 12th November 1797 to visit the Valley of Stones near Lynmouth. They proposed to meet the modest expenses of their walking-tour by writing a poem which might secure £5 from the editor of the *Monthly Magazine*. This poem was the *Ancient Mariner*, but it was not finished until March of the next year. Wordsworth withdrew from its composition early because he realized, as he told Miss Fenwick in later life, that he 'could only have been a clog' upon it.

By the time the poem was completed Coleridge was fairly well off, for the Wedgwood family had settled upon him an annuity of £150. Coleridge used his new-found independence to turn aside from the ballad poetry which had interested Wordsworth and himself in favour of his political odes. About this date he introduced Wordsworth to the Bristol bookseller and publisher, Joseph Cottle. In a letter dated the 9th May 1798, Wordsworth suggested to Cottle that he should publish *Salisbury Plain* and added, 'I have lately been busy about another plan, which I do not wish to mention till I see you.' This plan probably referred to *Lyrical Ballads*, for on the 31st May, Dorothy Wordsworth, in a letter to her brother Richard, wrote, 'William has now some poems in the Bristol press.' In September the Wordsworths were in London about to leave with Coleridge for a visit to Germany. On the 13th of that month Dorothy wrote to an unknown correspondent that the poems were printed but not yet published; they were to appear 'in one small volume, without the name of the author; their title is Lyrical Ballads, with other Poems'.

If it had not been for the Wedgwood annuity, very likely Coleridge would have had a more equal share in the volume, but even so, his influence was all-important. At this period the two poets were daily in each other's company and in later life Wordsworth spoke of 'the most unreserved intercourse between them'.[1] Coleridge's early poetry shows clearly how the poetic ambitions and ideals of the two men were shared. In 1793, before the two had even met, Coleridge had heard and admired Wordsworth's *An Evening Walk* and *Descriptive Sketches* when they were read at a literary society in Exeter, and by 1795, he himself had written *Reflections on having left a Place of Retirement*, in which the diction of lines such as the following, went a long way towards achieving the simplicity that Wordsworth was seeking:

> Low was our pretty Cot: our tallest rose
> Peeped at the chamber-window. We could hear
> At silent noon, and eve, and early morn,
> The sea's faint murmur.

In the next two years Coleridge also attempted ballad poetry and was engaged with both *Christabel* and *The Three Graves*, though he completed neither of them. In *Christabel* he was experimenting with an idiom which he perfected in the *Ancient Mariner*, though he himself in Chapter XIV of the *Biographia Literaria* speaks of the *Ancient Mariner* as falling short of what he had in mind, and says of *Christabel* that it was a poem 'in which I should have more nearly realized my ideal'. *The Three Graves* was very different. It is now known that Wordsworth wrote Parts I and II of this[2] and the whole poem is reminiscent of Wordsworth's *The Thorn*. In both

---

[1] *Reminiscences of the Hon. Mr. Justice Coleridge*, Grosart, iii. 42.

[2] *v.* de Selincourt, *The Early Wordsworth* (Presidential Address to the English Association, 1936). *v.* also Stephen Parrish's essay in *P.M.L.A.*, Vol. 73 (1958).

poems the ballad is put into the mouth of a dramatic personage. Coleridge's part is one of his least successful pieces of writing and demonstrates his weakness in the kind of ballad poetry which so attracted Wordsworth.[1] This probably explains the way in which they planned *Lyrical Ballads* and the division of labour between them which Coleridge describes in the *Biographia Literaria*.

'The thought suggested itself (to which of us I do not recollect)', writes Coleridge in Chapter XIV of the *Biographia Literaria*, 'that a series of poems might be composed of two sorts. In the one, the incidents and agents were to be, in part at least, supernatural; and the excellence aimed at was to consist in the interesting of the affections by the dramatic truth of such emotions, as would naturally accompany such situations, supposing them real. . . . For the second class, subjects were to be chosen from ordinary life; the characters and incidents were to be such as will be found in every village and its vicinity, where there is a meditative and feeling mind to seek after them, or to notice them, when they present themselves.'[2]

It was with this in mind, continues Coleridge, that they planned *Lyrical Ballads*. He himself was to write about 'persons and characters supernatural, or at least romantic', but though supernatural they had to possess 'a semblance of truth sufficient to procure . . . that willing suspension of disbelief for the moment, which constitutes poetic faith'. Wordsworth, for his part, was 'to give the charm of novelty to things of every day, and to excite a feeling analogous to the supernatural, by awakening the mind's attention to the lethargy of custom, and directing it to the loveliness and the wonders of the world before us'. Both of them were to observe what they considered to be 'the two cardinal points of poetry, the power of exciting the sympathy of the reader by a faithful adherence to the truth

---

[1] Coleridge later thought that Wordsworth, too, was least successful in this form. *v*. Notes to *The Thorn*.

[2] *Biog. Lit.*, ii. 5.

of nature, and the power of giving the interest of novelty by the modifying colours of imagination'.[1]

As far as the *Ancient Mariner* was concerned, Coleridge fulfilled his share of the bargain brilliantly. The supernatural events of the poem symbolize the pattern of sin, repentance, grace and expiation that is part of man's religious experience, but old and familiar things are presented in a new way. By investing a voyage of exploration and discovery with what he called 'the depth and height of the ideal world', he transforms it into a spiritual odyssey. The style – and this is truer of the poem in the 1798 version – was derived from Percy's *Reliques* and from the English translations of Bürger's *Lenore*[2]; but though ideally suited to its purpose, it was not the simple 'modern' style for which he and Wordsworth were looking. Nor, indeed, was the style of *The Foster-Mother's Tale* or *The Dungeon*, both taken from his tragedy *Osorio* and contributed by Coleridge to the original *Lyrical Ballads* volume. These poems, like *The Three Graves*, were written in the pseudo-ballad style of the eighteenth century, with Gothic sentimentality and melodrama.

The only other poem Coleridge contributed to the joint venture was *The Nightingale*, which bore the sub-title *A Conversational Poem*. This was more promising. It employs the simple idiom of *Reflections on having left a Place of Retirement* and *The Eolian Harp*, both of which were written in 1795, and of *This Lime-tree Bower my Prison*, which belongs to 1797. These poems, together with *Frost at Midnight*, written in 1798, are all 'conversational pieces', but in a different sense from that generally attributed to the term.

Humphry House[3] discerns in these poems the influence of Cowper, but recognizes in them a gravity which goes so far beyond Cowper's work as to make Coleridge's a new kind of poetry. Cowper, though meditative, plays only upon the surfaces of things, whereas these poems are deeply searching.

---

[1] *Biog. Lit.*, ii. 5-6.   [2] *v.* p. 275.
[3] *Coleridge: The Clark Lectures 1951-2*, pp. 71-2.

Their moralizing stems from acute introspection and leads to profound metaphysical speculation. The reciprocity of the mind of man and the world of nature, of which the Eolian Harp is the great emblem, manifests itself in passages which are more than descriptive, in which the changing face of nature reflects the changing state of the poet's mind. Here, if anywhere, we see the birth of Romantic poetry.

An insight into Coleridge's thought and poetic aspirations at the time when *Lyrical Ballads* was in preparation can be gained from a letter he wrote to his brother on the 10th March 1798. He describes his purpose in poetry as an endeavour 'to elevate the imagination & set the affections in right tune by the beauty of the inanimate impregnated, as with a living soul, by the presence of Life'. In prose he will seek to know 'with patience & a slow, very slow mind. . . . What our faculties are & what they are capable of becoming'. The letter also contains a tribute to nature and its power to heal the troubled mind:

> I love fields & woods & mounta[ins] with almost a visionary fondness–and because I have found benevolence & quietness growing within me as that fondness [has] increased, there-fore I should wish to be the means of implanting it in others.

The letter shows how close the two men were in their thinking, for this passage reads like a commentary upon, and, in places, is almost a paraphrase of *Tintern Abbey*.

In politics, too, Coleridge shared the views of Wordsworth. In the same letter he writes:

> . . . it is withheld from me to regret any thing: I therefore consent to be deemed a Democrat & a Seditionist . . . but I have snapped my squeaking baby-trumpet of Sedition & the fragments lie scattered in the lumber-room of Penitence . . . I have for some time past withdrawn myself almost totally from the consideration of *immediate* causes, which are infinitely complex & uncertain, to muse on fundamental & general causes – 'the 'causæ causarum'.[1]

Coleridge had been active in politics; in 1795 he had delivered lectures in Bristol against the government and the war with

[1] *C. Letters*, i. 397.

France. But his republicanism was not based upon a belief in revolution so much as upon the vision of a self-supporting community which should have all things in common. Such a vision had been at the centre of the ill-fated Pantisocratic scheme to found a society upon the banks of the Susquehanna, and had led him to settle at Nether Stowey, where he hoped to produce from his own plot of land enough to support his wife and family. His political views, in fact, were much closer to those of the Diggers of the seventeenth century than to those of the French Terror. He had left Clevedon, where he had set up his home on marriage, because he felt compelled to answer the question his conscience forced upon him:

> . . . Was it right,
> While my unnumber'd brethren toil'd and bled,
> That I should dream away the entrusted hours
> On rose-leaf beds, pampering the coward heart
> With feelings all too delicate for use?

But the struggle he anticipated for himself was not violent revolution:

> I therefore go, and join head, heart, and hand,
> Active and firm, to fight the bloodless fight
> Of Science, Freedom, and the Truth in Christ.[1]

Though the convictions of the two men were very similar, with Wordsworth the process which had brought him to accept them was a heart-searching and critical one. From the time when he left Cambridge, Wordsworth had followed no settled occupation, but there had grown within him the belief that he would achieve greatness as a poet. In the year 1791-2 he visited France at a time when the Revolution was at its height, when the monarchy was overthrown and the Republic established, and later described in *The Prelude* the impact of the Revolution upon him. In the beginning he experienced the intoxication of feeling that Freedom's banner was at last unfurled:

> Bliss was it in that dawn to be alive,
> But to be young was very Heaven . . .

---

[1] *Reflections on Having Left a Place of Retirement.*

From Paris, where he saw the ruins of the Bastille, he went on to Orléans and Blois. At Blois he met Beaupuy, a captain in the Republican army, and under his influence became a 'Democrat' or Republican. Also at Blois he met Annette Vallon, the French girl with whom he fell in love. Annette became the mother of his daughter, but Wordsworth was unable to marry her because lack of money forced him to return to England.

The next few years were utterly miserable for Wordsworth. He had no settled home and was separated from Annette and his child. His opinions were misunderstood in England and his own country declared war upon France. Finally his best hopes turned into his worst fears. His revolutionary ardour changed to a sense of betrayal as he learned of the excesses of the Jacobins. In *The Prelude* he writes of the nightmares in which, he said,

> . . . I pleaded
> Before unjust Tribunals, with a voice
> Labouring, a brain confounded, and a sense
> Of treachery and desertion in the place
> The holiest that I knew of, my own soul.[1]

During these desperate years which followed his return from France, Wordsworth experienced something approaching a mental breakdown. It was only when his friend Raisley Calvert left him a legacy of £900 that some relief came. With this help he settled with his sister Dorothy at Racedown in Dorset, and then, so as to be near Coleridge, at Alfoxden in Somerset. Here with the aid of his sister and his friend, in the peaceful countryside of the Quantocks, his mind recovered its normal balance and he turned to poetry once again.

Before starting on their German tour, Wordsworth and his sister spent some time in Bristol to see *Lyrical Ballads* through the press. They stayed at Shirehampton, across the Clifton Downs from Bristol. During the second week of their visit they crossed the Severn by ferry and walked up the Wye Valley, through Tintern to Monmouth and Goodrich, retracing the

[1] *Prelude*, x. 377-81 [1805].

steps taken by Wordsworth five years before on his return from France. *Tintern Abbey* was written during this visit to the Wye. They returned by boat to Aust on the Gloucestershire side of the Severn and Wordsworth composed the last passage of the poem as he and his sister walked, on the last evening of their tour, down the hill from Clifton to Bristol. That they should have walked into Bristol for William to write the poem down and give it to Cottle to include in *Lyrical Ballads*, indicates the importance he attached to it.

Tintern Abbey was the last poem to be written of the original *Lyrical Ballads* and it is the most considerable of Wordsworth's poems in the volume. It sums up Wordsworth's beliefs, formed over the five previous testing years. Curiously it echoes the first poem in the collection, Coleridge's major contribution, the *Ancient Mariner*. Coleridge's poem, though it probably has some personal reference, is narrative or dramatic in form, whereas Wordsworth's is directly autobiographical. But the two poems have a certain identity in the central experience they convey. Like the Ancient Mariner, Wordsworth had passed through a dark night of the soul and the visionary splendour he had experienced on the banks of the Wye had left him 'a sadder and a wiser man'. In both poems there is a stripping away of pretension and a new self-awareness gained through suffering. In both poems there is the belief, as Coleridge put it, 'that every Thing has a life of it's own, & that we are all *one Life*',[1] or as Wordsworth expressed it, that 'Nature never did betray/ The heart that loved her'. These two poems form a fitting introduction and conclusion to the 1798 volume, for the remainder of the poems are characterized by a stripping away of poetic ornament and a conviction that the natural piety which binds all men together is best sustained by a simple communion with nature.

2

The title of the 1798 volume is *Lyrical Ballads with a Few Other Poems*. The *Other Poems* in fact form a fairly large pro-

[1] Letter to Sotheby, *C. Letters*, ii. 864.

portion of the collection. If we disregard Coleridge's contribution – and it amounts to one-third of the total pages – we are even more aware of how few ballads there really are. *Goody Blake and Harry Gill*, *The Idiot Boy* and *The Thorn* are the only real ballads by Wordsworth. There are some songs, such as *The Mad Mother*, and *The Complaint of a Forsaken Indian Woman*, and some pieces such as *The Tables Turned*, *Lines Written at a Small Distance from My House* and *Lines Written in Early Spring*, which though lyrical could hardly be called ballads. The only other poems by Wordsworth which approximate to the ballad form are the narrative and anecdotal poems such as *The Female Vagrant*, *We are Seven*, *Simon Lee* and *The Last of the Flock*.

What is it then, we might ask, that gives unity to these poems of Wordsworth? The most obvious answer, of course, would be the simplicity of style and language, which characterizes them all. Wordsworth directs our attention to this in the *Advertisement* to the 1798 edition and defends it at length in the *Preface* he wrote for the 1800 edition. The poems were a conscious attempt to write in a new way, and much of the controversy about them has centred on this. Revolutions in poetic style, however, generally express a desire not only to write in a new way but to find the appropriate idiom for a new apprehension of the truth.

At first sight it might appear as if Wordsworth had failed to keep his part of the agreement recorded in *Biographia Literaria*. As a companion-piece to the *Ancient Mariner* he had written *Peter Bell* in which the supernatural narrative of Coleridge's poem was given its natural counterpart, but *Peter Bell* was not included in *Lyrical Ballads* and was not in fact published until 1819. Critics have tended to assume that the plans for a joint publication were never brought to a successful conclusion and that the poems sent to Cottle were written independently of them. But this is not in accordance with Coleridge's account in *Biographia Literaria*, and he writes very exactly. It is true that things did not run entirely according to plan, but this was because Coleridge failed to keep pace with Wordsworth, not because of any defection on Wordsworth's part. Some of Wordsworth's contributions to the collection had been written before the two men drew up their plan, but this again does not invalidate Coleridge's account, for the plan itself was not an *a priori* one but based upon work already in progress and a recognition of their respective talents and ideals. If Chapter XIV of *Biographia Literaria* means anything at all it means that we should expect to find in Wordsworth's poems in *Lyrical Ballads* – leaving out of account the 'two or three poems written in his own character, in the impassioned, lofty, and sustained diction, which is characteristic of his genius' – an endeavour 'to give the charm of novelty to things of every day, and to excite a feeling analogous to the supernatural, by awakening the mind's attention from the lethargy of custom'. We should expect to find 'characters and incidents such as will be found in every village and its vicinity, where there is a meditative and feeling mind to seek after them', and a stripping off of 'the film of familiarity and selfish solicitude'[1] which hides their significance from us. This in fact is what we do find.

By using the poem's subject as narrator, as in *The Female Vagrant*, for example, Wordsworth maintains some degree of naturalism. By allowing his rustic character free range over the felicities of his own language and by adapting to his purposes the elements of a basically simple poetic form, Wordsworth achieves something of the impersonal authenticity of the traditional ballad. In this way he brings together a bareness of language and an elementary poetic form to express the simple directness of his personal vision. His sense of man's solitary dignity depends largely on his personal faith in the reality of nature, but also on his conviction of the interdependence of man and nature. Clearly, in the *Preface* to the 1800 edition, he was not so much discussing poetic theory in general, as the particular techniques which he found it necessary to deploy in the attempt to find an objective formulation of an intensely

[1] *Biog. Lit.*, ii. 5-6.

personal faith. His *personae* are never allowed a dramatic life of their own and exist only in so far as they represent their creator's point of vision. The exception is *The Thorn* which, significantly, fails at just those points in the poem where the *persona* threatens to take on an independent dramatic existence.

These poems were written in a style unlike that of his previous work; they were, as Wordsworth informs the reader in his *Advertisement*, to be 'considered as experiments'. He had already achieved some success in the style which he was to bring to perfection in *Tintern Abbey*, but this was not the best medium for what he was trying to do. In attempting to get behind 'the lethargy of custom', in trying to make people see again with a freshness of vision what had lain before their eyes all the time, he had to avoid anything that smacked of poetic cliché. The 'poetry' was almost an obstacle to the process of communication; something Wilfred Owen must have felt when he wrote as a Preface to his own poems, 'Above all I am not concerned with Poetry. My subject is War, and the pity of War. The Poetry is in the pity.' For Wordsworth, too, the important thing was the emotion aroused by the poem and not the poem itself; as he put it in the *Preface* to the 1800 edition,

. . . the feeling therein developed gives importance to the action and situation and not the action and situation to the feeling.

The feeling aroused by these poems was to be so powerful and of such a kind that it would, as Coleridge describes it, be analogous to the supernatural, to have an almost religious quality; to be, to use a phrase of Keats (who owed so much to Wordsworth), a feeling of the 'holiness of the heart's affections'. As well as using language which was non-literary to the point of bathos, Wordsworth chose subjects that would reveal the workings of the human heart in all their elemental simplicity. This explains his turning to rustic people, and to idiots and children.

Rustic people were chosen not for their 'quaintness' nor

because Wordsworth was concerned with folk-lore and country customs, but for their lack of sophistication. He was not a dialect poet like Burns, though he admired and was moved by Burns. He explains his interest in idiots in a letter he wrote to John Wilson [Christopher North] in June 1802.[1] The letter is valuable for the light it throws upon the whole of *Lyrical Ballads*, but especially for what Wordsworth writes about *The Idiot Boy*. He realized that many people found the poem ridiculous or unpleasant, but these critics had misunderstood his purpose. The story of the idiot boy showed in a graphic manner the strength of maternal love:

> . . . the loathing and disgust which many people have at the sight of an idiot, is a feeling which . . . is owing in a great measure to a false delicacy, and . . . a certain want of comprehensiveness of thinking and feeling.

The well-to-do lack this comprehensiveness, but poor people act with the untutored response of their feelings:

> 'I have indeed', he writes, 'often looked upon the conduct of fathers and mothers of the lower classes of society towards idiots as the great triumph of the human heart.'

Wordsworth writes of the religious veneration which is given to idiots in some communities and declares:

> 'I have often applied to idiots, in my own mind, that sublime expression of Scripture, that *their life is hidden with God*.'[2]

He feels that idiots evoke in those who care for them a love which is unselfish and uncalculating. This is no prudential morality, but a love which gives freely and without thought of any reward. The spectacle of a mother's love for an idiot child produced in Wordsworth a realization of the mystery of original goodness.

The closest parallel to *Lyrical Ballads* is Blake's *Songs of Innocence* which had appeared in 1789. Blake's childhood poems are similar to Wordsworth's, for both poets felt that

---

[1] John Wilson's letter, to which Wordsworth's is a reply, is reproduced in Appendix C.

[2] *E.L.*, pp. 296-7.

children lacked sophistication and showed human nature un-
trammelled by the conventions of upbringing and education.
It is this childlike quality not only in the infant but in the
adult, that seizes their attention, and as with Blake, there are
political overtones to Wordsworth's vision of innocence. His
own childhood is important to every artist, but to Words-
worth, especially, its importance was paramount, a time of
freedom and joy, a time when, as he wrote at the beginning of
The Prelude:

> The earth is all before me: with a heart
> Joyous, nor scar'd at its own liberty,
> I look about, and should the guide I chuse
> Be nothing better than a wandering cloud,
> I cannot miss my way.[1]

But Man had exiled himself from this Paradise by his own
inhumanity, an inhumanity which showed itself politically and
economically in the exploitation of one man by another and in
the artificiality of convention. In the same passage Words-
worth rejoices in escaping from 'the vast city, where I long
had pined a discontented sojourner', and the city was to stand
in Book VII of *The Prelude* for the corrupting influence of
'self-destroying, transitory things' from which Wordsworth
fled in dismay:

> Oh, blank confusion ! true epitome
> Of what the mighty City is herself,
> To thousands upon thousands of her sons,
> Living amid the same perpetual whirl
> Of trivial objects.[2]

The passion for freedom and the longing for lost innocence
were given their greatest political emphasis in the poem which
was the earliest written of those in *Lyrical Ballads, The Female
Vagrant.*[3] Wordsworth had returned from France in December

[1] *Prelude*, i. 15-19 [1805].

[2] *Prelude*, vii. 722-726 [1850].

[3] This poem was later incorporated into a longer and quite early poem
which Wordsworth entitled *Salisbury Plain*. The final version, first
published in 1842, was called *Guilt and Sorrow. v.* Notes to the Poems.

1792, and in the following year he spent July with William Calvert in the Isle of Wight. From there the two friends travelled across Salisbury Plain. At Salisbury they separated and Wordsworth walked to Bath and Bristol before proceeding by the Wye valley to North Wales. This was the occasion of his first visit to Tintern Abbey when we know that he was in a state of great mental agitation. He had seen the English fleet off Portsmouth making ready for the war against France and was filled with foreboding of what he was later to describe in the Advertisement to *Guilt and Sorrow* as the 'calamities, principally those consequent upon war, to which, more than other classes of men, the poor are subject'. *The Female Vagrant* is undeniably pacifist and radical in its sentiments, but Wordsworth did not regard it as characteristic of *Lyrical Ballads* as a whole. In a letter written on the 9th April 1801 to Miss Taylor, who was an admirer of his work, he criticizes it for a lack of genuine simplicity:

> 'The diction of that Poem', he writes, 'is often vicious, and the descriptions are often false, giving proofs of a mind inattentive to the true nature of the subject on which it was employed.'[1]

Between 1795 and 1798 Wordsworth's political views suffered a change. Like Milton after the collapse of the Commonwealth, Wordsworth came to feel, as the Revolution changed into the Terror, that his lost Paradise could only be within his own soul. There was a revival of interest in politics at the death of Robespierre, but this was extinguished again with the emergence of Buonapartism.

His Christianity during all these years (and later) was merely a nominal one. Unlike Coleridge, whose cast of thought was always *animae naturaliter Christianae*, Wordsworth had pinned his hopes on the perfectibility of human nature and the rule of reason. When, in 1793, Godwin's *Political Justice* appeared, Wordsworth read it enthusiastically and by 1795, when the two

[1] *E.L.*, p. 270.

men first met, had become an ardent disciple of Godwin. Godwin disapproved of revolution as a political instrument; for him social justice would be achieved by the exercise of reason unfettered by emotion or by political, religious, or social conventions and institutions. To one, like Wordsworth, who was disillusioned with the Revolution but still retained his political idealism, this formula was at first attractive. But he soon began to realize its shortcomings and *The Borderers*, written in 1796, illustrates clearly this dissatisfaction.

By 1798, Wordsworth had rejected Godwin's dichotomy of reason and emotion. When he first came under the influence of Godwin's theories, Wordsworth was suffering from an emotional collapse or what, today, would be called a nervous breakdown. To suggest to one in this state that the emotions should be kept in the strict control of the reason might have seemed good advice. The explanation of a neurotic state in Godwinian terms would be that the emotions had overthrown the rule of reason. No doubt Wordsworth felt at first that this fitted his own case: he had been exposed to vicious influences and in France had been placed in a situation which had led to a loss of rational control. At Alfoxden the cheerful company of his sister and his friend had restored his peace of mind. But with the return of mental tranquility there came the conviction that his recovery had had little to do with the exercise of rational control in the Godwinian sense. The new environment had been all-important; it had allowed his spirit to drink at the deep, restorative springs which flowed from nature itself, but it had required very little in the way of intellectual activity.

Wordsworth concludes the Advertisement to the first edition of *Lyrical Ballads* with the following information:

> The lines entitled Expostulation and Reply, and those which follow, arose out of conversation with a friend who was somewhat unreasonably attached to modern books of moral philosophy.

The friend to whom he refers is Hazlitt and the moral philosophy is Godwin's. *Expostulation and Reply* speaks of the healing

effect of nature as something distinct from the conscious effort
of will or intellect:

> Nor less I deem that there are powers,
> Which of themselves our minds impress,
> That we can feed this mind of ours,
> In a wise passiveness.

> Think you, mid all this mighty sum
> Of things for ever speaking,
> That nothing of itself will come,
> But we must still be seeking?

The Tables Turned, the other poem to which Wordsworth
refers, is even more anti-intellectualist:

> One impulse from a vernal wood
> May teach you more of man;
> Of moral evil and of good,
> Than all the sages can.

> Sweet is the lore which nature brings;
> Our meddling intellect
> Misshapes the beauteous forms of things;
> – We murder to dissect.

> Enough of science and of art;
> Close up these barren leaves;
> Come forth, and bring with you a heart
> That watches and receives,

Tintern Abbey looks back upon the moral and intellectual quest
of the previous five years and celebrates the new-found con-
viction which has flooded Wordsworth's mind with light. He is
now

> . . . well pleased to recognize
> In nature and the language of the sense,
> The anchor of my purest thoughts, the nurse,
> The guide, the guardian of my heart, and soul
> Of all my moral being.

It is not the reason which gives the deepest insight but 'that
serene and blessed mood, / In which the affections gently lead

us on'; it is not by the intellect but 'the deep power of joy, / We see into the life of things'.

It was Hartley rather than Godwin who was able to give Wordsworth a satisfactory explanation of what had happened to him. By 1796 Coleridge had already transferred his allegiance from Godwin to Hartley, a change signalized in the September of that year by the naming of his new-born son Hartley.[1] Where Godwin put the emphasis on the reason, Hartley put it on environment. Hartley was an empiricist in the tradition of Locke, but his reputation rested on the plausibility with which he had restated in physiological terms the theory of the association of ideas. In its simplest form the theory of association stated that the order in which our ideas succeed one another is governed by the order in which the sensations (of which the ideas themselves are copies) occurred. The material of consciousness is made up, firstly, of sensations or (as modern philosophers would say) sense-data; secondly, simple ideas which are copies of sensations, or sensations which remain after the objects which cause them have been removed; and thirdly, complex ideas which are compounded of simple ideas. These three stages, as we may call them, correspond roughly to sensation, memory and thought. Within consciousness one idea will tend to call up another if the two ideas have been previously associated either in space or time and more especially so if this association has been frequently experienced. The process of thought will largely be governed by the association of ideas according to contiguity in space and time, and frequency. All this is commonplace in most theories of association; what gave Hartley's theory a certain novelty was his attempt to explain it physiologically. He believed that

[1] The philosophical interests of Coleridge at this period can be traced by the names he gave his children, for his next son (who was to live for less than a year) was Berkeley, born in May 1798. By the time *Lyrical Ballads* was published, Coleridge was growing dissatisfied with Hartley and within a year or so was to regard his doctrines as false as those of Godwin.

sensations are caused by vibrations in the nervous system and brain by external objects acting on the sense organs. Even when the external objects were removed, he thought that these vibrations continued with diminished force and would produce ideas in the mind.

Central to Hartley's restatement of association was the notion that the mind is passive in perception, a mere *tabula rasa* upon which the outside world writes its impressions. In accordance with this strict empiricism Hartley had stressed the importance of sensation as the basis of all our knowledge, including our moral principles. Morality, on such a view, was the product of experience, built up from the effects of environment upon one's personal development. This is of central importance in much of Wordsworth's poetry. The best known illustration of it is in the passage in Book I of *The Prelude*, which describes the theft of the boat and the feelings of guilt which arose in the poet's mind as a result of this. But other examples are met with in *Lyrical Ballads*. In *Ruth*, for instance, the treachery of the 'Youth from Georgia's Shore' is attributed to the influence of his surroundings in the New World:

> Whatever in those Climes he found
> Irregular in sight or sound
> Did to his mind impart
> A kindred impulse, . . .
>
> .   .   .   .   .   .
> His genius and his moral frame
> Were thus impaired, and he became
> The slave of low desires.

The *Preface* which Wordsworth wrote to the 1800 edition of *Lyrical Ballads* makes his debt to Hartley abundantly clear,[1]

---

[1] Wordsworth may have known Hartley's *Observations on Man* in the original edition of 1749 or in the condensed version to which Joseph Priestley gave the name *Hartley's Theory of the Human Mind*, the second edition of which appeared in 1790. For the fullest treatment of Wordsworth's indebtedness to Hartley the reader should consult Arthur Beatty, *William Wordsworth: His Doctrine and Art in Their Historical Relations*, University of Wisconsin Studies in Language and Literature, No. 24, Second Edition, Madison, 1927.

and many of the poems bear the marks of this influence. The *Anecdote for Fathers* is a particularly good example of how ideas are associated in a state of excitement, one of the aims, it will be remembered, which Wordsworth set himself in these poems. Perhaps Hartley may also throw some light on the psychological processes involved in the story of *Goody Blake and Harry Gill*. For Hartley a simple idea and a sensation are almost identical, the difference normally being that an idea is fainter than its corresponding sensation. But what if the idea were impressed upon the mind with great force? Might it not become, as with Harry Gill's feeling of cold, almost as permanent and vivid as a real sensation?

It is not difficult to see why Wordsworth found Hartley so attractive. Wordsworth's temperament had always caused him to rely more on sensory observation than rational principles, and his character had been influenced more by natural surroundings than formal education. At Racedown and Alfoxden, under the tutelage of his sister Dorothy and his friend Coleridge, he had found mental peace not by trying to find a rational solution to his problems but by 'a wise passiveness', by drinking deeply in the soul of things. Hartley's philosophy and psychology seemed to give warranty for what Wordsworth had proved by the truth of his own experience and what he expressed in *Expostulation and Reply* and in *The Tables Turned*.

It may be argued that the framework of *Tintern Abbey* derives from Hartley and presupposes an empiricist philosophy. The transition in the poem is certainly from a time when sensory pleasures were all important and

> . . . had no need of a remoter charm,
> By thought supplied, or any interest
> Unborrowed from the eye,

to a more mature wisdom when 'these wild ecstasies' have given way to 'a sober pleasure' which is the source of moral strength. In other words, Hartley's account of how the mind moves from sensation through perception to thought, is turned into an analogy of how the individual passes from childhood through youth to maturity.

And yet, attractive as this may be, we meet a difficulty in the lines where Wordsworth describes himself as

> . . . still
> A lover of the meadows and the woods,
> And mountains; and of all that we behold
> From this green earth; of all the mighty world
> Of eye and ear, *both what they half-create*,[1]
> *And what perceive*; well pleased to recognize
> In nature and the language of the sense,
> The anchor of my purest thoughts, the nurse,
> The guide, the guardian of my heart, and soul
> Of all my moral being.

The phrase in italics hardly suggests the rigorous empiricism of Hartley. It suggests rather a passage in *Biographia Literaria*, written many years later, in which Coleridge is criticizing Hartley's theory, and where he writes:

> There are evidently two powers at work [in the mind], which relatively to each other are active and passive; and this is not possible without an intermediate faculty, which is at once both active and passive. (In philosophical language, we must denominate this intermediate faculty in all its degrees and determinations, the IMAGINATION. . . .)
>
> (*Biog. Lit.*, i. 86)

Or, perhaps, the more famous lines in Coleridge's *Dejection* written in 1802:

> I may not hope from outward Forms to win
> The Passion and the Life, whose Fountains are within!

This passage in *Tintern Abbey* may have sprung from a new-found conviction which Wordsworth owed to Coleridge.

---

[1] Wordsworth added the following footnote to this line: 'This line has a close resemblance to an admirable line of Young, the exact expression of which I cannot recollect.' He had no time to look it up for he had hurried with the poem straight to Cottle's on arriving back in Bristol from the Wye valley. The line he had in mind was from Young's *Night Thoughts* (vi. 424) and ran: 'And half-create the wondrous world they see'.

Coleridge was already immersing himself in Berkeley; and in the later and more Platonic Berkeley, and in the seventeenth-century Platonists whom he had also been reading, he would have found a doctrine of the mind's creativity in perception.[1] Maybe it was simply Wordsworth's testimony to the facts of his own experience as he had now come to understand them. In either case *Tintern Abbey* expresses philosophical and religious beliefs which Wordsworth was later to abandon. Certainly his *Preface* to the 1800 edition of *Lyrical Ballads* shows, as we shall see, a renewed dependence upon Hartleian psychology and probably because of this, the first signs of serious disagreement between Wordsworth and Coleridge.

3

Having deposited *Lyrical Ballads* with Cottle, the Words-worths and Coleridge left England for Germany. They sailed from Yarmouth on the 16th September 1798, and four days later landed in Hamburg. The purpose of their visit was to learn the language and its literature, and to provide Coleridge with an opportunity of studying German philosophy and science. William and Dorothy returned to England early in May of the following year, Coleridge not until July. For most of the time the Wordsworths and Coleridge were separated; the Wordsworths spending the winter at Goslar, a small town near Brunswick, and Coleridge at Ratzeburg, from which he moved in February to the University of Göttingen. For Coleridge the German visit was a success. At Ratzeburg there was an enjoyable social life and at Göttingen he found the intellectual stimulus his mind needed. With the Wordsworths it was very different. They had no Wedgwood annuity and their resources were very few. Goslar was a small provincial town; they were cut off there by what Wordsworth described as the worst winter of the century and they were homesick. And yet the vein of creative ability which Wordsworth had tapped the

[1] *v.* R. L. Brett, 'Coleridge's Theory of the Imagination', *Essays and Studies* published for the English Association, John Murray, 1949.

previous summer seemed to flow again in abundance. Perhaps he had this period in mind when he wrote of poetry having its origin in 'emotion recollected in tranquillity', for the poetry he wrote at this time was not about his immediate surroundings, but about England and his childhood and youth. As with many other writers, exile fed the springs of his inspiration. It was at Goslar that Wordsworth wrote most of what later became the first two books of *The Prelude*, including the passages about nutting, skating, and the theft of the boat. And a good many of the poems Wordsworth was to include in the second edition of *Lyrical Ballads* were composed in Germany: *A Poet's Epitaph*, *The Two April Mornings*, *The Fountain*, *Ruth*, and the group of 'Lucy poems'.

Meanwhile the first edition of *Lyrical Ballads* had made its appearance. Mrs. Coleridge, writing to her husband on the 24th March 1799, speaks of its indifferent reception: 'The Lyrical Ballads are not esteemed well here.' Poor Mrs. Coleridge! She had never been very tactful and these remarks, inspired as they were by Southey, must have been very unwelcome to Coleridge, who had been on rather cool terms with his brother-in-law since their quarrel over Pantisocracy. Southey was one of the first to review the volume, in *The Critical Review*, October 1798. He was aware of the joint authorship of the poems and the knowledge of this must have added for Coleridge a certain offensiveness to his criticism. He was especially truculent over the *Ancient Mariner*:

'Many of the stanzas are laboriously beautiful;' he wrote, 'but in connection they are absurd or unintelligible. . . . We do not sufficiently understand the story to analyse it. It is a Dutch attempt at German sublimity. Genius has here been employed in producing a poem of little merit.'

But the *Idiot Boy* fared little better:

'No tale less deserved the labour that appears to have been bestowed upon this. It resembles a Flemish picture in the worthlessness of its design and excellence of its execution.'[1]

---

[1] For the full review see Appendix C.

Wordsworth seems to have been totally unaware of how his poems had been received while he was away. He returned to England with a renewed love for his own country; in the last of the 'Lucy' poems, written after his return, he cries out, with the relief of a man who recognizes at last what has been troubling him:

> I travelled among unknown men
> In lands beyond the sea;
> Nor, England! did I know till then
> What love I bore to thee.
>
> 'Tis past that melancholy dream!
> Nor will I quit thy shore
> A second time; for still I seem
> To love thee more and more.

But there is an element of withdrawal, almost perhaps of defeat, about the decision he was to make to return to his native mountains. It is the physical counterpart to that mood of passivity encountered in *Tintern Abbey*, a mood in which the poet is 'laid asleep in body', in which he ceases to struggle and allows the great restorative principle of nature to assert itself. This mood colours the poems he wrote in Germany and immediately after his return. We see it in the lines,

> A slumber did my spirit seal;
> I had no human fears . . .

and in the poem which describes the poet's ride to Lucy's cottage in the moonlight:

> In one of those sweet dreams I slept,
> Kind Nature's gentlest boon!

Before they moved to Grasmere and immediately on returning to England, Wordsworth and Dorothy stayed for seven months at Sockburn near Hurworth-on-Tees, the home of their friends the Hutchinsons. Coleridge on his return settled for a few months at Stowey, before moving with his wife and family to London, where he was to work on the *Morning Post*. But

before going to London he paid a visit to Sockburn, alarmed at
reports which had reached him of Wordsworth's ill-health.
Cottle had also been invited to Sockburn and the two of them
travelled together to the North from Bristol by post-chaise.
They reached Sockburn on the 26th October 1799 and found
Wordsworth not only well but fit enough to start the following
day on a walking tour to the Lakes. Cottle went only as far as
Greta Bridge; he was suffering from rheumatism and probably
felt that he could not keep up with his companions. He may
have felt this mentally as well as physically, for the two poets
had a great deal to discuss and were in fact at a turning point
in their careers.

It was during this walking-tour that Wordsworth showed
Coleridge for the first time the scenes of his boyhood and told
him of his decision to settle at Grasmere. We know from the
notebook which Coleridge kept, the impression this country-
side made upon his imagination. They stayed at Grasmere for
five days, exploring the neighbourhood in wintry weather that
gave the landscape an even greater sublimity than usual.
'Nature lived for us in all her grandest accidents', wrote
Coleridge to Dorothy Wordsworth from Keswick on the return
journey. By the end of the year the Wordsworths had left
Sockburn and moved into Dove Cottage at Grasmere. By the
middle of the next year, 1800, Coleridge had moved his wife
and family to Keswick to be near 'his god Wordsworth', as
Lamb called him. Coleridge had hoped to persuade his friend
to return to the Quantocks, so that he might enjoy the
company of both Wordsworth and Thomas Poole, his bene-
factor at Stowey, but it was not to be. Writing to Poole in
March 1800, Coleridge says: 'I would to God I could get
Wordsworth to retake Alfoxden. The society of so great a being
is of priceless value: but he will never quit the North of
England.'

On his return to England Wordsworth had at once begun to
think of a new edition of *Lyrical Ballads*, for the first edition

had sold out. He had got in touch with Cottle, who still retained the copyright though he had sold the first edition to the London bookseller, Arch. Wordsworth felt that the *Ancient Mariner* had been responsible for the lukewarm reception given to the poems on their first appearance. He proposed to Cottle that if there were a new edition he should substitute for Coleridge's poem some more of his own. In fact, when the new edition appeared it contained all Coleridge's original contributions together with an additional poem of his, *Love*, although the title was given as *Lyrical Ballads, by W. Wordsworth* and no reference was made to Coleridge.

Cottle on retiring from the publishing business at the end of 1799 had disposed of his copyrights to the London firm of Longman. They had considered the copyright of *Lyrical Ballads* worthless and so Cottle had asked for it back and presented it to Wordsworth. But more favourable reviews and, even more, the steady sale of the poems must have caused Longman to revise his opinion,[1] for on the 8th June Wordsworth wrote to his brother Richard that Longman had offered £80 'for the right of printing two editions of 750 each of this vol. of poems, and of printing two editions, one of 1000 and another of 750 of another volume of the same size'.[2] The new edition was printed at Bristol by the firm of Biggs and Co., and published in London by Longman. Wordsworth himself was at Grasmere and he asked Coleridge's friend Humphry Davy, the distinguished chemist, who lived in Bristol, to see the poems through the press. Indeed, Wordsworth left a great deal of the work to Coleridge and Davy. With such divided responsibility, it is no wonder that the poems were not published until January 1801, although the title-page bore the date 1800. It was intended to include *Christabel*, but Coleridge never managed to finish it and wrote to Davy on the 9th

---

[1] Not only was a new edition called for in 1800, but further editions appeared in 1802 and 1805.

[2] *E.L.*, p. 243.

October 1800, that it was 'in direct opposition to the very purpose for which the *Lyrical Ballads* were published'. For the same reason (though it was little more than a rationalization of Wordsworth's belief that the poem had aroused prejudice in the readers' minds) the *Ancient Mariner* was removed from the beginning of the first volume and placed at the end. The archaic spellings were all changed and Wordsworth added a note to the poem, apologizing for its 'strangeness'. Coleridge, the most humble of men, never objected to this treatment, though his later letters make it clear that it produced in him a loss of confidence in his powers as a poet.[1] Wordsworth himself must have realized the error of judgment he had made over the *Ancient Mariner* and the note was dropped from subsequent editions.

Wordsworth seems to have become intent on showing in the new edition that poetry should depict 'incidents of common life' and demonstrate the workings of our 'primary passions'. The importance of Coleridge's contribution, that is, poems based upon the supernatural, faded from his mind. If in Wordsworth's estimation *The Idiot Boy* was the chief poem of volume one, then *Michael* was the most important poem in volume two. His conviction that the elemental passions of human nature are best seen in the simple environment of country-life was strengthened by his settling at Grasmere. The notion in the earlier volume that contact with nature brings emotional stability and virtue, is deepened in the later volume to the belief that character, the settled disposition of our sentiments and consequent actions, is conditioned more by environment than by rational *a priori* principles of the kind advanced by Godwin.

There is an increased assurance in many of the poems in the second volume which seems to spring from Wordsworth's new-found sense of security. The patriotism he had felt in Germany had become a very personal thing since his return to England. He had a home of his own and had found a new sense of

[1] *v. C. Letters*, i. 631n.

independence. In a letter to Thomas Poole, in which he says
that Poole is the prototype of Michael, he writes:

> I have attempted to give a picture of a man, of strong mind
> and lively sensibility, agitated by two of the most powerful
> affections of the human heart; the parental affection, and the
> love of property, *landed* property, including the feelings of
> inheritance, home and personal and family independence.[1]

Wordsworth was now a man with a stake in the country, not
only in the political but in a psychological sense. He had put
down his roots in their native soil.

All this is reflected in the radicalism of many of the poems in
the second volume, in their belief that virtue is nurtured by
simplicity of living, family affection, and economic independ-
ence. Coupled with this belief is his compassion for individuals
who have been made the victims of industrialization and
officialdom. One of those to whom Wordsworth sent a
presentation copy of the new edition of *Lyrical Ballads* was
Charles James Fox and with the two volumes he sent a long
letter (dated 14th January 1801) in which he wrote:

> But recently by the spreading of manufactures through every
> part of the country, by the heavy taxes upon postage, by work-
> houses, Houses of Industry, and the invention of Soup-shops
> &c. &c. superadded to the encreasing disproportion between
> the price of labour and that of the necessaries of life, the
> bonds of domestic feeling among the poor, as far as the
> influence of these things has extended, have been weakened,
> and in innumerable instances entirely destroyed . . .

He goes on to describe how the new institutions have broken up
family life:

> . . . parents are separated from their children, and children
> from their parents; the wife no longer prepares with her own
> hands a meal for her husband, the produce of his labour;
> there is little doing in his house in which his affections can be
> interested, and but little left in it which he can love.'[2]

An important feature of the second edition of *Lyrical*

---

[1] *E.L.*, p. 266.
[2] *E.L.*, pp. 260-1.

Ballads was the *Preface*, which replaced the *Advertisement* of
1798. Wordsworth always maintained that he disliked writing
of this kind and that it was written only to please Coleridge,
but it is hard to believe that he wrote six thousand words for
this reason alone. There was talk of Coleridge himself under-
taking the task, for on the 13th July 1802 in a letter to his
friend Sotheby, he wrote, '. . . the f[irst pass]ages were indeed
partly taken from notes of mine for it was at first intended that
the Preface should be written by me'.[1] If Wordsworth did
write only to please Coleridge, he failed in his purpose, for
long before his critique of Wordsworth's theories in the
Biographia Literaria, Coleridge expressed his disagreement with
the *Preface*. Within a fortnight of writing to Sotheby he con-
fided to Southey also his dissatisfaction with Wordsworth's
work. '. . . altho' Wordsworth's Preface is half a child of my
own Brain', he wrote, '. . . yet I am far from going all lengths
with Wordsworth'.[2] In the letter to Sotheby he had gone so far
as to say of himself and Wordsworth, '. . . we begin to suspect,
that there is, somewhere or other, a *radical* Difference [in our]
opinions'.

Many readers have believed Wordsworth's views about
poetic diction to be the main point in Coleridge's criticism of
the *Preface*. Those chapters of *Biographia Literaria* which
refer specifically to *Lyrical Ballads* certainly concentrate very
largely on this topic, but the remaining chapters, too, are
written with the *Preface* in mind. Indeed, *Biographia Literaria*
as a whole can be seen as Coleridge's reply to Wordsworth. It
was not only Wordsworth's views on poetic diction, but his
conception of poetry itself, which raised doubts in Coleridge's
mind and at the centre of their disagreement lies Coleridge's
belief that Wordsworth's conception of poetry relied too much
on Hartley.

The immediate purpose of the *Preface* was, of course, to
disarm criticism. The *Advertisement* to the 1798 edition had

[1] *C. Letters*, ii. 811.
[2] *Ibid.*, ii. 830.

spoken of the *Ballads* as 'experiments' and had asked for an unprejudiced hearing for them, but it was clear that a good many readers were confused and uncertain in their judgments. The very term *ballad* was ambiguous; as well as the traditional ballad, there were many contemporary poems called ballads, which did not seem to belong firmly to any one recognisable kind. Robert Mayo accurately describes the situation when he writes, 'By 1798 almost anything might be called a "ballad" and very often it was.'[1] Wordsworth's own poems might have seemed to many of his readers not unlike the ballads they already knew in the magazines of the day. Why, then, did Wordsworth describe them as 'experiments', and what was the peculiar significance of the adjective *Lyrical* he and Coleridge had used in the title of their volume? It was to answer these and similiar questions that the *Preface* was written.

To accomplish his purpose, Wordsworth felt that it was necessary to start at the beginning and to define the nature of poetry. His account of poetry is a psychological one which describes the genesis of poetry in the poet's mind. 'Poetry', he tells us in a famous passage of the *Preface*, 'is the spontaneous overflow of powerful feelings.' These feelings do not at once lead to the creation of poetry; they are recalled by the poet after the actual situation which first aroused them is past. Poetry, he continues,

> . . . takes its origin from emotion recollected in tranquillity: the emotion is contemplated till by a species of reaction the tranquillity gradually disappears, and an emotion, similar to that which was before the subject of contemplation, is gradually produced, and does itself actually exist in the mind[2].

This recollected emotion is not absolutely identical with the original, for whatever its original character, it produces when turned into poetic channels, a feeling of pleasure. Even if the

[1] R. Mayo, *The Contemporaneity of the 'Lyrical Ballads'*, P.M.L.A., LXIX (1954), p. 507.

[2] The phrase 'emotion recollected in tranquillity' may have come from Coleridge (*v. C. Notebooks*, i. 787 and 787n).

original feelings were painful, its recollection as part of artistic creation is such that 'the mind will upon the whole be in a state of enjoyment'. This process of *katharsis* should also occur in the reader, and the poet, according to Wordsworth, has a duty to see that it does:

> ... the Poet ... ought especially to take care, that whatever passions he communicates to his Reader, those passions, if his Reader's mind be sound and vigorous, should always be accompanied with an overbalance of pleasure.

By 'feeling' or 'emotion' in these and other passages of the *Preface* Wordsworth does not mean pure feeling or emotion, for, as he tells us in Hartleian language, 'our continued influxes of feeling are modified and directed by our thoughts' and our thoughts 'are indeed the representatives of all our past feelings'. He is concerned with states of mind in which strong emotion accompanies or is accompanied by some idea or ideas. These feelings and ideas are more important than the stories recounted in his poems; this, no doubt, explains why the poems are called not simply ballads, but *Lyrical Ballads*.

> 'I should mention one other circumstance', he writes, 'which distinguishes these Poems from the popular Poetry of the day; it is this, that the feeling therein developed gives importance to the action and situation and not the action and situation to the feeling.'

Not only does Wordsworth give a psychological description of the nature of poetry, but the purpose of the poems in *Lyrical Ballads* is put in psychological terms derived from Hartley:

> 'The principal object then which I proposed to myself in these Poems', he writes, 'was to make the incidents of common life interesting by tracing in them, truly though not ostentatiously, the primary laws of our nature: chiefly as far as regards the manner in which we associate ideas in a state of excitement.'

Wordsworth believed that human behaviour may be observed

more clearly in moments of crisis (a state of excitement), because on such occasions men do not react with a stock response or hide behind a façade of convention. He expresses himself more clearly, perhaps, a little later on when he re-defines his purpose as being 'to follow the fluxes and refluxes of the mind when agitated by the great and simple affections of our nature'. The risk he has run, he thinks, in choosing such subjects, is to have been too particular or idiosyncratic. Even this fear is expressed in Hartleian terms: 'I am sensible that my associations must have sometimes been particular instead of general.' But on the whole he thinks that simple and rustic people will best serve his purpose because in them human nature stands more clearly revealed and is less corrupted by social convention:

> 'Low and rustic life was generally chosen,' he explains to the reader, 'because in that situation the essential passions of the heart find a better soil in which they can attain their maturity, are less under restraint, and speak a plainer and more emphatic language; because in that situation our elementary feelings exist in a state of greater simplicity, and consequently may be more accurately contemplated.'

There is much here that was to be challenged, but the most important assumption (so far as his own poems are concerned) was that concerning the language of rustic people:

> The language too of these men is adopted (purified indeed from what appear to be its real defects, from all lasting and rational causes of dislike or disgust) because such men hourly communicate with the best objects from which the best part of language is originally derived.

Coleridge pointed out the ambiguity of the phrase 'best objects'. Did this mean natural objects, or perhaps the Bible, which had played a part in shaping the speech of Wordsworth's neighbours? Presumably Wordsworth had in mind natural objects, for in the same passage he asserts that 'the passions of men are incorporated with the beautiful and permanent forms of nature', and if their passions, then perhaps their language which is the expression of these passions, would reveal the influence of nature. But if this is so, what are the defects he refers to? Why should the speech of men in hourly communion with the beauty of nature, have features that disgust us?

One thing is clear, Wordsworth was not attempting dialect poetry. The poems in *Lyrical Ballads* do not try to capture the atmosphere or style of folk poetry. They use rather a 'selection of language really used by men' so as to avoid the literary and artificial language of much eighteenth-century poetry, and because this will bring them closer to human behaviour. Coleridge was at one with Wordsworth in wanting to cut through the artificiality of a good deal of poetic diction, but he remained unpersuaded that a style based upon rustic speech was the formula to use for achieving 'a more permanent and a far more philosophical language'.

To those who might ask Wordsworth why he should bother to write in verse when he believed that 'between the language of prose and metrical composition . . . there neither is nor can be any essential difference', he has a double answer. At first sight the two parts of his argument seem to contradict each other. Rhythm, he tells us, will 'have great efficacy in temper-ing and restraining the passion' which is aroused by poetry. But if our passions have not been sufficiently stimulated by 'the Poet's words', their metre 'will greatly contribute to impart passion to the words'. What Wordsworth is saying is not self-contradictory, but contains a valuable insight into the part played by metre in poetry. Rhythm arouses emotion but it also controls it; it subordinates it to the whole aesthetic experience and also has a therapeutic value.

Throughout the *Preface* there runs this thread of psycho-logical interest and explanation. Wordsworth was deeply interested in the processes of the poetic mind. Unfortunately the only psychological theory he could find to explain these processes was Hartley's and at the centre of Hartley's theory, the key concept of his thought, was the association of ideas. Here was what dissatisfied Coleridge, for as he was to argue so strenuously in the *Biographia Literaria*, association can only lead to works of fancy. 'The Fancy', as he was to write in Chapter XIII of that work, 'is indeed no other than a mode of Memory emancipated from the order of time and space . . . the Fancy must receive all its materials ready made from the law of association.'[1] This did not explain Wordsworth's own poetry. Coleridge was convinced that Wordsworth's work was the product not of fancy but of imagination, a creative and not merely an associative faculty. Wordsworth himself had not explained this and so Coleridge continued with those 'repeated meditations' he refers to in Chapter IV of *Biographia Literaria*, in the effort to distinguish properly between the fancy and the imagination.

No doubt Coleridge told Wordsworth of his disagreement with the 1800 *Preface*, for when a new edition of *Lyrical Ballads* was called for in 1802, Wordsworth, as well as making minor amendments, took the opportunity of adding a passage of some three thousand words. This passage is devoted to the question, 'What is a Poet?', and to a discussion of poetic pleasure which approximates in some degree to the views Coleridge held. Wordsworth may be influenced by Hartley as when, for instance, he writes of the poet as one who above all possesses the power of expressing 'especially those thoughts and feelings which, by his own choice, or from the structure of his own mind, arise in him without immediate external excitement'. But when he discusses the relation of science and poetry he writes in terms which must have met with Coleridge's approval, for they anticipate the language of *Biographia Literaria*.

Wordsworth believes with Aristotle that poetry is more philosophical than history '. . . its object is truth, not individual and local, but general, and operative'. But he also makes claims for poetry that would raise it above science. The disciplines of

[1] *Biog. Lit.*, i. 202.

discursive thought, he maintains, are all abstractions, they reflect only a part of human nature, whereas poetry is a reflection of the whole mind of man:

> The Poet writes under one restriction only, namely, that of the necessity of giving immediate pleasure to a human being possessed of that information which may be expected from him, not as a lawyer, a physician, a mariner, an astronomer or a natural philosopher, but as a Man. Except this one restriction, there is no object standing between the Poet and the image of things.

This is close to what Coleridge wrote later in *Biographia Literaria*:

> A poem is that species of composition, which is opposed to works of science, by proposing for its *immediate* object pleasure, not truth.[1]

And

> The poet, described in *ideal* perfection, brings the whole soul of man into activity, with the subordination of its faculties to each other, according to their relative worth and dignity.[2]

But whereas Coleridge went on to give an impressive analysis of the poetic imagination and its relation to the reasoning power of man's mind, Wordsworth's views remain the expression of a rather confused anti-intellectualism. Coleridge set himself no less a task than to explain poetry as part of a man's whole intellectual and spiritual endeavour, Wordsworth is intent only on expressing the convictions which grew from his own personal experience. This was always the difference between the two men; the great philosophical poem which Coleridge was always urging on Wordsworth remained unfinished, his great achievement was to be *The Prelude*, the poem on the growth of his own mind. Wordsworth's poetic vision remained a personal one which even his own *Preface* could not wholly explain.

[1] *Biog. Lit.*, ii. 10.
[2] *Ibid.*, ii. 12.

Poems in the 1798 edition of Lyrical Ballads in the order in which they were printed

The number in brackets gives the order in the first volume of the 1800 edition.

1. (23) *The Rime of the Ancyent Marinere*
   (The title in the 1800 edition was *The Ancient Mariner: A Poet's Reverie.*)
2. (7) *The Foster-Mother's Tale*
3. (6) *Lines left upon a Seat in a Yew-tree which stands near the Lake of Esthwaite*
4. (17) *The Nightingale, a Conversational Poem*
   (In most copies this took the place of *Lewti* while the poems were going through the press.)
5. (13) *The Female Vagrant*
6. (8) *Goody Blake and Harry Gill*
7. (12) *Lines written at a small distance from my House, and sent by my little Boy to the Person to whom they are addressed*
8. (15) *Simon Lee, the old Huntsman*
9. (11) *Anecdote for Fathers*
10. (10) *We are seven*
11. (16) *Lines written in early spring*
12. (9) *The Thorn*
13. (5) *The last of the Flock*
14. (14) *The Dungeon*
15. (22) *The Mad Mother*
16. (20) *The Idiot Boy*

Poems in the 1800 *edition of* Lyrical Ballads *in the order in which they were printed*

VOLUME ONE

The poems in this first volume were substantially the same as those in the 1798 edition. For details of the order in which they were printed and the changes in the titles of some of the poems, see the list of Poems in the 1798 edition. *The Convict* was omitted, but the following poem of Coleridge's was added:

– (21) *Love*

VOLUME TWO

1. *Hart-leap Well*
2. *There was a Boy, &c.*
3. *The Brothers, a Pastoral Poem*
4. *Ellen Irwin, or the Braes of Kirtle*
5. *Strange fits of passion I have known, &c.*
6. *Song*
7. *A slumber did my spirit seal, &c.*
8. *The Waterfall and the Eglantine*
9. *The Oak and the Broom, a Pastoral*
10. *Lucy Gray*
11. *The Idle Shepherd-Boys, or Dungeon-Gill Force, a Pastoral*
12. *'Tis said that some have died for love, &c.*
13. *Poor Susan*
14. *Inscription for the Spot where the Hermitage stood on St. Herbert's Island, Derwent-Water*

Wordsworth is inconsistent in his use of titles and some of the above titles differ from those which head the poems.

LYRICAL BALLADS,

WITH

A FEW OTHER POEMS.

BRISTOL:

PRINTED BY BIGGS AND COTTLE,

FOR T. N. LONGMAN, PATERNOSTER-ROW, LONDON.

1798.

Advertisement

It is the honourable characteristic of Poetry that its materials are to be found in every subject which can interest the human mind. The evidence of this fact is to be sought, not in the writings of Critics, but in those of Poets themselves.

The majority of the following poems are to be considered as experiments. They were written chiefly with a view to ascertain how far the language of conversation in the middle and lower classes of society is adapted to the purposes of poetic pleasure. Readers accustomed to the gaudiness and inane phraseology of many modern writers, if they persist in reading this book to its conclusion, will perhaps frequently have to struggle with feelings of strangeness and aukwardness: they will look round for poetry, and will be induced to enquire by what species of courtesy these attempts can be permitted to assume that title. It is desirable that such readers, for their own sakes, should not suffer the solitary word Poetry, a word of very disputed meaning, to stand in the way of their gratification; but that, while they are perusing this book, they should ask themselves if it contains a natural delineation of human passions, human characters, and human incidents; and if the answer be favourable to the author's wishes, that they should consent to be pleased in spite of that most dreadful enemy to our pleasures, our own pre-established codes of decision.

Readers of superior judgment may disapprove of the style in which many of these pieces are executed it must be expected that many lines and phrases will not exactly suit their taste. It will perhaps appear to them, that wishing to avoid the prevalent fault of the day, the author has sometimes descended too low, and that many of his expressions are too familiar, and not of sufficient dignity. It is apprehended, that the more conversant the reader is with our elder writers, and with those in modern times who have been the most successful in painting manners and passions, the fewer complaints of this kind will he have to make.

An accurate taste in poetry, and in all the other arts, Sir Joshua Reynolds has observed, is an acquired talent, which can only be produced by severe thought, and a long continued intercourse with the best models of composition. This is mentioned not with so ridiculous a purpose as to prevent the most inexperienced reader from judging for himself; but merely to temper the rashness of decision, and to suggest that if poetry be a subject on which much time has not been bestowed, the judgment may be erroneous, and that in many cases it necessarily will be so.

The tale of Goody Blake and Harry Gill is founded on a well-authenticated fact which happened in Warwickshire. Of the other poems in the collection, it may be proper to say that they are either absolute inventions of the author, or facts which took place within his personal observation or that of his friends. The poem of the Thorn, as the reader will soon discover, is not supposed to be spoken in the author's own person: the character of the loquacious narrator will sufficiently shew itself in the course of the story. The Rime of the Ancyent Marinere was professedly written in imitation of the *style*, as well as of the spirit of the elder poets; but with a few exceptions, the Author believes that the language adopted in it has been equally intelligible for these three last centuries. The lines entitled Expostulation and Reply, and those which follow, arose out of conversation with a friend who was somewhat unreasonably attached to modern books of moral philosophy.

ARGUMENT

How a Ship having passed the Line was driven by Storms to
the cold Country towards the South Pole; and how from
thence she made her course to the tropical Latitude of the
Great Pacific Ocean; and of the strange things that befell;
and in what manner the Ancyent Marinere came back to
his own Country.

The Rime of the Ancyent Marinere,

IN SEVEN PARTS

I

It is an ancyent Marinere,
    And he stoppeth one of three:
"By thy long grey beard and thy glittering eye
    "Now wherefore stoppest me?

"The Bridegroom's doors are open'd wide
    "And I am next of kin;
"The Guests are met, the Feast is set, –
    "May'st hear the merry din. –

Argument: How a Ship, having first sailed to the Equator, was driven
  by Storms, to the cold Country towards the South Pole; how the
  Ancient Mariner cruelly, and in contempt of the laws of hospitality,
  killed a Sea-bird; and how he was followed by many and strange
  Judgements; and in what manner he came back to his own Country.
  [1800].
Om. 1802: 1805: 1817 & sub.
Title: The Ancient Mariner. A Poet's Reverie. [1800]. *v.* Notes.

  1. ancyent] ancient [1800].
    Marinere] Mariner [1800].

But still he holds the wedding-guest –
    There was a Ship, quoth he –   10
"Nay, if thou'st got a laughsome tale,
    "Marinere ! come with me."

He holds him with his skinny hand,
    Quoth he, there was a Ship –
"Now get thee hence, thou grey-beard Loon !
    "Or my Staff shall make thee skip.

He holds him with his glittering eye –
    The wedding guest stood still
And listens like a three year's child;
    The Marinere hath his will.   20

The wedding-guest sate on a stone,
    He cannot chuse but hear:
And thus spake on that ancyent man,
    The bright-eyed Marinere.

The Ship was cheer'd, the Harbour clear'd –
    Merrily did we drop
Below the Kirk, below the Hill,
    Below the Light-house top.

The Sun came up upon the left,
    Out of the Sea came he: 30
And he shone bright, and on the right
    Went down into the Sea.

Higher and higher every day,
    Till over the mast at noon –
The wedding-guest here beat his breast,
    For he heard the loud bassoon.

13–16. He holds him with his skinny hand,
      'There was a ship,' quoth he.
      'Hold off! unhand me, grey-beard loon!'
      Eftsoons his hand dropt he.
      The preceding stanza is omitted.
                  [*P. of C.*]

The Bride hath pac'd into the Hall,
　　Red as a rose is she;
Nodding their heads before her goes
　　The merry Minstralsy.　　　　　　　　　　40

The wedding-guest he beat his breast,
　　Yet he cannot chuse but hear:
And thus spake on that ancyent Man,
　　The bright-eyed Marinere.

Listen, Stranger! Storm and Wind,
　　A Wind and Tempest strong!
For days and weeks it play'd us freaks –
　　Like Chaff we drove along.

Listen, Stranger! Mist and Snow,
　　And it grew wond'rous cauld:　　　　　　　　50
And Ice mast-high came floating by
　　As green as Emerauld.

45–52. 'And now the STORM-BLAST came, and he
Was tyrannous and strong:
He struck with his o'ertaking wings,
And chased us south along.

With sloping masts and dipping prow,
As who pursued with yell and blow
Still treads the shadow of his foe,
And forward bends his head,
The ship drove fast, loud roared the blast,
And southward aye we fled.

And now there came both mist and snow,
And it grew wondrous cold:
And ice, mast-high, came floating by,
As green as emerald. [*P. of C.*]

45–48. But now the Northwind came more fierce,
There came a Tempest strong!
And Southward still for days and weeks
Like Chaff we drove along. [1800].

49. And now there came both Mist and Snow, [1800].

And thro' the drifts the snowy clifts
    Did send a dismal sheen;
Ne shapes of men ne beasts we ken –
    The Ice was all between.

The Ice was here, the Ice was there,
    The Ice was all around:
It crack'd and growl'd, and roar'd and howl'd –
    Like noises of a swound.   60

At length did cross an Albatross,
    Thorough the Fog it came;
And an it were a Christian Soul,
    We hail'd it in God's name.

The Marineres gave it biscuit-worms,
    And round and round it flew:
The Ice did split with a Thunder-fit;
    The Helmsman steer'd us thro'.

And a good south wind sprung up behind,
    The Albatross did follow;   70
And every day for food or play
    Came to the Marinere's hollo !

In mist or cloud on mast or shroud
    It perch'd for vespers nine,
Whiles all the night thro' fog-smoke white
    Glimmer'd the white moon-shine.

"God save thee, ancyent Marinere !
    "From the fiends that plague thee thus –

---

60. A wild and ceaseless sound. [1800].
65. It ate the food it ne'er had eat, [*P. of C.*]
75. fog-smoke white] fog smoke-white [1798 amend. errat.].

"Why look'st thou so?" – with my cross bow
   I shot the Albatross.   80

II

The Sun came up upon the right,
   Out of the Sea came he;
And broad as a weft upon the left
   Went down into the Sea.

And the good south wind still blew behind,
   But no sweet Bird did follow
Ne any day for food or play
   Came to the Marinere's hollo !

And I had done an hellish thing
   And it would work 'em woe: 90
For all averr'd, I had kill'd the Bird
   That made the Breeze to blow.

Ne dim ne red, like God's own head,
   The glorious Sun uprist:
Then all averr'd, I had kill'd the Bird
   That brought the fog and mist.
'Twas right, said they, such birds to slay
   That bring the fog and mist.

The breezes blew, the white foam flew,
   The furrow follow'd free: 100

---

81. The Sun now rose [1800].
83. Still hid in mist; and on the left [1800].
87 & 93 & 118. Ne] Nor [1800].
93. like an Angel's head, [1800].

We were the first that ever burst
  Into that silent Sea.

Down dropt the breeze, the Sails dropt down,
  'Twas sad as sad could be
And we did speak only to break
  The silence of the Sea.

All in a hot and copper sky
  The bloody sun at noon,
Right up above the mast did stand,
  No bigger than the moon.   110

Day after day, day after day,
  We stuck, ne breath ne motion,
As idle as a painted Ship
  Upon a painted Ocean.

Water, water, every where
  And all the boards did shrink;
Water, water, every where
  Ne any drop to drink.

The very deeps did rot: O Christ!
  That ever this should be!   120
Yea, slimy things did crawl with legs
  Upon the slimy Sea.

About, about, in reel and rout
  The Death-fires danc'd at night;
The water, like a witch's oils,
  Burnt green and blue and white.

And some in dreams assured were
  Of the Spirit that plagued us so:

Nine fathom deep he had follow'd us
    From the Land of Mist and Snow.   130

And every tongue thro' utter drouth
    Was wither'd at the root;
We could not speak no more than if
    We had been choked with soot.

Ah wel-a-day! what evil looks
    Had I from old and young;
Instead of the Cross the Albatross
    About my neck was hung.

III

I saw a something in the Sky
    No bigger than my fist;   140
At first it seem'd a little speck
    And then it seem'd a mist:
It mov'd and mov'd, and took at last
    A certain shape, I wist.

A speck, a mist, a shape, I wist!
    And still it ner'd and ner'd;
And, an it dodg'd a water-sprite,
    It plung'd and tack'd and veer'd.

139–140. So past a weary time; each throat
        Was parch'd, and glaz'd each eye,
        When, looking westward, I beheld
        A something in the sky. [1800].

        There passed a weary time. Each throat
        Was parched, and glazed each eye.
        A weary time! A weary time!
        How glazed each weary eye,
        When looking westward, I beheld
        A something in the sky. [P. of C.]

With throat unslack'd, with black lips bak'd
   Ne could we laugh, ne wail: 150
Then while thro' drouth all dumb they stood
I bit my arm and suck'd the blood
   And cry'd, A sail! a sail!

With throat unslack'd, with black lips bak'd
   Agape they hear'd me call:
Gramercy! they for joy did grin
And all at once their breath drew in
   As they were drinking all.

She doth not tack from side to side –
   Hither to work us weal   160
Withouten wind, withouten tide
   She steddies with upright keel.

The western wave was all a flame,
   The day was well nigh done!
Almost upon the western wave
   Rested the broad bright Sun;
When that strange shape drove suddenly
   Betwixt us and the Sun.

And strait the Sun was fleck'd with bars
   (Heaven's mother send us grace)   170
As if thro' a dungeon grate he peer'd
   With broad and burning face.

Alas! (thought I, and my heart beat loud)
   How fast she neres and neres!

149–152. With throat unslack'd, with black lips bak'd,
       We could nor laugh nor wail;
       Thro' utter drouth all dumb we stood
       Till I bit my arm and suck'd the blood, [1800].
   154. With throats unslaked etc., [P. of C.]
149–162. See! See! (I cry'd) she tacks no more!
       Hither to work us weal
       Without a breeze, without a tide
       She steddies with upright keel! [1800].

Are those *her* Sails that glance in the Sun
 Like restless gossameres?

Are these *her* naked ribs, which fleck'd
 The sun that did behind them peer?
And are these two all, all the crew,
 That woman and her fleshless Pheere?   180

His bones were black with many a crack,
 All black and bare, I ween;
Jet-black and bare, save where with rust
Of mouldy damps and charnel crust
 They're patch'd with purple and green.

Her lips are red, *her* looks are free,
 Her locks are yellow as gold:
Her skin is as white as leprosy,
And she is far liker Death than he;
 Her flesh makes the still air cold.   190

177-185. Are those *her* ribs through which the Sun
           Did peer, as through a grate?
           And is that Woman all her crew?
           Is that a DEATH? and are there two?
           Is DEATH that woman's mate? [*P. of C.*]

           Are those *her* Ribs, thro' which the Sun
           Did peer as thro' a grate?
           And are those two all, all her crew,
           That Woman, and her Mate?

           His bones were black with many a crack

           .   .   .   .   .   .

           They were patch'd with purple and green. [1800].

186-190. *Her* lips were red, *her* looks were free,
           Her locks were yellow as gold:
           Her skin was as white as leprosy,
           The Night-mare LIFE-IN-DEATH was she,
           Who thicks man's blood with cold. [*P. of C.*]

           Her lips were red, *her* looks were free,
           Her locks were as yellow as gold:
           Her skin was as white as leprosy,
           And she was far liker Death than he;
           Her flesh made the still air cold. [1800].

The naked Hulk alongside came
  And the Twain were playing dice;
"The Game is done! I've won, I've won!"
  Quoth she, and whistled thrice.

A gust of wind sterte up behind
  And whistled thro' his bones;
Thro' the holes of his eyes and the hole of his mouth
  Half-whistles and half-groans.

With never a whisper in the Sea
  Off darts the Spectre-ship;   200
While clombe above the Eastern bar
The horned Moon, with one bright Star
  Almost atween the tips.

One after one by the horned Moon
  (Listen, O Stranger! to me)
Each turn'd his face with a ghastly pang
  And curs'd me with his ee.

195–207. The Sun's rim dips; the stars rush out:
        At one stride comes the dark;
        With far-heard whisper, o'er the sea,
        Off shot the spectre-bark.

        We listened and looked sideways up!
        Fear at my heart, as at a cup,
        My life-blood seemed to sip!
        The stars were dim, and thick the night,
        The steersman's face by his lamp gleamed white;
        From the sails the dew did drip –
        Till clomb above the eastern bar
        The hornéd Moon, with one bright star
        Within the nether tip.

        One after one, by the star-dogged Moon,
        Too quick for groan or sigh,
        Each turned his face with a ghastly pang,
        And cursed me with his eye. [*P. of C.*]

Four times fifty living men,
  With never a sigh or groan,
With heavy thump, a lifeless lump   210
  They dropp'd down one by one.

Their souls did from their bodies fly, –
  They fled to bliss or woe;
And every soul it pass'd me by,
  Like the whiz of my Cross-bow.

IV

"I fear thee, ancyent Marinere !
  "I fear thy skinny hand;
"And thou art long and lank and brown
  "As is the ribb'd Sea-sand.

"I fear thee and thy glittering eye   220
  "And thy skinny hand so brown –
Fear not, fear not, thou wedding guest !
  This body dropt not down.

Alone, alone, all all alone
  Alone on the wide wide Sea;
And Christ would take no pity on
  My soul in agony.

The many men so beautiful,
  And they all dead did lie !
And a million million slimy things   230
  Liv'd on – and so did I.

---

209. (And I heard nor sigh nor groan) [*P. of C.*]
225–227. Alone on a wide, wide sea!
     And never a saint took pity on
     My soul in agony. [*P. of C.*]
230. And a thousand thousand slimy things [*P. of C.*]

I look'd upon the rotting Sea,
    And drew my eyes away;
I look'd upon the eldritch deck,
    And there the dead men lay.

I look'd to Heaven, and try'd to pray;
    But or ever a prayer had gusht,
A wicked whisper came and made
    My heart as dry as dust.

I clos'd my lids and kept them close,   240
    Till the balls like pulses beat;
For the sky and the sea, and the sea and the sky
Lay like a load on my weary eye,
    And the dead were at my feet.

The cold sweat melted from their limbs,
    Ne rot, ne reek did they;
The look with which they look'd on me,
    Had never pass'd away.

An orphan's curse would drag to Hell
    A spirit from on high: 250
But O! more horrible than that
    Is the curse in a dead man's eye!
Seven days, seven nights I saw that curse,
    And yet I could not die.

The moving Moon went up the sky
    And no where did abide:
Softly she was going up
    And a star or two beside –

---

234. eldritch] ghastly [1800] rotting [*P. of C.*]
246. Ne ... ne] Nor ... nor [1800].

Her beams bemock'd the sultry main
   Like morning frosts yspread;   260
But where the ship's huge shadow lay,
The charmed water burnt alway
   A still and awful red.

Beyond the shadow of the ship
   I watch'd the water-snakes:
They mov'd in tracks of shining white;
And when they rear'd, the elfish light
   Fell off in hoary flakes.

Within the shadow of the ship
   I watch'd their rich attire: 270
Blue, glossy green, and velvet black
They coil'd and swam; and every track
   Was a flash of golden fire.

O happy living things! no tongue
   Their beauty might declare:
A spring of love gusht from my heart,
   And I bless'd them unaware!
Sure my kind saint took pity on me,
   And I bless'd them unaware.

The self-same moment I could pray;   280
   And from my neck so free
The Albatross fell off, and sank
   Like lead into the sea.

V

O sleep, it is a gentle thing
   Belov'd from pole to pole!
To Mary-queen the praise be yeven
She sent the gentle sleep from heaven
   That slid into my soul.

---

260. Like April hoar-frost spread; [1800].
286. yeven] given [1800].

The silly buckets on the deck
   That had so long remain'd,   290
I dreamt that they were fill'd with dew
   And when I awoke it rain'd.

My lips were wet, my throat was cold,
   My garments all were dank;
Sure I had drunken in my dreams
   And still my body drank.

I mov'd and could not feel my limbs,
   I was so light, almost
I thought that I had died in sleep,
   And was a blessed Ghost.   300

The roaring wind! it roar'd far off,
   It did not come anear;
But with its sound it shook the sails
   That were so thin and sere.

The upper air bursts into life,
   And a hundred fire-flags sheen
To and fro they are hurried about;
And to and fro, and in and out
   The stars dance on between.

The coming wind doth roar more loud;   310
   The sails do sigh, like sedge:
The rain pours down from one black cloud
   And the Moon is at its edge.

Hark! hark! the thick black cloud is cleft,
   And the Moon is at its side:

---

301. And soon I heard a roaring wind, [1800].
309. The wan stars danc'd between. [1800].
310–315. And the coming wind did roar more loud,
     And the sails did sigh like sedge:
     And the rain pour'd down from one black cloud;
     The moon was at its edge.

     The thick black cloud was cleft, and still
     The Moon was at its side: [1800].

Like waters shot from some high crag,
The lightning falls with never a jag
    A river steep and wide.

The strong wind reach'd the ship: it roar'd
    And dropp'd down, like a stone!   320
Beneath the lightning and the moon
    The dead men gave a groan.

They groan'd, they stirr'd, they all uprose,
    Ne spake, ne mov'd their eyes:
It had been strange, even in a dream
    To have seen those dead men rise.

The helmsman steerd, the ship mov'd on;
    Yet never a breeze up-blew;
The Marineres all 'gan work the ropes,
    Where they were wont to do: 330
They rais'd their limbs like lifeless tools —
    We were a ghastly crew.

The body of my brother's son
    Stood by me knee to knee:
The body and I pull'd at one rope,
    But he said nought to me —
And I quak'd to think of my own voice
    How frightful it would be!

The day-light dawn'd — they dropp'd their arms,
    And cluster'd round the mast: 340

319–320. The loud wind never reached the Ship,
            Yet now the Ship mov'd on! [1800].
    324. Ne . . . ne] Nor . . . nor [1800].
337–338. Om. 1800.
338–339. I fear thee, ancient Mariner!
            Be calm, thou wedding guest!
            'Twas not those souls, that fled in pain,
            Which to their corses came again,
            But a troop of Spirits blest: [1800].
    339. For when it dawn'd [1800].

Sweet sounds rose slowly thro' their mouths
   And from their bodies pass'd.

Around, around, flew each sweet sound,
   Then darted to the sun:
Slowly the sounds came back again
   Now mix'd, now one by one.

Sometimes a dropping from the sky
   I heard the Lavrock sing;
Sometimes all little birds that are
How they seem'd to fill the sea and air   350
   With their sweet jargoning,

And now 'twas like all instruments,
   Now like a lonely flute;
And now it is an angel's song
   That makes the heavens be mute.

It ceas'd: yet still the sails made on
   A pleasant noise till noon,
A noise like of a hidden brook
   In the leafy month of June,
That to the sleeping woods all night   360
   Singeth a quiet tune.

Listen, O listen, thou Wedding-guest !
   "Marinere ! thou hast thy will:
"For that, which comes out of thine eye, doth make
   "My body and soul to be still."

Never sadder tale was told
   To a man of woman born:
Sadder and wiser thou wedding-guest !
   Thou'lt rise to morrow morn.

---

348. Lavrock] Sky-lark [1800].

Never sadder tale was heard   370
   By a man of woman born:
The Marineres all return'd to work
   As silent as beforne.

The Marineres all 'gan pull the ropes,
   But look at me they n'old:
Thought I, I am as thin as air –
   They cannot me behold.

Till noon we silently sail'd on
   Yet never a breeze did breathe:
Slowly and smoothly went the ship   380
   Mov'd onward from beneath.

Under the keel nine fathom deep
   From the land of mist and snow
The spirit slid: and it was He
   That made the Ship to go.
The sails at noon left off their tune
   And the Ship stood still also.

The sun right up above the mast
   Had fix'd her to the ocean:
But in a minute she 'gan stir   390
   With a short uneasy motion –
Backwards and forwards half her length
   With a short uneasy motion.

Then, like a pawing horse let go,
   She made a sudden bound:
It flung the blood into my head,
   And I fell into a swound.

362–377. Om. 1800.

How long in that same fit I lay,
  I have not to declare;
But ere my living life return'd,   400
I heard and in my soul discern'd
  Two voices in the air,

"Is it he? quoth one, "Is this the man?
  "By him who died on cross,
"With his cruel bow he lay'd full low
  "The harmless Albatross.

"The spirit who 'bideth by himself
  "In the land of mist and snow,
"He lov'd the bird that lov'd the man
  "Who shot him with his bow.   410

The other was a softer voice,
  As soft as honey-dew:
Quoth he the man hath penance done,
  And penance more will do.

VI

FIRST VOICE

"But tell me, tell me! speak again,
  "Thy soft response renewing –
"What makes that ship drive on so fast?
  "What is the Ocean doing?

SECOND VOICE

"Still as a Slave before his Lord,
  "The Ocean hath no blast: 420
"His great bright eye most silently
  "Up to the moon is cast –

"If he may know which way to go,
  "For she guides him smooth or grim,
"See, brother, see! how graciously
  "She looketh down on him.

"But why drives on that ship so fast
"Withouten wave or wind?

"The air is cut away before,
"And closes from behind.   430

"Fly, brother, fly! more high, more high,
"Or we shall be belated:
"For slow and slow that ship will go,
"When the Marinere's trance is abated."

I woke, and we were sailing on
As in a gentle weather:
'Twas night, calm night, the moon was high:
The dead men stood together.

All stood together on the deck,
For a charnel-dungeon fitter: 440
All fix'd on me their stony eyes
That in the moon did glitter.

The pang, the curse, with which they died,
Had never pass'd away:
I could not draw my een from theirs
Ne turn them up to pray.

And in its time the spell was snapt,
And I could move my een:
I look'd far-forth, but little saw
Of what might else be seen.   450

428. Without or wave or wind? [1800].
445. een] eyes [1800].
446. Ne] Nor [1800].
447-450. And now this spell was snapt: once more
         I view'd the ocean green,
         And look'd far forth, yet little saw
         Of what had else been seen – [1800].

Like one, that on a lonely road
   Doth walk in fear and dread,
And having once turn'd round, walks on
   And turns no more his head:
Because he knows, a frightful fiend
   Doth close behind him tread.

But soon there breath'd a wind on me,
   Ne sound ne motion made:
Its path was not upon the sea
   In ripple or in shade.   460

It rais'd my hair, it fann'd my cheek,
   Like a meadow-gale of spring –
It mingled strangely with my fears,
   Yet it felt like a welcoming.

Swiftly, swiftly flew the ship,
   Yet she sail'd softly too:
Sweetly, sweetly blew the breeze –
   On me alone it blew.

O dream of joy! is this indeed
   The light-house top I see?   470
Is this the Hill? Is this the Kirk?
   Is this mine own countrée?

We drifted o'er the Harbour-bar,
   And I with sobs did pray –
"O let me be awake, my God!
   "Or let me sleep alway!"

The harbour-bay was clear as glass,
   So smoothly it was strewn!
And on the bay the moon light lay,
   And the shadow of the moon.   480

---

451. lonely] lonesome [1800].
458. Ne . . . ne] Nor . . . nor [1800].

The moonlight bay was white all o'er,
    Till rising from the same,
Full many shapes, that shadows were,
    Like as of torches came.

A little distance from the prow
    Those dark-red shadows were;
But soon I saw that my own flesh
    Was red as in a glare.

I turn'd my head in fear and dread,
    And by the holy rood,   490
The bodies had advanc'd, and now
    Before the mast they stood.

They lifted up their stiff right arms,
    They held them strait and tight;
And each right-arm burnt like a torch,
    A torch that's borne upright.
Their stony eye-balls glitter'd on
    In the red and smoky light.

I pray'd and turn'd my head away
    Forth looking as before.   500
There was no breeze upon the bay,
    No wave against the shore.

The rock shone bright, the kirk no less
    That stands above the rock:
The moonlight steep'd in silentness
    The steady weathercock.

And the bay was white with silent light,
    Till rising from the same
Full many shapes, that shadows were,
    In crimson colours came.   510

_____

481–502. Om. 1800.

A little distance from the prow
　　Those crimson shadows were:
I turn'd my eyes upon the deck –
　　O Christ! what saw I there?

Each corse lay flat, lifeless and flat;
　　And by the Holy rood
A man all light, a seraph-man,
　　On every corse there stood.

This seraph-band, each wav'd his hand:
　　It was a heavenly sight: 520
They stood as signals to the land,
　　Each one a lovely light:

This seraph-band, each wav'd his hand,
　　No voice did they impart –
No voice; but O! the silence sank,
　　Like music on my heart.

Eftsones I heard the dash of oars,
　　I heard the pilot's cheer:
My head was turn'd perforce away
　　And I saw a boat appear.   530

Then vanish'd all the lovely lights;
　　The bodies rose anew:
With silent pace, each to his place,
　　Came back the ghastly crew.
The wind, that shade nor motion made,
　　On me alone it blew.

---

527. Eftsones] But soon [1800].
531–536. Om. 1800.

The pilot, and the pilot's boy
   I heard them coming fast:
Dear Lord in Heaven! it was a joy,
   The dead men could not blast.   540

I saw a third – I heard his voice:
   It is the Hermit good!
He singeth loud his godly hymns
   That he makes in the wood.
He'll shrieve my soul, he'll wash away
   The Albatross's blood.

VII

This Hermit good lives in that wood
   Which slopes down to the Sea.
How loudly his sweet voice he rears!
He loves to talk with Marineres   550
   That come from a far Contrée.

He kneels at morn and noon and eve –
   He hath a cushion plump:
It is the moss, that wholly hides
   The rotted old Oak-stump.

The Skiff-boat ne'rd: I heard them talk,
   "Why, this is strange, I trow!
"Where are those lights so many and fair
   "That signal made but now?

"Strange, by my faith! the Hermit said –   560
   "And they answer'd not our cheer.
"The planks look warp'd, and see those sails
   "How thin they are and sere!
"I never saw aught like to them
   "Unless perchance it were

"The skeletons of leaves that lag
  "My forest brook along:
"When the Ivy-tod is heavy with snow,
"And the Owlet whoops to the wolf below
  "That eats the she-wolf's young.   570

"Dear Lord! it has a fiendish look –
  (The Pilot made reply)
"I am a-fear'd. – "Push on, push on!
  "Said the Hermit cheerily.

The Boat came closer to the Ship,
  But I ne spake ne stirr'd!
The Boat came close beneath the Ship,
  And strait a sound was heard!

Under the water it rumbled on,
  Still louder and more dread: 580
It reach'd the Ship, it split the bay;
  The Ship went down like lead.

Stunn'd by that loud and dreadful sound,
  Which sky and ocean smote:
Like one that hath been seven days drown'd
  My body lay afloat:
But, swift as dreams, myself I found
  Within the Pilot's boat.

Upon the whirl, where sank the Ship,
  The boat spun round and round: 590
And all was still, save that the hill
  Was telling of the sound.

I mov'd my lips: the Pilot shriek'd
  And fell down in a fit.
The Holy Hermit rais'd his eyes
  And pray'd where he did sit.

---

566. The] Brown [*P. of C.*]
576. ne . . . ne] nor . . . nor [1800].

I took the oars: the Pilot's boy,
　Who now doth crazy go,
Laugh'd loud and long, and all the while
　His eyes went to and fro,   600
"Ha ! ha !" quoth he – "full plain I see,
　"The devil knows how to row."

And now all in mine own Countrée
　I stood on the firm land !
The Hermit stepp'd forth from the boat,
　And scarcely he could stand.

"O shrieve me, shrieve me, holy Man !
　The Hermit cross'd his brow –
"Say quick," quoth he, "I bid thee say
　"What manner man art thou?   610

Forthwith this frame of mine was wrench'd
　With a woeful agony,
Which forc'd me to begin my tale
　And then it left me free.

Since then at an uncertain hour
　Now oftimes and now fewer,
That anguish comes and makes me tell
　My ghastly aventure.

I pass, like night, from land to land;
　I have strange power of speech;   620
The moment that his face I see
I know the man that must hear me;
　To him my tale I teach.

615-618. Since then, at an uncertain hour,
　　　　　　　　That agency returns; agency] agony [1802].
　　　　　　　　And till my ghastly tale is told,
　　　　　　　　This heart within me burns. [1800].

What loud uproar bursts from that door!
   The Wedding-guests are there;
But in the Garden-bower the Bride
   And Bride-maids singing are:
And hark the little Vesper-bell
   Which biddeth me to prayer.

O Wedding-guest! this soul hath been   630
   Alone on a wide wide sea
So lonely 'twas, that God himself
   Scarce seemed there to be.

O sweeter than the Marriage-feast,
   'Tis sweeter far to me
To walk together to the Kirk
   With a goodly company.

To walk together to the Kirk
   And all together pray,
While each to his great father bends,   640
Old men, and babes, and loving friends,
   And Youths, and Maidens gay.

Farewel, farewell! but this I tell
   To thee, thou wedding-guest!
He prayeth well who loveth well
   Both man and bird and beast.

He prayeth best who loveth best,
   All things both great and small:
For the dear God, who loveth us,
   He made and loveth all.   650

The Marinere, whose eye is bright,
   Whose beard with age is hoar,
Is gone; and now the wedding-guest
   Turn'd from the bridegroom's door.

He went, like one that hath been stunn'd
    And is of sense forlorn:
A sadder and a wiser man
    He rose the morrow morn.

The Foster-Mother's Tale,

A DRAMATIC FRAGMENT

FOSTER-MOTHER

I never saw the man whom you describe.

MARIA

'Tis strange! he spake of you familiarly
As mine and Albert's common Foster-mother.

FOSTER-MOTHER

Now blessings on the man, whoe'er he be,
That joined your names with mine! O my sweet lady,
As often as I think of those dear times
When you two little ones would stand at eve
On each side of my chair, and make me learn
All you had learnt in the day; and how to talk
In gentle phrase, then bid me sing to you –   10
'Tis more like heaven to come than what *has* been.

MARIA

O my dear Mother! this strange man has left me
Troubled with wilder fancies, than the moon
Breeds in the love-sick maid who gazes at it,
Till lost in inward vision, with wet eye
She gazes idly! – But that entrance, Mother!

Title: *The Foster-mother's Tale. A Narration in Dramatic Blank Verse*
    [1800].
  1-16. Om. 1800 which begins: 'But that entrance, Mother!'
    In *Remorse* (*v.* Notes) *dramatis personae* renamed Teresa and
    Selma.

FOSTER-MOTHER

Can no one hear? It is a perilous tale!

MARIA

No one.

FOSTER-MOTHER

My husband's father told it me,
Poor old Leoni! – Angels rest his soul!   20
He was a woodman, and could fell and saw
With lusty arm. You know that huge round beam
Which props the hanging wall of the old chapel?
Beneath that tree, while yet it was a tree
He found a baby wrapt in mosses, lined
With thistle-beards, and such small locks of wool
As hang on brambles. Well, he brought him home,
And reared him at the then Lord Velez' cost
And so the babe grew up a pretty boy,
A pretty boy, but most unteachable –   30
And never learnt a prayer, nor told a bead,
But knew the names of birds, and mocked their notes,
And whistled, as he were a bird himself:
And all the autumn 'twas his only play
To get the seeds of wild flowers, and to plant them
With earth and water, on the stumps of trees.
A Friar, who gathered simples in the wood,
A grey-haired man – he loved this little boy,
The boy loved him – and, when the Friar taught him,
He soon could write with the pen: and from that time, 40
Lived chiefly at the Convent or the Castle.
So he became a very learned youth.
But Oh! poor wretch! – he read, and read, and read,
'Till his brain turned – and ere his twentieth year,
He had unlawful thoughts of many things:

35. get the] gather [1802].
37. gathered] sought for [1802].

And though he prayed, he never loved to pray
With holy men, nor in a holy place –
But yet his speech, it was so soft and sweet,
The late Lord Velez ne'er was wearied with him.
And once, as by the north side of the Chapel   50
They stood together, chained in deep discourse,
The earth heaved under them with such a groan,
That the wall tottered, and had well-nigh fallen
Right on their heads. My Lord was sorely frightened;
A fever seized him, and he made confession
Of all the heretical and lawless talk
Which brought this judgment: so the youth was seized
And cast into that hole. My husband's father
Sobbed like a child – it almost broke his heart:
And once as he was working in the cellar,   60
He heard a voice distinctly; 'twas the youth's,
Who sung a doleful song about green fields,
How sweet it were on lake or wild savannah,
To hunt for food, and be a naked man,
And wander up and down at liberty.
He always doted on the youth, and now
His love grew desperate; and defying death,
He made that cunning entrance I described:
And the young man escaped.

MARIA

'Tis a sweet tale: 70
Such as would lull a listening child to sleep,
His rosy face besoiled with unwiped tears. –
And what became of him?

FOSTER-MOTHER

He went on ship-board

---

49. Velez] Valdez [*Remorse*].
58. hole] cell [1800].
60. in the cellar] near the cell [1802].
66. He always] Leoni [1800].
71–72. Om. 1800.

With those bold voyagers, who made discovery
Of golden lands. Leoni's younger brother
Went likewise, and when he returned to Spain,
He told Leoni, that the poor mad youth,
Soon after they arrived in that new world,
In spite of his dissuasion, seized a boat,   80
And all alone, set sail by silent moonlight
Up a great river, great as any sea,
And ne'er was heard of more: but 'tis supposed,
He lived and died among the savage men.

Lines

*left upon a Seat in a Yew-tree which stands near
the Lake of Esthwaite, on a desolate part of the shore,
yet commanding a beautiful prospect*

—————

— Nay, Traveller ! rest. This lonely yew-tree stands
Far from all human dwelling: what if here
No sparkling rivulet spread the verdant herb;
What if these barren boughs the bee not loves;
Yet, if the wind breathe soft, the curling waves,
That break against the shore, shall lull thy mind
By one soft impulse saved from vacancy.

          Who he was
That piled these stones, and with the mossy sod
First covered o'er, and taught this aged tree,   10

10–19.   and taught this aged tree
          With its dark arms to form a circling bower,
          I well remember. – He was one who owned
          No common soul. In youth by science nursed,
          And led by nature into a wild scene   5
          Of lofty hopes, he to the world went forth,
          A favored being, knowing no desire
          Which genius did not hallow, 'gainst the taint
          Of dissolute tongues, and jealousy, and hate
          And scorn, against all enemies prepared,   10

Now wild, to bend its arms in circling shade,
I well remember. – He was one who own'd
No common soul. In youth, by genius nurs'd,
And big with lofty views, he to the world
Went forth, pure in his heart, against the taint
Of dissolute tongues, 'gainst jealousy, and hate,
And scorn, against all enemies prepared,
All but neglect: and so, his spirit damped
At once, with rash disdain he turned away,
And with the food of pride sustained his soul   20
In solitude. – Stranger ! these gloomy boughs
Had charms for him; and here he loved to sit,
His only visitants a straggling sheep,
The stone-chat, or the glancing sand-piper;
And on these barren rocks, with juniper,
And heath, and thistle, thinly sprinkled o'er,
Fixing his downward eye, he many an hour
A morbid pleasure nourished, tracing here
An emblem of his own unfruitful life:
And lifting up his head, he then would gaze   30
On the more distant scene; how lovely 'tis
Thou seest, and he would gaze till it became
Far lovelier, and his heart could not sustain
The beauty still more beauteous. Nor, that time,
Would he forget those beings, to whose minds,

All but neglect. The world, for so it thought,
Owed him no service: he was like a plant
Fair to the sun, the darling of the winds,
But hung with fruit which no one, that passed by,
Regarded, and, his spirit damped at once,   15
With indignation did he turn away, [1800].

(11).   The world, for so it thought,
Owed him no service: wherefore he at once
With indignation turned himself away, [1805].

27. downward] downcast [1800].

34.   Nor, that time,
When Nature had subdued him to herself,
Would he forget those beings, [1800].

Warm from the labours of benevolence,
The world, and man himself, appeared a scene
Of kindred loveliness: then he would sigh
With mournful joy, to think that others felt
What he must never feel: and so, lost man !   40
On visionary views would fancy feed,
Till his eye streamed with tears. In this deep vale
He died, this seat his only monument.

If thou be one whose heart the holy forms
Of young imagination have kept pure,
Stranger ! henceforth be warned; and know, that pride,
Howe'er disguised in its own majesty,
Is littleness; that he, who feels contempt
For any living thing, hath faculties
Which he has never used; that thought with him   50
Is in its infancy. The man, whose eye
Is ever on himself, doth look on one,
The least of nature's works, one who might move
The wise man to that scorn which wisdom holds
Unlawful, ever. O, be wiser thou !
Instructed that true knowledge leads to love,
True dignity abides with him alone
Who, in the silent hour of inward thought,
Can still suspect, and still revere himself,
In lowliness of heart.   60

The Nightingale;

A CONVERSATIONAL POEM,
Written in April, 1798

No cloud, no relique of the sunken day
Distinguishes the West, no long thin slip
Of sullen Light, no obscure trembling hues.

Sub-title: A Conversational Poem] om. 1800.

Come, we will rest on this old mossy Bridge!
You see the glimmer of the stream beneath,
But hear no murmuring: it flows silently
O'er its soft bed of verdure. All is still,
A balmy night! and tho' the stars be dim,
Yet let us think upon the vernal showers
That gladden the green earth, and we shall find   10
A pleasure in the dimness of the stars.
And hark! the Nightingale begins its song,
"Most musical, most melancholy"* Bird!
A melancholy Bird? O idle thought!
In nature there is nothing melancholy.
– But some night-wandering Man, whose heart was pierc'd
With the remembrance of a grievous wrong,
Or slow distemper or neglected love,
(And so, poor Wretch! fill'd all things with himself
And made all gentle sounds tell back the tale   20
Of his own sorrows) he and such as he
First nam'd these notes a melancholy strain;
And many a poet echoes the conceit,
Poet, who hath been building up the rhyme
When he had better far have stretch'd his limbs
Beside a brook in mossy forest-dell
By sun or moonlight, to the influxes
Of shapes and sounds and shifting elements
Surrendering his whole spirit, of his song
And of his fame forgetful! so his fame   30
Should share in nature's immortality,
A venerable thing! and so his song
Should make all nature lovelier, and itself

---

* '*Most musical, most melancholy.*' This passage in Milton possesses
an excellence far superior to that of mere description: it is spoken in the
character of the melancholy Man, and has therefore a *dramatic* propriety.
The Author makes this remark, to rescue himself from the charge of
having alluded with levity to a line in Milton: a charge than which none
could be more painful to him, except perhaps that of having ridiculed
his Bible.

Be lov'd, like nature! – But 'twill not be so;
And youths and maidens most poetical
Who lose the deep'ning twilights of the spring
In ball-rooms and hot theatres, they still
Full of meek sympathy must heave their sighs
O'er Philomela's pity-pleading strains.
My Friend, and my Friend's Sister! we have learnt   40
A different lore: we may not thus profane
Nature's sweet voices always full of love
And joyance! 'Tis the merry Nightingale
That crowds, and hurries, and precipitates
With fast thick warble his delicious notes,
As he were fearful, that an April night
Would be too short for him to utter forth
His love-chant, and disburthen his full soul
Of all its music! And I know a grove
Of large extent, hard by a castle huge   50
Which the great lord inhabits not: and so
This grove is wild with tangling underwood,
And the trim walks are broken up, and grass,
Thin grass and king-cups grow within the paths.
But never elsewhere in one place I knew
So many Nightingales: and far and near
In wood and thicket over the wide grove
They answer and provoke each other's songs –
With skirmish and capricious passagings,
And murmurs musical and swift jug jug   60
And one low piping sound more sweet than all –
Stirring the air with such an harmony,
That should you close your eyes, you might almost
Forget it was not day! On moonlight bushes,
Whose dewy leafits are but half disclos'd,
You may perchance behold them on the twigs,
Their bright, bright eyes, their eyes both bright and full,

64–69. On moonlight . . . love-torch om. 1800.

Glistning, while many a glow-worm in the shade
Lights up her love-torch.

         A most gentle maid
Who dwelleth in her hospitable home   70
Hard by the Castle, and at latest eve,
(Even like a Lady vow'd and dedicate
To something more than nature in the grove)
Glides thro' the pathways; she knows all their notes,
That gentle Maid! and oft, a moment's space,
What time the moon was lost behind a cloud,
Hath heard a pause of silence: till the Moon
Emerging, hath awaken'd earth and sky
With one sensation, and those wakeful Birds
Have all burst forth in choral minstrelsy,   80
As if one quick and sudden Gale had swept
An hundred airy harps! And she hath watch'd
Many a Nightingale perch giddily
On blosmy twig still swinging from the breeze,
And to that motion tune his wanton song,
Like tipsy Joy that reels with tossing head.

Farewell, O Warbler! till to-morrow eve,
And you, my friends! farewell, a short farewell!
We have been loitering long and pleasantly,
And now for our dear homes. – That strain again!   90
Full fain it would delay me! – My dear Babe,
Who, capable of no articulate sound,
Mars all things with his imitative lisp,
How he would place his hand beside his ear,
His little hand, the small forefinger up,
And bid us listen! And I deem it wise
To make him Nature's playmate. He knows well
The evening star: and once when he awoke
In most distressful mood (some inward pain
Had made up that strange thing, an infant's dream)   100

I hurried with him to our orchard plot,
And he beholds the moon, and hush'd at once
Suspends his sobs, and laughs most silently,
While his fair eyes that swam with undropt tears
Did glitter in the yellow moon-beam! Well –
It is a father's tale. But if that Heaven
Should give me life, his childhood shall grow up
Familiar with these songs, that with the night
He may associate Joy! Once more farewell,
Sweet Nightingale! once more, my friends! farewell.   110

The Female Vagrant

By Derwent's side my Father's cottage stood,
(The Woman thus her artless story told)
One field, a flock, and what the neighbouring flood
Supplied, to him were more than mines of gold.
Light was my sleep; my days in transport roll'd:
With thoughtless joy I stretch'd along the shore
My father's nets, or watched, when from the fold
High o'er the cliffs I led my fleecy store,
A dizzy depth below! his boat and twinkling oar.

My father was a good and pious man,   10
An honest man by honest parents bred,
And I believe that, soon as I began

---

1. St. om. 1802.
7.   Or from the mountain fold
     Saw on the distant lake his twinkling oar
     Or watch'd his lazy boat less'ning more and more. [1800].

To lisp, he made me kneel beside my bed,
And in his hearing there my prayers I said:
And afterwards, by my good father taught,
I read, and loved the books in which I read;
For books in every neighbouring house I sought,
And nothing to my mind a sweeter pleasure brought.

Can I forget what charms did once adorn
My garden, stored with pease, and mint, and thyme,   20
And rose and lilly for the sabbath morn?
The sabbath bells, and their delightful chime;
The gambols and wild freaks at shearing time;
My hen's rich nest through long grass scarce espied;
The cowslip-gathering at May's dewy prime;
The swans, that, when I sought the water-side,
From far to meet me came, spreading their snowy pride.

The staff I yet remember which upbore
The bending body of my active sire;
His seat beneath the honeyed sycamore   30
When the bees hummed, and chair by winter fire;
When market-morning came, the neat attire
With which, though bent on haste, myself I deck'd;
My watchful dog, whose starts of furious ire,
When stranger passed, so often I have check'd;
The red-breast known for years, which at my casement peck'd.

The suns of twenty summers danced along, –
Ah! little marked, how fast they rolled away:
Then rose a mansion proud our woods among,
And cottage after cottage owned its sway,   40
No joy to see a neighbouring house, or stray
Through pastures not his own, the master took;

---

19. St. om. 1802.
28. St. om. 1802.
39. mansion proud] stately hall [1800].

My Father dared his greedy wish gainsay;
He loved his old hereditary nook,
And ill could I the thought of such sad parting brook.

But, when he had refused the proffered gold,
To cruel injuries he became a prey,
Sore traversed in whate'er he bought and sold.
His troubles grew upon him day by day,
Till all his substance fell into decay.   50
His little range of water was denied;*
All but the bed where his old body lay,
All, all was seized, and weeping, side by side,
We sought a home where we uninjured might abide.

Can I forget that miserable hour,
When from the last hill-top, my sire surveyed,
Peering above the trees, the steeple tower,
That on his marriage-day sweet music made?
Till then he hoped his bones might there be laid,
Close by my mother in their native bowers: 60
Bidding me trust in God, he stood and prayed, –
I could not pray: – through tears that fell in showers,
Glimmer'd our dear-loved home, alas! no longer ours!

There was a youth whom I had loved so long,
That when I loved him not I cannot say.
'Mid the green mountains many and many a song
We two had sung, like little birds in May.

* Several of the Lakes in the north of England are let out to different
Fishermen, in parcels marked out by imaginary lines drawn from rock
to rock. [*note omitted* 1802]

---

51. They dealt most hardly with him, and he tried
    To move their hearts – but it was vain – for they
    Seized all he had; and, weeping side by side,
    We sought a home where we uninjured might abide. [1802].
55. It was in truth a lamentable hour [1802].
63. I saw our own dear home, that was no longer ours. [1802].
67. little] gladsome [1800].

When we began to tire of childish play
We seemed still more and more to prize each other:
We talked of marriage and our marriage day;⠀⠀⠀⠀⠀⠀70
And I in truth did love him like a brother,
For never could I hope to meet with such another.

His father said, that to a distant town
He must repair, to ply the artist's trade.
What tears of bitter grief till then unknown!
What tender vows our last sad kiss delayed!
To him we turned: – we had no other aid.
Like one revived, upon his neck I wept,
And her whom he had loved in joy, he said
He well could love in grief: his faith he kept;⠀⠀⠀⠀80
And in a quiet home once more my father slept.

Four years each day with daily bread was blest,
By constant toil and constant prayer supplied.
Three lovely infants lay upon my breast;
And often, viewing their sweet smiles, I sighed,
And knew not why. My happy father died
When sad distress reduced the children's meal:
Thrice happy! that from him the grave did hide
The empty loom, cold hearth, and silent wheel,
And tears that flowed for ills which patience could not heal.⠀⠀90

'Twas a hard change, an evil time was come;
We had no hope, and no relief could gain.
But soon, with proud parade, the noisy drum
Beat round, to sweep the streets of want and pain.
My husband's arms now only served to strain
Me and his children hungering in his view:

---

73. Two years were pass'd, since to a distant Town
⠀⠀⠀⠀He had repair'd, to ply the artist's trade. [1802].
82. We lived in peace and comfort; and were blest
⠀⠀⠀⠀With daily bread, by constant toil supplied. [1802].
93. But soon, day after day, the noisy drum [1802].

In such dismay my prayers and tears were vain:
To join those miserable men he flew;
And now to the sea-coast, with numbers more, we drew.

There foul neglect for months and months we bore,   100
Nor yet the crowded fleet its anchor stirred.
Green fields before us and our native shore,
By fever, from polluted air incurred,
Ravage was made, for which no knell was heard.
Fondly we wished, and wished away, nor knew,
'Mid that long sickness, and those hopes deferr'd,
That happier days we never more must view:
The parting signal streamed, at last the land withdrew,

But from delay the summer calms were past.
On as we drove, the equinoctial deep   110
Ran mountains-high before the howling blast.
We gazed with terror on the gloomy sleep
Of them that perished in the whirlwind's sweep,
Untaught that soon such anguish must ensue,
Our hopes such harvest of affliction reap,
That we the mercy of the waves should rue.
We reached the western world, a poor, devoted crew.

Oh! dreadful price of being to resign
All that is dear *in* being! better far

100–106. There, long were we neglected, and we bore
       Much sorrow ere the fleet its anchor weigh'd;
       Green fields before us and our native shore,
       We breath'd a pestilential air that made
       Ravage for which no knell was heard. We pray'd
       For our departure; wish'd and wish'd – nor knew
       'Mid that long sickness, and those hopes delay'd, [1802].
109–113. But the calm summer season now was past.
       On as we drove, the equinoctial Deep
       Ran mountains-high before the howling blast;
       And many perish'd in the whirlwind's sweep. [1802].
   118. St. om. 1802.

In Want's most lonely cave till death to pine,   120
Unseen, unheard, unwatched by any star;
Or in the streets and walks where proud men are,
Better our dying bodies to obtrude,
Than dog-like, wading at the heels of war,
Protract a curst existence, with the brood
That lap (their very nourishment!) their brother's blood.

The pains and plagues that on our heads came down,
Disease and famine, agony and fear,
In wood or wilderness, in camp or town,
It would thy brain unsettle even to hear.   130
All perished – all, in one remorseless year,
Husband and children! one by one, by sword
And ravenous plague, all perished: every tear
Dried up, despairing, desolate, on board
A British ship I waked, as from a trance restored.

Peaceful as some immeasurable plain
By the first beams of dawning light impress'd,
In the calm sunshine slept the glittering main.
The very ocean has its hour of rest,
That comes not to the human mourner's breast.   140
Remote from man, and storms of mortal care,
A heavenly silence did the waves invest;
I looked and looked along the silent air,
Until it seemed to bring a joy to my despair.

Ah! how unlike those late terrific sleeps!
And groans, that rage of racking famine spoke,

140–144. I too was calm, though heavily distress'd!
　　　　Oh me, how quiet sky and ocean were!
　　　　My heart was healed within me, I was bless'd,
　　　　And looked, and looked along the silent air,
　　　　Until it seemed to bring a joy to my despair. [1802].

Where looks inhuman dwelt on festering heaps !
The breathing pestilence that rose like smoke !
The shriek that from the distant battle broke !
The mine's dire earthquake, and the pallid host   150
Driven by the bomb's incessant thunder-stroke
To loathsome vaults, where heart-sick anguish toss'd,
Hope died, and fear itself in agony was lost !

Yet does that burst of woe congeal my frame,
When the dark streets appeared to heave and gape,
While like a sea the storming army came,
And Fire from Hell reared his gigantic shape,
And Murder, by the ghastly gleam, and Rape
Seized their joint prey, the mother and the child !
But from these crazing thoughts my brain, escape !   160
– For weeks the balmy air breathed soft and mild,
And on the gliding vessel Heaven and Ocean smiled.

Some mighty gulph of separation past,
I seemed transported to another world: –
A thought resigned with pain, when from the mast
The impatient mariner the sail unfurl'd,
And whistling, called the wind that hardly curled
The silent sea. From the sweet thoughts of home,
And from all hope I was forever hurled.
For me – farthest from earthly port to roam   170
Was best, could I but shun the spot where man might come.

---

147. The unburied dead that lay in festering heaps. [1800].
154–162. At midnight once the storming Army came,
          Yet do I see the miserable sight,
          The Bayonet, the Soldier, and the Flame
          They followed us and faced us in our flight;
          When Rape and Murder by the ghastly light
          Seized their joint prey, the Mother and the Child!
          But I must leave these thoughts. – From night to night,
          From day to day, the air breathed soft and mild;
          And on the gliding vessel Heaven and Ocean smiled. [1802].

And oft, robb'd of my perfect mind, I thought
At last my feet a resting-place had found:
Here will I weep in peace, (so fancy wrought,)
Roaming the illimitable waters round;
Here watch, of every human friend disowned,
All day, my ready tomb the ocean-flood –
To break my dream the vessel reached its bound:
And homeless near a thousand homes I stood,
And near a thousand tables pined, and wanted food.   180

By grief enfeebled was I turned adrift,
Helpless as sailor cast on desart rock;
Nor morsel to my mouth that day did lift,
Nor dared my hand at any door to knock.
I lay, where with his drowsy mates, the cock
From the cross timber of an out-house hung;
How dismal tolled, that night, the city clock!
At morn my sick heart hunger scarcely stung,
Nor to the beggar's language could I frame my tongue.

So passed another day, and so the third: 190
Then did I try, in vain, the crowd's resort,
In deep despair by frightful wishes stirr'd,
Near the sea-side I reached a ruined fort:
There, pains which nature could no more support,
With blindness linked, did on my vitals fall;
Dizzy my brain, with interruption short
Of hideous sense; I sunk, nor step could crawl,
And thence was borne away to neighbouring hospital.

172–177. And oft I thought (my fancy was so strong)
        That I at last a resting-place had found;
        "Here will I dwell," said I, "my whole life-long,
        Roaming the illimitable waters round:
        Here will I live: – of every friend disown'd,
        Here will I roam about the ocean flood." [1802].
   187. Dismally tolled, that night, the city clock! [1802].
196–198. And I had many interruptions short
        Of hideous sense; I sank, nor step could crawl,
        And thence was carried to a neighbouring Hospital. [1802].

Recovery came with food: but still, my brain
Was weak, nor of the past had memory.   200
I heard my neighbours, in their beds, complain
Of many things which never troubled me;
Of feet still bustling round with busy glee,
Of looks where common kindness had no part,
Of service done with careless cruelty,
Fretting the fever round the languid heart,
And groans, which, as they said, would make a dead man start.

These things just served to stir the torpid sense,
Nor pain nor pity in my bosom raised.
Memory, though slow, returned with strength; and thence   210
Dismissed, again on open day I gazed,
At houses, men, and common light, amazed.
The lanes I sought, and as the sun retired,
Came, where beneath the trees a faggot blazed;
The wild brood saw me weep, my fate enquired,
And gave me food, and rest, more welcome, more desired.

My heart is touched to think that men like these,
The rude earth's tenants, were my first relief:
How kindly did they paint their vagrant ease !
And their long holiday that feared not grief,   220
For all belonged to all, and each was chief.
No plough their sinews strained; on grating road
No wain they drove, and yet, the yellow sheaf
In every vale for their delight was stowed:
For them, in nature's meads, the milky udder flowed.

Semblance, with straw and panniered ass, they made
Of potters wandering on from door to door:

----

210. My memory and my strength returned; and thence [1802].
215. wild brood] Travellers [1802].
218. The rude earth's tenants] Wild houseless Wanderers [1802].
225. In every field, with milk their dairy overflow'd. [1802].
226. They with their pannier'd Asses semblance made [1802].

But life of happier sort to me pourtrayed,
And other joys my fancy to allure;
The bag-pipe dinning on the midnight moor   230
In barn uplighted, and companions boon
Well met from far with revelry secure,
In depth of forest glade, when jocund June
Rolled fast along the sky his warm and genial moon.

But ill it suited me, in journey dark
O'er moor and mountain, midnight theft to hatch;
To charm the surly house-dog's faithful bark,
Or hang on tiptoe at the lifted latch;
The gloomy lantern, and the dim blue match,
The black disguise, the warning whistle shrill,   240
And ear still busy on its nightly watch,
Were not for me, brought up in nothing ill;
Besides, on griefs so fresh my thoughts were brooding still.

What could I do, unaided and unblest?
Poor Father! gone was every friend of thine:
And kindred of dead husband are at best
Small help, and, after marriage such as mine,
With little kindness would to me incline.
Ill was I then for toil or service fit:
With tears whose course no effort could confine,   250
By high-way side forgetful would I sit
Whole hours, my idle arms in moping sorrow knit.

I lived upon the mercy of the fields,
And oft of cruelty the sky accused;

---

233. In depth of forest glade] Among the forest glades [1802].
235. But ill they suited me; those journeys dark [1802].
245. Poor] My [1802].
251. high-way side] the road-side [1802].
253–257. I led a wandering life among the fields;
Contentedly, yet sometimes self-accused,
I liv'd upon what casual bounty yields,
Now coldly given, now utterly refused.
The ground I for my bed have often used: [1802].

On hazard, or what general bounty yields,
Now coldly given, now utterly refused.
The fields I for my bed have often used:
But, what afflicts my peace with keenest ruth
Is, that I have my inner self abused,
Foregone the home delight of constant truth,   260
And clear and open soul, so prized in fearless youth.

Three years a wanderer, often have I view'd,
In tears, the sun towards that country tend
Where my poor heart lost all its fortitude:
And now across this moor my steps I bend –
Oh! tell me whither – for no earthly friend
Have I. – She ceased, and weeping turned away,
As if because her tale was at an end
She wept; – because she had no more to say
Of that perpetual weight which on her spirit lay.   270

Goody Blake, and Harry Gill,

A TRUE STORY

Oh! what's the matter? what's the matter?
What is't that ails young Harry Gill?
That evermore his teeth they chatter,
Chatter, chatter, chatter still.
Of waistcoats Harry has no lack,
Good duffle grey, and flannel fine;
He has a blanket on his back,
And coats enough to smother nine.

In March, December, and in July,
'Tis all the same with Harry Gill;   10
The neighbours tell, and tell you truly,

262. a wanderer,] thus wandering, [1802].

His teeth they chatter, chatter still.
At night, at morning, and at noon,
'Tis all the same with Harry Gill;
Beneath the sun, beneath the moon,
His teeth they chatter, chatter still.

Young Harry was a lusty drover,
And who so stout of limb as he?
His cheeks were red as ruddy clover,
His voice was like the voice of three.   20
Auld Goody Blake was old and poor,
Ill fed she was, and thinly clad;
And any man who pass'd her door,
Might see how poor a hut she had.

All day she spun in her poor dwelling,
And then her three hours' work at night!
Alas! 'twas hardly worth the telling,
It would not pay for candle-light.
– This woman dwelt in Dorsetshire,
Her hut was on a cold hill-side,   30
And in that country coals are dear,
For they come far by wind and tide.

By the same fire to boil their pottage,
Two poor old dames, as I have known,
Will often live in one small cottage,
But she, poor woman, dwelt alone.
'Twas well enough when summer came,
The long, warm, lightsome summer-day,
Then at her door the *canty* dame
Would sit, as any linnet gay.   40

But when the ice our streams did fetter,
Oh! then how her old bones would shake!
You would have said, if you had met her,

21. Auld Goody Blake] Old Goody Blake [1802].

'Twas a hard time for Goody Blake.
Her evenings then were dull and dead;
Sad case it was, as you may think,
For very cold to go to bed,
And then for cold not sleep a wink.

Oh joy for her! when e'er in winter
The winds at night had made a rout,   50
And scatter'd many a lusty splinter,
And many a rotten bough about.
Yet never had she, well or sick,
As every man who knew her says,
A pile before-hand, wood or stick,
Enough to warm her for three days.

Now, when the frost was past enduring,
And made her poor old bones to ache,
Could any thing be more alluring,
Than an old hedge to Goody Blake?   60
And now and then, it must be said,
When her old bones were cold and chill,
She left her fire, or left her bed,
To seek the hedge of Harry Gill.

Now Harry he had long suspected
This trespass of old Goody Blake,
And vow'd that she should be detected,
And he on her would vengeance take.
And oft from his warm fire he'd go,
And to the fields his road would take,   70
And there, at night, in frost and snow,
He watch'd to seize old Goody Blake.

And once, behind a rick of barley,
Thus looking out did Harry stand;
The moon was full and shining clearly,

And crisp with frost the stubble-land.
– He hears a noise – he's all awake –
Again? – on tip-toe down the hill
He softly creeps – 'Tis Goody Blake,
She's at the hedge of Harry Gill.   80

Right glad was he when he beheld her:
Stick after stick did Goody pull,
He stood behind a bush of elder,
Till she had filled her apron full.
When with her load she turned about,
The bye-road back again to take,
He started forward with a shout,
And sprang upon poor Goody Blake.

And fiercely by the arm he took her,
And by the arm he held her fast,   90
And fiercely by the arm he shook her,
And cried, "I've caught you then at last!"
Then Goody, who had nothing said,
Her bundle from her lap let fall;
And kneeling on the sticks, she pray'd
To God that is the judge of all.

She pray'd, her wither'd hand uprearing,
While Harry held her by the arm –
"God! who art never out of hearing,
"O may he never more be warm!"   100
The cold, cold moon above her head,
Thus on her knees did Goody pray,
Young Harry heard what she had said,
And icy-cold he turned away.

He went complaining all the morrow
That he was cold and very chill:
His face was gloom, his heart was sorrow,

Alas! that day for Harry Gill!
That day he wore a riding-coat,
But not a whit the warmer he: 110
Another was on Thursday brought,
And ere the Sabbath he had three.

'Twas all in vain, a useless matter,
And blankets were about him pinn'd;
Yet still his jaws and teeth they clatter,
Like a loose casement in the wind.
And Harry's flesh it fell away;
And all who see him say 'tis plain,
That, live as long as live he may,
He never will be warm again.   120

No word to any man he utters,
A-bed or up, to young or old;
But ever to himself he mutters,
"Poor Harry Gill is very cold."
A-bed or up, by night or day;
His teeth they chatter, chatter still.
Now think, ye farmers all, I pray,
Of Goody Blake and Harry Gill.

Lines

*written at a small distance from my House,
and sent by my little Boy to the
Person to whom they are
addressed*

It is the first mild day of March:
Each minute sweeter than before,
The red-breast sings from the tall larch
That stands beside our door.

There is a blessing in the air,
Which seems a sense of joy to yield
To the bare trees, and mountains bare,
And grass in the green field.

My Sister! ('tis a wish of mine)
Now that our morning meal is done,⁣   10
Make haste, your morning task resign;
Come forth and feel the sun.

Edward will come with you, and pray,
Put on with speed your woodland dress,
And bring no book, for this one day
We'll give to idleness.

No joyless forms shall regulate
Our living Calendar:
We from to-day, my friend, will date
The opening of the year.⁣   20

Love, now an universal birth,
From heart to heart is stealing,
From earth to man, from man to earth,
– It is the hour of feeling.

One moment now may give us more
Than fifty years of reason;
Our minds shall drink at every pore
The spirit of the season.

Some silent laws our hearts may make,
Which they shall long obey;⁣   30
We for the year to come may take
Our temper from to-day.

And from the blessed power that rolls
About, below, above;
We'll frame the measure of our souls,
They shall be tuned to love.

Then come, my sister! come, I pray,
With speed put on your woodland dress,
And bring no book; for this one day
We'll give to idleness.   40

Simon Lee,

the Old Huntsman, with an incident
in which he was concerned

In the sweet shire of Cardigan,
Not far from pleasant Ivor-hall,
An old man dwells, a little man,
I've heard he once was tall.
Of years he has upon his back,
No doubt, a burthen weighty;
He says he is three score and ten,
But others say he's eighty.

A long blue livery-coat has he,
That's fair behind, and fair before;   10
Yet, meet him where you will, you see
At once that he is poor.
Full five and twenty years he lived
A running huntsman merry;
And, though he has but one eye left,
His cheek is like a cherry.

No man like him the horn could sound,
And no man was so full of glee;
To say the least, four counties round

Had heard of Simon Lee;   20
His master's dead, and no one now
Dwells in the hall of Ivor;
Men, dogs, and horses, all are dead;
He is the sole survivor.

His hunting feats have him bereft
Of his right eye, as you may see:
And then, what limbs those feats have left
To poor old Simon Lee!
He has no son, he has no child,
His wife, an aged woman,   30
Lives with him, near the waterfall,
Upon the village common.

And he is lean and he is sick,
His little body's half awry
His ancles they are swoln and thick
His legs are thin and dry.
When he was young he little knew
Of husbandry or tillage;
And now he's forced to work, though weak,
– The weakest in the village.   40

He all the country could outrun,
Could leave both man and horse behind;
And often, ere the race was done,
He reeled and was stone-blind.
And still there's something in the world
At which his heart rejoices;
For when the chiming hounds are out,
He dearly loves their voices!

Old Ruth works out of doors with him,
And does what Simon cannot do;   50

25-32. St. 6 [1802].
  34. little] dwindled [1800].

For she, not over stout of limb,
Is stouter of the two.
And though you with your utmost skill
From labour could not wean them,
Alas! 'tis very little, all
Which they can do between them.

Beside their moss-grown hut of clay,
Not twenty paces from the door,
A scrap of land they have, but they
Are poorest of the poor.   60
This scrap of land he from the heath
Enclosed when he was stronger;
But what avails the land to them,
Which they can till no longer?

Few months of life has he in store,
As he to you will tell,
For still, the more he works, the more
His poor old ancles swell.
My gentle reader, I perceive
How patiently you've waited,   70
And I'm afraid that you expect
Some tale will be related.

O reader! had you in your mind
Such stores as silent thought can bring,
O gentle reader! you would find
A tale in every thing.
What more I have to say is short,
I hope you'll kindly take it;
It is no tale; but should you think,
Perhaps a tale you'll make it.   80

One summer-day I chanced to see
This old man doing all he could

About the root of an old tree,
A stump of rotten wood.
The mattock totter'd in his hand
So vain was his endeavour
That at the root of the old tree
He might have worked for ever.

"You're overtasked, good Simon Lee,
Give me your tool" to him I said;   90
And at the word right gladly he
Received my proffer'd aid.
I struck, and with a single blow
The tangled root I sever'd,
At which the poor old man so long
And vainly had endeavour'd.

The tears into his eyes were brought,
And thanks and praises seemed to run
So fast out of his heart, I thought
They never would have done.   100
– I've heard of hearts unkind, kind deeds
With coldness still returning.
Alas! the gratitude of men
Has oftner left me mourning.

Anecdote for Fathers,

*shewing how the art of lying may be
taught*

I have a boy of five years old,
His face is fair and fresh to see;
His limbs are cast in beauty's mould,
And dearly he loves me.
One morn we stroll'd on our dry walk,
Our quiet house all full in view,
And held such intermitted talk
As we are wont to do.

My thoughts on former pleasures ran;
I thought of Kilve's delightful shore,   10
My pleasant home, when spring began,
A long, long year before.

A day it was when I could bear
To think, and think, and think again;
With so much happiness to spare,
I could not feel a pain.

My boy was by my side, so slim
And graceful in his rustic dress !
And oftentimes I talked to him,
In very idleness.   20

The young lambs ran a pretty race;
The morning sun shone bright and warm;

Title: *art*] *practice* [1800].
  6. house] home [1802].
  11. My] Our [1802].

"Kilve," said I, "was a pleasant place,
"And so is Liswyn farm.

"My little boy, which like you more,"
I said and took him by the arm –
"Our home by Kilve's delightful shore,
"Or here at Liswyn farm?"

"And tell me, had you rather be,"
I said and held him by the arm,
"At Kilve's smooth shore by the green sea,
"Or here at Liswyn farm?

In careless mood he looked at me,
While still I held him by the arm,
And said, "At Kilve I'd rather be
"Than here at Liswyn farm."

"Now, little Edward, say why so;
My little Edward, tell me why;"
"I cannot tell, I do not know."
"Why this is strange," said I.

"For, here are woods and green-hills warm;
"There surely must some reason be
"Why you would change sweet Liswyn farm
"For Kilve by the green sea."

At this, my boy, so fair and slim,
Hung down his head, nor made reply;
And five times did I say to him,
"Why? Edward, tell me why?"

30

40

45–48. At this, my boy hung down his head,
He blush'd with shame, nor made reply;
And five times to the child I said,
"Why, Edward, tell me why?" [1800].

His head he raised – there was in sight,
It caught his eye, he saw it plain –   50
Upon the house-top, glittering bright,
A broad and gilded vane.

Then did the boy his tongue unlock,
And thus to me he made reply;
"At Kilve there was no weather-cock,
"And that's the reason why."

Oh dearest, dearest boy! my heart
For better lore would seldom yearn,
Could I but teach the hundredth part
Of what from thee I learn.   60

We are seven

A simple child, dear brother Jim,
That lightly draws its breath,
And feels its life in every limb,
What should it know of death?

I met a little cottage girl,
She was eight years old, she said;
Her hair was thick with many a curl
That cluster'd round her head.

She had a rustic, woodland air,
And she was wildly clad;   10
Her eyes were fair, and very fair,
– Her beauty made me glad.

"Sisters and brothers, little maid,
"How many may you be?"
"How many? seven in all," she said,
And wondering looked at me.

"And where are they, I pray you tell?"
She answered, "Seven are we,
"And two of us at Conway dwell,
"And two are gone to sea.   20

"Two of us in the church-yard lie,
"My sister and my brother,
"And in the church-yard cottage, I
"Dwell near them with my mother."

"You say that two at Conway dwell,
"And two are gone to sea,
"Yet you are seven; I pray you tell
"Sweet Maid, how this may be?"

Then did the little Maid reply,
"Seven boys and girls are we;   30
"Two of us in the church-yard lie,
"Beneath the church-yard tree."

"You run about, my little maid,
"Your limbs they are alive;
"If two are in the church-yard laid,
"Then ye are only five."

"Their graves are green, they may be seen,"
The little Maid replied,
"Twelve steps or more from my mother's door,
"And they are side by side.   40

"My stockings there I often knit,
"My 'kerchief there I hem;
"And there upon the ground I sit –
"I sit and sing to them.

"And often after sunset, Sir,
"When it is light and fair,
"I take my little porringer,
"And eat my supper there.

"The first that died was little Jane;
"In bed she moaning lay,   50
"Till God released her of her pain,
"And then she went away.

"So in the church-yard she was laid,
"And all the summer dry,
"Together round her grave we played,
"My brother John and I.

"And when the ground was white with snow,
"And I could run and slide,
"My brother John was forced to go,
"And he lies by her side."   60

"How many are you then," said I,
"If they two are in Heaven?"
The little Maiden did reply,
"O Master! we are seven."

"But they are dead; those two are dead!
"Their spirits are in heaven!"
'Twas throwing words away; for still
The little Maid would have her will,
And said, "Nay, we are seven!"

Lines
written in early spring

———

I heard a thousand blended notes,
While in a grove I sate reclined,
In that sweet mood when pleasant thoughts
Bring sad thoughts to the mind.

To her fair works did nature link
The human soul that through me ran;
And much it griev'd my heart to think
What man has made of man.

Through primrose-tufts, in that sweet bower,
The periwinkle trail'd its wreathes;   10
And 'tis my faith that every flower
Enjoys the air it breathes.

The birds around me hopp'd and play'd:
Their thoughts I cannot measure,
But the least motion which they made,
It seem'd a thrill of pleasure.

The budding twigs spread out their fan,
To catch the breezy air;
And I must think, do all I can,
That there was pleasure there.   20

If I these thoughts may not prevent,
If such be of my creed the plan,
Have I not reason to lament
What man has made of man?

The Thorn

I

There is a thorn; it looks so old,
In truth you'd find it hard to say,
How it could ever have been young,
It looks so old and grey.
Not higher than a two-years' child,
It stands erect this aged thorn;
No leaves it has, no thorny points;
It is a mass of knotted joints,
A wretched thing forlorn.
It stands erect, and like a stone   10
With lichens it is overgrown.

II

Like rock or stone, it is o'ergrown
With lichens to the very top,
And hung with heavy tufts of moss,
A melancholy crop:
Up from the earth these mosses creep,
And this poor thorn they clasp it round
So close, you'd say that they were bent
With plain and manifest intent,
To drag it to the ground;   20
And all had joined in one endeavour
To bury this poor thorn for ever.

III

High on a mountain's highest ridge,
Where oft the stormy winter gale
Cuts like a scythe, while through the clouds

It sweeps from vale to vale;
Not five yards from the mountain-path,
This thorn you on your left espy;
And to the left, three yards beyond,
You see a little muddy pond   30
Of water, never dry;
I've measured it from side to side:
'Tis three feet long, and two feet wide.

IV

And close beside this aged thorn,
There is a fresh and lovely sight,
A beauteous heap, a hill of moss,
Just half a foot in height.
All lovely colours there you see,
All colours that were ever seen,
And mossy network too is there,   40
As if by hand of lady fair
The work had woven been,
And cups, the darlings of the eye
So deep is their vermilion dye.

V

Ah me! what lovely tints are there!
Of olive-green and scarlet bright,
In spikes, in branches, and in stars,
Green, red, and pearly white.
This heap of earth o'ergrown with moss
Which close beside the thorn you see,   50
So fresh in all its beauteous dyes,
Is like an infant's grave in size
As like as like can be:
But never, never any where,
An infant's grave was half so fair.

VI

Now would you see this aged thorn,
This pond and beauteous hill of moss,
You must take care and chuse your time
The mountain when to cross.
For oft there sits, between the heap   60
That's like an infant's grave in size,
And that same pond of which I spoke,
A woman in a scarlet cloak,
And to herself she cries,
"Oh misery! oh misery!
"Oh woe is me! oh misery!"

VII

At all times of the day and night
This wretched woman thither goes,
And she is known to every star,
And every wind that blows;   70
And there beside the thorn she sits
When the blue day-light's in the skies,
And when the whirlwind's on the hill,
Or frosty air is keen and still,
And to herself she cries,
"Oh misery! oh misery!
"Oh woe is me! oh misery!"

VIII

"Now wherefore thus, by day and night,
"In rain, in tempest, and in snow,
"Thus to the dreary mountain-top   80
"Does this poor woman go?
"And why sits she beside the thorn
"When the blue day-light's in the sky,
"Or when the whirlwind's on the hill,
"Or frosty air is keen and still,
"And wherefore does she cry? –

"Oh wherefore? wherefore? tell me why
"Does she repeat that doleful cry?"

IX

I cannot tell; I wish I could;
For the true reason no one knows,   90
But if you'd gladly view the spot,
The spot to which she goes;
The heap that's like an infant's grave,
The pond – and thorn, so old and grey,
Pass by her door – 'tis seldom shut –
And if you see her in her hut,
Then to the spot away ! –
I never heard of such as dare
Approach the spot when she is there.

X

"But wherefore to the mountain-top   100
"Can this unhappy woman go,
"Whatever star is in the skies,
"Whatever wind may blow?"
Nay rack your brain – 'tis all in vain,
I'll tell you every thing I know;
But to the thorn, and to the pond
Which is a little step beyond,
I wish that you would go:
Perhaps when you are at the place
You something of her tale may trace.   110

XI

I'll give you the best help I can:
Before you up the mountain go,
Up to the dreary mountain-top,
I'll tell you all I know.
'Tis now some two and twenty years,
Since she (her name is Martha Ray)

Gave with a maiden's true good will
Her company to Stephen Hill;
And she was blithe and gay,
And she was happy, happy still   120
Whene'er she thought of Stephen Hill.

XII

And they had fix'd the wedding-day,
The morning that must wed them both;
But Stephen to another maid
Had sworn another oath;
And with this other maid to church
Unthinking Stephen went –
Poor Martha! on that woful day
A cruel, cruel fire, they say,
Into her bones was sent: 130
It dried her body like a cinder,
And almost turn'd her brain to tinder.

XIII

They say, full six months after this,
While yet the summer-leaves were green,
She to the mountain-top would go,
And there was often seen.
'Tis said, a child was in her womb,
As now to any eye was plain;
She was with child, and she was mad,
Yet often she was sober sad   140
From her exceeding pain.
Oh me! ten thousand times I'd rather
That he had died, that cruel father!

XIV

Sad case for such a brain to hold
Communion with a stirring child!
Sad case, as you may think, for one
Who had a brain so wild!

Last Christmas when we talked of this,
Old Farmer Simpson did maintain,
That in her womb the infant wrought   150
About its mother's heart, and brought
Her senses back again:
And when at last her time drew near,
Her looks were calm, her senses clear.

XV

No more I know, I wish I did,
And I would tell it all to you;
For what became of this poor child
There's none that ever knew:
And if a child was born or no,
There's no one that could ever tell;   160
And if 'twas born alive or dead,
There's no one knows, as I have said,
But some remember well,
That Martha Ray about this time
Would up the mountain often climb.

XVI

And all that winter, when at night
The wind blew from the mountain-peak,
'Twas worth your while, though in the dark,
The church-yard path to seek:
For many a time and oft were heard   170
Cries coming from the mountain-head,
Some plainly living voices were,
And others, I've heard many swear,
Were voices of the dead:
I cannot think, whate'er they say,
They had to do with Martha Ray.

XVII

But that she goes to this old thorn,
The thorn which I've described to you,
And there sits in a scarlet cloak,
I will be sworn is true.   180
For one day with my telescope,
To view the ocean wide and bright,
When to this country first I came,
Ere I had heard of Martha's name,
I climbed the mountain's height:
A storm came on, and I could see
No object higher than my knee.

XVIII

'Twas mist and rain, and storm and rain,
No screen, no fence could I discover,
And then the wind! in faith, it was   190
A wind full ten times over.
I looked around, I thought I saw
A jutting crag, and off I ran,
Head-foremost, through the driving rain,
The shelter of the crag to gain,
And, as I am a man,
Instead of jutting crag, I found
A woman seated on the ground.

XIX

I did not speak – I saw her face,
Her face it was enough for me;   200
I turned about and heard her cry,
"O misery! O misery!"
And there she sits, until the moon
Through half the clear blue sky will go,
And when the little breezes make
The waters of the pond to shake,
As all the country know,

She shudders and you hear her cry,
"Oh misery! oh misery!

XX

"But what's the thorn? and what's the pond?   210
"And what's the hill of moss to her?
"And what's the creeping breeze that comes
"The little pond to stir?"
I cannot tell; but some will say
She hanged her baby on the tree,
Some say she drowned it in the pond,
Which is a little step beyond,
But all and each agree,
The little babe was buried there,
Beneath that hill of moss so fair.   220

XXI

I've heard the scarlet moss is red
With drops of that poor infant's blood;
But kill a new-born infant thus!
I do not think she could.
Some say, if to the pond you go,
And fix on it a steady view,
The shadow of a babe you trace,
A baby and a baby's face,
And that it looks at you;
Whene'er you look on it, 'tis plain   230
The baby looks at you again.

XXII

And some had sworn an oath that she
Should be to public justice brought;
And for the little infant's bones
With spades they would have sought.
But then the beauteous hill of moss

Before their eyes began to stir;
And for full fifty yards around,
The grass it shook upon the ground;
But all do still aver   240
The little babe is buried there,
Beneath that hill of moss so fair.

XXIII

I cannot tell how this may be,
But plain it is, the thorn is bound
With heavy tufts of moss, that strive
To drag it to the ground.
And this I know, full many a time,
When she was on the mountain high,
By day, and in the silent night,
When all the stars shone clear and bright,   250
That I have heard her cry,
"Oh misery! oh misery!
"O woe is me! oh misery!"

The Last of the Flock

In distant countries I have been,
And yet I have not often seen
A healthy man, a man full grown
Weep in the public roads alone.
But such a one, on English ground,
And in the broad high-way, I met;
Along the broad high-way he came,
His cheeks with tears were wet.
Sturdy he seemed, though he was sad;
And in his arms a lamb he had.   10

He saw me, and he turned aside,
As if he wished himself to hide:
Then with his coat he made essay
To wipe those briny tears away.
I follow'd him, and said, "My friend
"What ails you? wherefore weep you so?"
– "Shame on me, Sir! this lusty lamb,
He makes my tears to flow.
To-day I fetched him from the rock;
He is the last of all my flock.   20

When I was young, a single man,
And after youthful follies ran,
Though little given to care and thought,
Yet, so it was, a ewe I bought;
And other sheep from her I raised,
As healthy sheep as you might see,
And then I married, and was rich
As I could wish to be;
Of sheep I number'd a full score,
And every year encreas'd my store.   30

Year after year my stock it grew,
And from this one, this single ewe,
Full fifty comely sheep I raised,
As sweet a flock as ever grazed!
Upon the mountain did they feed;
They throve, and we at home did thrive.
– This lusty lamb of all my store
Is all that is alive:
And now I care not if we die,
And perish all of poverty.   40

Ten children, Sir! had I to feed,
Hard labour in a time of need!
My pride was tamed, and in our grief
I of the parish ask'd relief.
They said I was a wealthy man;
My sheep upon the mountain fed,
And it was fit that thence I took
Whereof to buy us bread:"
"Do this; how can we give to you,"
They cried, "what to the poor is due?"   50

I sold a sheep as they had said,
And bought my little children bread,
And they were healthy with their food;
For me it never did me good.
A woeful time it was for me,
To see the end of all my gains,
The pretty flock which I had reared
With all my care and pains,
To see it melt like snow away!
For me it was a woeful day.   60

Another still! and still another!
A little lamb, and then its mother!
It was a vein that never stopp'd,
Like blood-drops from my heart they dropp'd.
Till thirty were not left alive
They dwindled, dwindled, one by one,
And I may say that many a time
I wished they all were gone:
They dwindled one by one away;
For me it was a woeful day.   70

41. Ten] Six [1800].

To wicked deeds I was inclined,
And wicked fancies cross'd my mind,
And every man I chanc'd to see,
I thought he knew some ill of me.
No peace, no comfort could I find,
No ease, within doors or without,
And crazily, and wearily,
I went my work about.
Oft-times I thought to run away;
For me it was a woeful day.   80

Sir! 'twas a precious flock to me,
As dear as my own children be;
For daily with my growing store
I loved my children more and more.
Alas! it was an evil time;
God cursed me in my sore distress,
I prayed, yet every day I thought
I loved my children less;
And every week, and every day,
My flock, it seemed to melt away.   90

They dwindled, Sir, sad sight to see!
From ten to five, from five to three,
A lamb, a weather, and a ewe;
And then at last, from three to two;
And of my fifty, yesterday
I had but only one,
And here it lies upon my arm,
Alas! and I have none;
To-day I fetched it from the rock
It is the last of all my flock."   100

The Dungeon

And this place our forefathers made for man!
This is the process of our love and wisdom,
To each poor brother who offends against us –
Most innocent, perhaps – and what if guilty?
Is this the only cure? Merciful God?
Each pore and natural outlet shrivell'd up
By ignorance and parching poverty,
His energies roll back upon his heart,
And stagnate and corrupt; till changed to poison,
They break out on him, like a loathsome plague-spot;　10
Then we call in our pamper'd mountebanks –
And this is their best cure! uncomforted
And friendless solitude, groaning and tears,
And savage faces, at the clanking hour,
Seen through the steams and vapour of his dungeon,
By the lamp's dismal twilight! So he lies
Circled with evil, till his very soul
Unmoulds its essence, hopelessly deformed
By sights of ever more deformity!

With other ministrations thou, O nature!　20
Healest thy wandering and distempered child:
Thou pourest on him thy soft influences,
Thy sunny hues, fair forms, and breathing sweets,
Thy melodies of woods, and winds, and waters,
Till he relent, and can no more endure
To be a jarring and a dissonant thing,
Amid this general dance and minstrelsy;

---

1. our] my [*Osorio*. V. i. 107.].
   man] men [*Osorio*. V. i. 107.].
15. steams and vapour] steaming vapours [*Osorio*. V. i. 121.].

But, bursting into tears, wins back his way,
His angry spirit healed and harmonized
By the benignant touch of love and beauty.   30

The Mad Mother

Her eyes are wild, her head is bare,
The sun has burnt her coal-black hair,
Her eye-brows have a rusty stain,
And she came far from over the main.
She has a baby on her arm,
Or else she were alone;
And underneath the hay-stack warm,
And on the green-wood stone,
She talked and sung the woods among;
And it was in the English tongue.   10

"Sweet babe! they say that I am mad,
But nay, my heart is far too glad;
And I am happy when I sing
Full many a sad and doleful thing:
Then, lovely baby, do not fear!
I pray thee have no fear of me,
But, safe as in a cradle, here
My lovely baby! thou shalt be,
To thee I know too much I owe;
I cannot work thee any woe.   20

A fire was once within my brain;
And in my head a dull, dull pain;
And fiendish faces one, two, three,
Hung at my breasts, and pulled at me.
But then there came a sight of joy;

It came at once to do me good;
I waked, and saw my little boy,
My little boy of flesh and blood;
Oh joy for me that sight to see!
For he was here, and only he.   30

Suck, little babe, oh suck again!
It cools my blood; it cools my brain;
Thy lips I feel them, baby! they
Draw from my heart the pain away.
Oh! press me with thy little hand;
It loosens something at my chest;
About that tight and deadly band
I feel thy little fingers press'd.
The breeze I see is in the tree;
It comes to cool my babe and me.   40

Oh! love me, love me, little boy!
Thou art thy mother's only joy;
And do not dread the waves below,
When o'er the sea-rock's edge we go;
The high crag cannot work me harm,
Nor leaping torrents when they howl;
The babe I carry on my arm,
He saves for me my precious soul;
Then happy lie, for blest am I;
Without me my sweet babe would die.   50

Then do not fear, my boy! for thee
Bold as a lion I will be;
And I will always be thy guide,
Through hollow snows and rivers wide
I'll build an Indian bower; I know
The leaves that make the softest bed:
And if from me thou wilt not go,
But still be true 'till I am dead,

My pretty thing! then thou shalt sing,
As merry as the birds in spring. 60

Thy father cares not for my breast,
'Tis thine, sweet baby, there to rest:
'Tis all thine own! and if its hue
Be changed, that was so fair to view,
'Tis fair enough for thee, my dove!
My beauty, little child, is flown;
But thou wilt live with me in love,
And what if my poor cheek be brown?
'Tis well for me; thou canst not see
How pale and wan it else would be. 70

Dread not their taunts, my little life!
I am thy father's wedded wife;
And underneath the spreading tree
We two will live in honesty.
If his sweet boy he could forsake,
With me he never would have stay'd:
From him no harm my babe can take,
But he, poor man! is wretched made,
And every day we two will pray
For him that's gone and far away. 80

I'll teach my boy the sweetest things;
I'll teach him how the owlet sings.
My little babe! thy lips are still,
And thou hast almost suck'd thy fill.
– Where art thou gone my own dear child?
What wicked looks are those I see?
Alas! alas! that look so wild,
It never, never came from me:
If thou art mad, my pretty lad,
Then I must be for ever sad. 90

Oh! smile on me, my little lamb!
For I thy own dear mother am.
My love for thee has well been tried:
I've sought thy father far and wide.
I know the poisons of the shade,
I know the earth-nuts fit for food;
Then, pretty dear, be not afraid;
We'll find thy father in the wood.
Now laugh and be gay, to the woods away!
And there, my babe; we'll live for aye.   100

The Idiot Boy

'Tis eight o'clock, – a clear March night,
The moon is up – the sky is blue,
The owlet in the moonlight air,
He shouts from nobody knows where;
He lengthens out his lonely shout,
Halloo! halloo! a long halloo!

– Why bustle thus about your door,
What means this bustle, Betty Foy?
Why are you in this mighty fret?
And why on horseback have you set   10
Him whom you love, your idiot boy?

Beneath the moon that shines so bright,
Till she is tired, let Betty Foy
With girt and stirrup fiddle-faddle;
But wherefore set upon a saddle
Him whom she loves, her idiot boy?

There's scarce a soul that's out of bed;
Good Betty! put him down again;
His lips with joy they burr at you,
But, Betty! what has he to do   20
With stirrup, saddle, or with rein?

The world will say 'tis very idle,
Bethink you of the time of night;
There's not a mother, no not one,
But when she hears what you have done,
Oh! Betty she'll be in a fright.

But Betty's bent on her intent,
For her good neighbour, Susan Gale,
Old Susan, she who dwells alone,
Is sick, and makes a piteous moan,   30
As if her very life would fail.

There's not a house within a mile,
No hand to help them in distress:
Old Susan lies a bed in pain,
And sorely puzzled are the twain,
For what she ails they cannot guess.
And Betty's husband's at the wood,
Where by the week he doth abide,
A woodman in the distant vale;
There's none to help poor Susan Gale,   40
What must be done? what will betide?

And Betty from the lane has fetched
Her pony, that is mild and good,
Whether he be in joy or pain,
Feeding at will along the lane,
Or bringing faggots from the wood.

And he is all in travelling trim,
And by the moonlight, Betty Foy
Has up upon the saddle set,
The like was never heard of yet,   50
Him whom she loves, her idiot boy.

And he must post without delay
Across the bridge that's in the dale,
And by the church, and o'er the down,
To bring a doctor from the town,
Or she will die, old Susan Gale.

There is no need of boot or spur,
There is no need of whip or wand,
For Johnny has his holly-bough,
And with a hurly-burly now   60
He shakes the green bough in his hand.

And Betty o'er and o'er has told
The boy who is her best delight,
Both what to follow, what to shun,
What do, and what to leave undone,
How turn to left, and how to right.

And Betty's most especial charge,
Was, "Johnny! Johnny! mind that you
"Come home again, nor stop at all,
"Come home again, whate'er befal,   70
"My Johnny do, I pray you do."

To this did Johnny answer make,
Both with his head, and with his hand,
And proudly shook the bridle too,
And then! his words were not a few,
Which Betty well could understand.

And now that Johnny is just going,
Though Betty's in a mighty flurry,
She gently pats the pony's side,
On which her idiot boy must ride,   80
And seems no longer in a hurry.

But when the pony moved his legs,
Oh! then for the poor idiot boy!
For joy he cannot hold the bridle,
For joy his head and heels are idle,
He's idle all for very joy.

And while the pony moves his legs,
In Johnny's left-hand you may see,
The green bough's motionless and dead;
The moon that shines above his head   90
Is not more still and mute than he.

His heart it was so full of glee,
That till full fifty yards were gone,
He quite forgot his holly whip,
And all his skill in horsemanship,
Oh! happy, happy, happy John.

And Betty's standing at the door,
And Betty's face with joy o'erflows,
Proud of herself, and proud of him,
She sees him in his travelling trim;   100
How quietly her Johnny goes.

The silence of her idiot boy,
What hopes it sends to Betty's heart!
He's at the guide-post – he turns right,
She watches till he's out of sight,
And Betty will not then depart.

Burr, burr – now Johnny's lips they burr,
As loud as any mill, or near it,
Meek as a lamb the pony moves,
And Johnny makes the noise he loves,   110
And Betty listens, glad to hear it.

Away she hies to Susan Gale:
And Johnny's in a merry tune,
The owlets hoot, the owlets curr,
And Johnny's lips they burr, burr, burr,
And on he goes beneath the moon.

His steed and he right well agree,
For of this pony there's a rumour,
That should he lose his eyes and ears,
And should he live a thousand years,   120
He never will be out of humour.

But then he is a horse that thinks!
And when he thinks his pace is slack;
Now, though he knows poor Johnny well,
Yet for his life he cannot tell
What he has got upon his back.

So through the moonlight lanes they go,
And far into the moonlight dale,
And by the church, and o'er the down,
To bring a doctor from the town,   130
To comfort poor old Susan Gale.

And Betty, now at Susan's side,
Is in the middle of her story,
What comfort Johnny soon will bring,
With many a most diverting thing,
Of Johnny's wit and Johnny's glory.

And Betty's still at Susan's side:
By this time she's not quite so flurried;
Demure with porringer and plate
She sits, as if in Susan's fate   140
Her life and soul were buried.

But Betty, poor good woman! she,
You plainly in her face may read it,
Could lend out of that moment's store
Five years of happiness or more,
To any that might need it.

But yet I guess that now and then
With Betty all was not so well,
And to the road she turns her ears,
And thence full many a sound she hears,   150
Which she to Susan will not tell.

Poor Susan moans, poor Susan groans,
"As sure as there's a moon in heaven,"
Cries Betty, "he'll be back again;
"They'll both be here, 'tis almost ten,
"They'll both be here before eleven."

Poor Susan moans, poor Susan groans,
The clock gives warning for eleven;
'Tis on the stroke – "If Johnny's near,"
Quoth Betty "he will soon be here,   160
"As sure as there's a moon in heaven."

The clock is on the stroke of twelve,
And Johnny is not yet in sight,
The moon's in heaven, as Betty sees,
But Betty is not quite at ease;
And Susan has a dreadful night.

And Betty, half an hour ago,
On Johnny vile reflections cast;
"A little idle sauntering thing!"
With other names, an endless string, 　　　　170
But now that time is gone and past.

And Betty's drooping at the heart,
That happy time all past and gone,
"How can it be he is so late?
"The doctor he has made him wait,
"Susan! they'll both be here anon."

And Susan's growing worse and worse,
And Betty's in a sad quandary;
And then there's nobody to say
If she must go or she must stay: 　　　　180
– She's in a sad quandary.

The clock is on the stroke of one;
But neither Doctor nor his guide
Appear along the moonlight road,
There's neither horse nor man abroad,
And Betty's still at Susan's side.

And Susan she begins to fear
Of sad mischances not a few,
That Johnny may perhaps be drown'd,
Or lost perhaps, and never found; 　　　　190
Which they must both for ever rue.

She prefaced half a hint of this
With, "God forbid it should be true!"
At the first word that Susan said
Cried Betty, rising from the bed,
"Susan, I'd gladly stay with you.

"I must be gone, I must away,
"Consider, Johnny's but half-wise;
"Susan, we must take care of him,
"If he is hurt in life or limb" –   200
"Oh God forbid!" poor Susan cries.

"What can I do?" says Betty, going,
"What can I do to ease your pain?
"Good Susan tell me, and I'll stay;
"I fear you're in a dreadful way,
"But I shall soon be back again."

"Good Betty go, good Betty go,
"There's nothing that can ease my pain."
Then off she hies, but with a prayer
That God poor Susan's life would spare,   210
Till she comes back again.

So, through the moonlight lane she goes,
And far into the moonlight dale;
And how she ran, and how she walked,
And all that to herself she talked,
Would surely be a tedious tale.

In high and low, above, below,
In great and small, in round and square,
In tree and tower was Johnny seen,
In bush and brake, in black and green,   220
'Twas Johnny, Johnny, every where.

She's past the bridge that's in the dale,
And now the thought torments her sore,
Johnny perhaps his horse forsook,
To hunt the moon that's in the brook,
And never will be heard of more.

And now she's high upon the down,
Alone amid a prospect wide;
There's neither Johnny nor his horse,
Among the fern or in the gorse;   230
There's neither doctor nor his guide.

"Oh saints! what is become of him?
"Perhaps he's climbed into an oak,
"Where he will stay till he is dead;
"Or sadly he has been misled,
"And joined the wandering gypsey-folk.

"Or him that wicked pony's carried
"To the dark cave, the goblins' hall,
"Or in the castle he's pursuing,
"Among the ghosts, his own undoing;   240
"Or playing with the waterfall."

At poor old Susan then she railed,
While to the town she posts away;
"If Susan had not been so ill,
"Alas! I should have had him still,
"My Johnny, till my dying day."

Poor Betty! in this sad distemper,
The doctor's self would hardly spare,
Unworthy things she talked and wild,
Even he, of cattle the most mild,   250
The pony had his share.

And now she's got into the town,
And to the doctor's door she hies;
'Tis silence all on every side;
The town so long, the town so wide,
Is silent as the skies.

And now she's at the doctor's door,
She lifts the knocker, rap, rap, rap,
The doctor at the casement shews,
His glimmering eyes that peep and doze;   260
And one hand rubs his old night-cap.

"Oh Doctor! Doctor! where's my Johnny?"
"I'm here, what is't you want with me?"
"Oh Sir! you know I'm Betty Foy,
"And I have lost my poor dear boy,
"You know him – him you often see;

"He's not so wise as some folks be."
"The devil take his wisdom!" said
The Doctor, looking somewhat grim,
"What, woman! should I know of him?"   270
And, grumbling, he went back to bed.

"O woe is me! O woe is me!
"Here will I die; here will I die;
"I thought to find my Johnny here,
"But he is neither far nor near,
"Oh! what a wretched mother I!"

She stops, she stands, she looks about,
Which way to turn she cannot tell.
Poor Betty! it would ease her pain
If she had heart to knock again;   280
– The clock strikes three – a dismal knell!

Then up along the town she hies,
No wonder if her senses fail,
This piteous news so much it shock'd her,
She quite forgot to send the Doctor,
To comfort poor old Susan Gale.

And now she's high upon the down,
And she can see a mile of road,
"Oh cruel! I'm almost three-score;
"Such night as this was ne'er before,
"There's not a single soul abroad."

She listens, but she cannot hear
The foot of horse, the voice of man;
The streams with softest sound are flowing,
The grass you almost hear it growing,
You hear it now if e'er you can.

The owlets through the long blue night
Are shouting to each other still:
Fond lovers, yet not quite hob nob,
They lengthen out the tremulous sob,
That echoes far from hill to hill.

Poor Betty now has lost all hope,
Her thoughts are bent on deadly sin;
A green-grown pond she just has pass'd,
And from the brink she hurries fast,
Lest she should drown herself therein.

And now she sits her down and weeps;
Such tears she never shed before;
"Oh dear, dear pony! my sweet joy!
"Oh carry back my idiot boy!
"And we will ne'er o'erload thee more."

A thought is come into her head;
"The pony he is mild and good,
"And we have always used him well;
"Perhaps he's gone along the dell,
"And carried Johnny to the wood."

290

300

310

Then up she springs as if on wings;
She thinks no more of deadly sin;
If Betty fifty ponds should see,
The last of all her thoughts would be,   320
To drown herself therein.

Oh reader! now that I might tell
What Johnny and his horse are doing
What they've been doing all this time,
Oh could I put it into rhyme,
A most delightful tale pursuing!

Perhaps, and no unlikely thought!
He with his pony now doth roam
The cliffs and peaks so high that are,
To lay his hands upon a star,   330
And in his pocket bring it home.

Perhaps he's turned himself about,
His face unto his horse's tail,
And still and mute, in wonder lost,
All like a silent horseman-ghost,
He travels on along the vale.

And now, perhaps, he's hunting sheep,
A fierce and dreadful hunter he!
Yon valley, that's so trim and green,
In five months' time, should he be seen,   340
A desart wilderness will be.

Perhaps, with head and heels on fire,
And like the very soul of evil,
He's galloping away, away,
And so he'll gallop on for aye,
The bane of all that dread the devil.

I to the muses have been bound,
These fourteen years, by strong indentures;
Oh gentle muses! let me tell
But half of what to him befel,   350
For sure he met with strange adventures.

Oh gentle muses! is this kind?
Why will ye thus my suit repel?
Why of your further aid bereave me?
And can ye thus unfriended leave me?
Ye muses! whom I love so well.

Who's yon, that, near the waterfall,
Which thunders down with headlong force,
Beneath the moon, yet shining fair,
As careless as if nothing were,   360
Sits upright on a feeding horse?

Unto his horse, that's feeding free,
He seems, I think, the rein to give;
Of moon or stars he takes no heed;
Of such we in romances read,
– 'Tis Johnny! Johnny! as I live.

And that's the very pony too.
Where is she, where is Betty Foy?
She hardly can sustain her fears;
The roaring water-fall she hears,   370
And cannot find her idiot boy.

Your pony's worth his weight in gold,
Then calm your terrors, Betty Foy!
She's coming from among the trees,
And now, all full in view, she sees
Him whom she loves, her idiot boy.

And Betty sees the pony too:
Why stand you thus Good Betty Foy?
It is no goblin, 'tis no ghost,
'Tis he whom you so long have lost,   380
He whom you love, your idiot boy.

She looks again – her arms are up –
She screams – she cannot move for joy;
She darts as with a torrent's force,
She almost has o'erturned the horse,
And fast she holds her idiot boy.

And Johnny burrs and laughs aloud,
Whether in cunning or in joy,
I cannot tell; but while he laughs,
Betty a drunken pleasure quaffs,   390
To hear again her idiot boy.

And now she's at the pony's tail,
And now she's at the pony's head,
On that side now, and now on this,
And almost stifled with her bliss,
A few sad tears does Betty shed.

She kisses o'er and o'er again,
Him whom she loves, her idiot boy,
She's happy here, she's happy there,
She is uneasy every where;   400
Her limbs are all alive with joy.

She pats the pony, where or when
She knows not, happy Betty Foy!
The little pony glad may be,
But he is milder far than she,
You hardly can perceive his joy.

"Oh! Johnny, never mind the Doctor;
"You've done your best, and that is all."
She took the reins, when this was said,
And gently turned the pony's head   410
From the loud water-fall.

By this the stars were almost gone,
The moon was setting on the hill,
So pale you scarcely looked at her:
The little birds began to stir,
Though yet their tongues were still.

The pony, Betty, and her boy,
Wind slowly through the woody dale:
And who is she, be-times abroad.
That hobbles up the steep rough road?   420
Who is it, but old Susan Gale?

Long Susan lay deep lost in thought,
And many dreadful fears beset her,
Both for her messenger and nurse;
And as her mind grew worse and worse,
Her body it grew better.

She turned, she toss'd herself in bed,
On all sides doubts and terrors met her;
Point after point did she discuss;
And while her mind was fighting thus,   430
Her body still grew better.

"Alas! what is become of them?
"These fears can never be endured,
"I'll to the wood." – The word scarce said,
Did Susan rise up from her bed,
As if by magic cured.

Away she posts up hill and down,
And to the wood at length is come,
She spies her friends, she shouts a greeting;
Oh me! it is a merry meeting,   440
As ever was in Christendom.

The owls have hardly sung their last,
While our four travellers homeward wend;
The owls have hooted all night long,
And with the owls began my song,
And with the owls must end.

For while they all were travelling home,
Cried Betty, "Tell us Johnny, do,
"Where all this long night you have been,
"What you have heard, what you have seen,   450
"And Johnny, mind you tell us true."

Now Johnny all night long had heard
The owls in tuneful concert strive;
No doubt too he the moon had seen;
For in the moonlight he had been
From eight o'clock till five.

And thus to Betty's question, he
Made answer, like a traveller bold,
(His very words I give to you,)
"The cocks did crow to-whoo, to-whoo,   460
"And the sun did shine so cold."
– Thus answered Johnny in his glory,
And that was all his travel's story.

Lines

written near Richmond, upon the Thames,
*at Evening**

How rich the wave, in front, imprest
With evening-twilight's summer hues,
While, facing thus the crimson west,
The boat her silent path pursues!
And see how dark the backward stream!
A little moment past, so smiling!
And still, perhaps, with faithless gleam,
Some other loiterer beguiling.

Such views the youthful bard allure,
But, heedless of the following gloom,   10
He deems their colours shall endure
'Till peace go with him to the tomb.
– And let him nurse his fond deceit,

And what if he must die in sorrow!
Who would not cherish dreams so sweet,
Though grief and pain may come to-morrow?

Glide gently, thus for ever glide,
O Thames! that other bards may see,
As lovely visions by thy side
As now, fair river! come to me.   20

---

* In 1800 this poem was divided after the second stanza and
printed as two separate poems. The first [stanzas 1 and 2 above]
was entitled "Lines / written when sailing in a boat at evening."
The second [stanzas 3, 4, 5] was entitled "Lines / written near
Richmond upon the Thames" which title, in 1805, was changed
to "Remembrance of Collins, / written upon the Thames near
Richmond". [See notes.]

4. path] course [1802].

Oh glide, fair stream ! for ever so;
Thy quiet soul on all bestowing,
'Till all our minds for ever flow,
As thy deep waters now are flowing.

Vain thought ! yet be as now thou art,
That in thy waters may be seen
The image of a poet's heart,
How bright, how solemn, how serene !
Such heart did once the poet bless,
Who, pouring here a *later ditty,   30
Could find no refuge from distress,
But in the milder grief of pity.

Remembrance ! as we glide along,
For him suspend the dashing oar,
And pray that never child of Song
May know his freezing sorrows more.
How calm ! how still ! the only sound,
The dripping of the oar suspended !
– The evening darkness gathers round
By virtue's holiest powers attended.   40

* Collins's Ode on the death of Thomson, the last written, I believe
of the poems which were published during his life-time. This Ode is also
alluded to in the next stanza.

---

29. Such heart did once] Such as did once [1800].
33. Now let us, as we float along, [1802].
36. May know that Poet's sorrows more [1802].

Expostulation and Reply

"Why William, on that old grey stone,
"Thus for the length of half a day,
"Why William, sit you thus alone,
"And dream your time away?

"Where are your books? that light bequeath'd
"To beings else forlorn and blind!
"Up! Up! and drink the spirit breath'd
"From dead men to their kind.

"You look round on your mother earth,
"As if she for no purpose bore you;   10
"As if you were her first-born birth,
"And none had lived before you!"

One morning thus, by Esthwaite lake,
When life was sweet I knew not why,
To me my good friend Matthew spake,
And thus I made reply.

"The eye it cannot chuse but see,
"We cannot bid the ear be still;
"Our bodies feel, where'er they be,
"Against, or with our will.   20

"Nor less I deem that there are powers,
"Which of themselves our minds impress,
"That we can feed this mind of ours,
"In a wise passiveness.

"Think you, mid all this mighty sum
"Of things for ever speaking,
"That nothing of itself will come,
"But we must still be seeking?

" – Then ask not wherefore, here, alone,
"Conversing as I may,   30
"I sit upon this old grey stone,
"And dream my time away."

The Tables Turned;

AN EVENING SCENE, ON THE SAME SUBJECT

Up! up! my friend, and clear your looks,
Why all this toil and trouble?
Up! up! my friend, and quit your books,
Or surely you'll grow double.

The sun above the mountain's head,
A freshening lustre mellow,
Through all the long green fields has spread,
His first sweet evening yellow.

Books! 'tis a dull and endless strife,
Come, hear the woodland linnet,   10
How sweet his music; on my life
There's more of wisdom in it.

And hark! how blithe the throstle sings!
And he is no mean preacher;
Come forth into the light of things,
Let Nature be your teacher.

She has a world of ready wealth,
Our minds and hearts to bless –
Spontaneous wisdom breathed by health,
Truth breathed by chearfulness.   20

One impulse from a vernal wood
May teach you more of man;
Of moral evil and of good,
Than all the sages can.

Sweet is the lore which nature brings;
Our meddling intellect
Misshapes the beauteous forms of things;
– We murder to dissect.

Enough of science and of art;
Close up these barren leaves;   30
Come forth, and bring with you a heart
That watches and receives.

Old Man Travelling;

ANIMAL TRANQUILLITY AND DECAY,

A SKETCH

The little hedge-row birds,
That peck along the road, regard him not.
He travels on, and in his face, his step,
His gait, is one expression; every limb,
His look and bending figure, all bespeak
A man who does not move with pain, but moves
With thought – He is insensibly subdued

Title: In 1800 the sub-title was made the title and the words "Old Man
Travelling" discarded.

To settled quiet: he is one by whom
All effort seems forgotten, one to whom
Long patience has such mild composure given, 10
That patience now doth seem a thing, of which
He hath no need. He is by nature led
To peace so perfect, that the young behold
With envy, what the old man hardly feels.
– I asked him whither he was bound, and what
The object of his journey; he replied
"Sir! I am going many miles to take
"A last leave of my son, a mariner,
"Who from a sea-fight has been brought to
      Falmouth,
And there is dying in an hospital." 20

17–20. That he was going many miles to take
        A last leave of his son, a mariner,
        Who from a sea-fight had been brought to Falmouth,
        And there was lying in an hospital. [1800].
  (20). lying] dying [1802].
15–20. om. [1815].

The Complaint
of a forsaken Indian Woman

———

[*When a Northern Indian, from sickness, is unable to continue
his journey with his companions; he is left behind, covered
over with Deer-skins, and is supplied with water, food, and
fuel if the situation of the place will afford it. He is informed
of the track which his companions intend to pursue, and if he
is unable to follow, or overtake them, he perishes alone in the
Desart; unless he should have the good fortune to fall in with
some other Tribes of Indians. It is unnecessary to add that
the females are equally, or still more, exposed to the same fate.**
See that very interesting work*, Hearne's Journey *from*
Hudson's Bay *to the* Northern Ocean. *When the Northern
Lights, as the same writer informs us*,† *vary their position in
the air, they make a rustling and a crackling noise. This
circumstance is alluded to in the first stanza of the following
poem.*]

Before I see another day,
Oh let my body die away!
In sleep I heard the northern gleams;
The stars they were among my dreams;
In sleep did I behold the skies,
I saw the crackling flashes drive;
And yet they are upon my eyes,
And yet I am alive.

---

* The females are equally, or still more, exposed to the same fate
[1802.]

† In the high Northern Latitudes, as the same writer informs us.
when the Northern Lights, etc.; [1800].

Before I see another day,
Oh let my body die away! 10

My fire is dead: it knew no pain;
Yet is it dead, and I remain.
All stiff with ice the ashes lie;
And they are dead, and I will die.
When I was well, I wished to live,
For clothes, for warmth, for food, and fire;
But they to me no joy can give,
No pleasure now, and no desire.
Then here contented will I lie;
Alone I cannot fear to die. 20

Alas! you might have dragged me on
Another day, a single one!
Too soon despair o'er me prevailed;
Too soon my heartless spirit failed;
When you were gone my limbs were stronger,
And Oh how grievously I rue,
That, afterwards, a little longer,
My friends, I did not follow you!
For strong and without pain I lay,
My friends, when you were gone away. 30

My child! they gave thee to another,
A woman who was not thy mother.
When from my arms my babe they took,
On me how strangely did he look!
Through his whole body something ran,
A most strange something did I see;
– As if he strove to be a man,
That he might pull the sledge for me.
And then he stretched his arms, how wild
Oh mercy! like a little child. 40

My little joy! my little pride!
In two days more I must have died.
Then do not weep and grieve for me;
I feel I must have died with thee.
Oh wind that o'er my head art flying,
The way my friends their course did bend,
I should not feel the pain of dying,
Could I with thee a message send.
Too soon, my friends, you went away;
For I had many things to say.   50

I'll follow you across the snow,
You travel heavily and slow:
In spite of all my weary pain,
I'll look upon your tents again.
My fire is dead, and snowy white
The water which beside it stood;
The wolf has come to me to-night,
And he has stolen away my food.
For ever left alone am I,
Then wherefore should I fear to die?   60

My journey will be shortly run,
I shall not see another sun,
I cannot lift my limbs to know
If they have any life or no.
My poor forsaken child! if I
For once could have thee close to me,
With happy heart I then would die,
And my last thoughts would happy be.
I feel my body die away,
I shall not see another day.   70

The Convict

The glory of evening was spread through the west;
  – On the slope of a mountain I stood,
While the joy that precedes the calm season of rest
  Rang loud through the meadow and wood.

'And must we then part from a dwelling so fair?"
  In the pain of my spirit I said,
And with a deep sadness I turned, to repair
  To the cell where the convict is laid.

The thick-ribbed walls that o'ershadow the gate
  Resound; and the dungeons unfold: 10
I pause; and at length, through the glimmering grate,
  That outcast of pity behold.

His black matted head on his shoulder is bent,
  And deep is the sigh of his breath,
And with stedfast dejection his eyes are intent
  On the fetters that link him to death.

'Tis sorrow enough on that visage to gaze,
  That body dismiss'd from his care;
Yet my fancy has pierced to his heart, and **pourtrays**
  More terrible images there.   20

His bones are consumed, and his life-blood **is dried**,
  With wishes the past to undo;
And his crime, through the pains that o'**erwhelm him**, descried,
  Still blackens and grows on his view.

When from the dark synod, or blood-reeking field,
    To his chamber the monarch is led,
All soothers of sense their soft virtue shall yield,
    And quietness pillow his head.

But if grief, self-consumed, in oblivion would doze,
    And conscience her tortures appease,   30
'Mid tumult and uproar this man must repose;
    In the comfortless vault of disease.

When his fetters at night have so press'd on his limbs,
    That the weight can no longer be borne,
If, while a half-slumber his memory bedims,
    The wretch on his pallet should turn,

While the jail-mastiff howls at the dull clanking chain,
    From the roots of his hair there shall start
A thousand sharp punctures of cold-sweating pain,
    And terror shall leap at his heart.   40

But now he half-raises his deep-sunken eye,
    And the motion unsettles a tear;
The silence of sorrow it seems to supply,
    And asks of me why I am here.

"Poor victim! no idle intruder has stood
    "With o'erweening complacence our state to compare,
"But one, whose first wish is the wish to be good,
    "Is come as a brother thy sorrows to share.

"At thy name though compassion her nature resign,
    "Though in virtue's proud mouth thy report be a stain,   50
"My care, if the arm of the mighty were mine,
    "Would plant thee where yet thou might'st blossom again.'

Lines

written a few miles above Tintern Abbey,

ON REVISITING THE BANKS OF THE WYE
DURING A TOUR,

July 13, 1798

Five years have passed; five summers, with the length
Of five long winters! and again I hear
These waters, rolling from their mountain-springs
With a sweet inland murmur.* – Once again
Do I behold these steep and lofty cliffs,
Which on a wild secluded scene impress
Thoughts of more deep seclusion; and connect
The landscape with the quiet of the sky.
The day is come when I again repose
Here, under this dark sycamore, and view   10
These plots of cottage-ground, these orchard-tufts,
Which, at this season, with their unripe fruits,
Among the woods and copses lose themselves,
Nor, with their green and simple hue, disturb
The wild green landscape. Once again I see
These hedge-rows, hardly hedge-rows, little lines
Of sportive wood run wild; these pastoral farms
Green to the very door; and wreathes of smoke
Sent up, in silence, from among the trees,
With some uncertain notice, as might seem,   20

* The river is not affected by the tides a few miles above Tintern.

13–15. Are clad in one green hue, and lose themselves
          Among the woods and copses, nor disturb
          The wild green landscape. [1802].
19–20. And the low copses – coming from the trees. [1798 cancel. in errat.].

Of vagrant dwellers in the houseless woods,
Or of some hermit's cave, where by his fire
The hermit sits alone.

                    Though absent long,
These forms of beauty have not been to me,
As is a landscape to a blind man's eye:
But oft, in lonely rooms, and mid the din
Of towns and cities, I have owed to them,
In hours of weariness, sensations sweet,
Felt in the blood, and felt along the heart,
And passing even into my purer mind   30
With tranquil restoration: – feelings too
Of unremembered pleasure; such, perhaps,
As may have had no trivial influence
On that best portion of a good man's life;
His little, nameless, unremembered acts
Of kindness and of love. Nor less, I trust,
To them I may have owed another gift,
Of aspect more sublime; that blessed mood,
In which the burthen of the mystery,
In which the heavy and the weary weight   40
Of all this unintelligible world
Is lighten'd: – that serene and blessed mood,
In which the affections gently lead us on,
Until, the breath of this corporeal frame,
And even the motion of our human blood
Almost suspended, we are laid asleep
In body, and become a living soul:
While with an eye made quiet by the power
Of harmony, and the deep power of joy,
We see into the life of things.

23–24.   These beauteous forms,
        Through a long absence, have not been to me [1827].

If this   50
Be but a vain belief, yet, oh ! how oft,
In darkness, and amid the many shapes
Of joyless day-light; when the fretful stir
Unprofitable, and the fever of the world,
Have hung upon the beatings of my heart,
How oft, in spirit, have I turned to thee
O sylvan Wye ! Thou wanderer through the woods,
How often has my spirit turned to thee !

And now, with gleams of half-extinguish'd thought,
With many recognitions dim and faint,   60
And somewhat of a sad perplexity,
The picture of the mind revives again:
While here I stand, not only with the sense
Of present pleasure, but with pleasing thoughts
That in this moment there is life and food
For future years. And so I dare to hope
Though changed, no doubt, from what I was, when first
I came among these hills; when like a roe
I bounded o'er the mountains, by the sides
Of the deep rivers, and the lonely streams,   70
Wherever nature led; more like a man
Flying from something that he dreads, than one
Who sought the thing he loved. For nature then
(The coarser pleasures of my boyish days,
And their glad animal movements all gone by,)
To me was all in all. – I cannot paint
What then I was. The sounding cataract
Haunted me like a passion: the tall rock,
The mountain, and the deep and gloomy wood,
Their colours and their forms, were then to me   80
An appetite: a feeling and a love,
That had no need of a remoter charm,
By thought supplied, or any interest

Unborrowed from the eye. – That time is past,
And all its aching joys are now no more,
And all its dizzy raptures. Not for this
Faint I, nor mourn nor murmur: other gifts
Have followed, for such loss, I would believe,
Abundant recompence. For I have learned
To look on nature, not as in the hour　　　　　　　　90
Of thoughtless youth, but hearing oftentimes
The still, sad music of humanity,
Not harsh nor grating, though of ample power
To chasten and subdue. And I have felt
A presence that disturbs me with the joy
Of elevated thoughts; a sense sublime
Of something far more deeply interfused,
Whose dwelling is the light of setting suns,
And the round ocean, and the living air,
And the blue sky, and in the mind of man,　　　　　100
A motion and a spirit, that impels
All thinking things, all objects of all thought,
And rolls through all things. Therefore am I still
A lover of the meadows and the woods,
And mountains; and of all that we behold
From this green earth; of all the mighty world
Of eye and ear, both what they half-create,*
And what perceive; well pleased to recognize
In nature and the language of the sense,
The anchor of my purest thoughts, the nurse,　　　110
The guide, the guardian of my heart, and soul
Of all my moral being.

　　　　　　　　　　　Nor, perchance,
If I were not thus taught, should I the more
Suffer my genial spirits to decay:
For thou art with me, here, upon the banks

* This line has a close resemblance to an admirable line of Young, the exact expression of which I cannot recollect.

Of this fair river; thou, my dearest Friend,
My dear, dear Friend, and in thy voice I catch
The language of my former heart, and read
My former pleasures in the shooting lights
Of thy wild eyes. Oh! yet a little while   120
May I behold in thee what I was once,
My dear, dear Sister! And this prayer I make,
Knowing that Nature never did betray
The heart that loved her; 'tis her privilege,
Through all the years of this our life, to lead
From joy to joy: for she can so inform
The mind that is within us, so impress
With quietness and beauty, and so feed
With lofty thoughts, that neither evil tongues,
Rash judgments, nor the sneers of selfish men,   130
Nor greetings where no kindness is, nor all
The dreary intercourse of daily life,
Shall e'er prevail against us, or disturb
Our chearful faith that all which we behold
Is full of blessings. Therefore let the moon
Shine on thee in thy solitary walk;
And let the misty mountain winds be free
To blow against thee: and in after years,
When these wild ecstasies shall be matured
Into a sober pleasure, when thy mind   140
Shall be a mansion for all lovely forms,
Thy memory be as a dwelling-place
For all sweet sounds and harmonies; Oh! then,
If solitude, or fear, or pain, or grief,
Should be thy portion, with what healing thoughts
Of tender joy wilt thou remember me,
And these my exhortations! Nor, perchance,
If I should be, where I no more can hear
Thy voice, nor catch from thy wild eyes these gleams
Of past existence, wilt thou then forget   150
That on the banks of this delightful stream

We stood together; and that I, so long
A worshipper of Nature, hither came,
Unwearied in that service: rather say
With warmer love, oh! with far deeper zeal
Of holier love. Nor wilt thou then forget,
That after many wanderings, many years
Of absence, these steep woods and lofty cliffs,
And this green pastoral landscape, were to me
More dear, both for themselves, and for thy sake.   160

Love

All Thoughts, all Passions, all Delights,
Whatever stirs this mortal Frame,
All are but Ministers of Love,
    And feed his sacred flame.

Oft in my waking dreams do I   5
Live o'er again that happy hour,
When midway on the Mount I lay
    Beside the Ruin'd Tower.

Title: In the first version which appeared in the *Morning Post* (*v.* Notes) the title was *Introduction to the Tale of the Dark Ladie.* The opening stanzas of the poem as it appeared in the *Morning Post* were

O leave the Lilly on its stem;
    O leave the Rose upon the spray;
O leave the Elder-bloom, fair Maids!
    And listen to my lay.

A Cypress and a Myrtle bough,
    This morn around my harp you twin'd,
Because it fashion'd mournfully
    Its murmurs in the wind.

And now a Tale of Love and Woe,
    A woeful Tale of Love I sing:
Hark, gentle Maidens, hark! it sighs
    And trembles on the string.

But most, my own dear Genevieve!
    It sighs and trembles most for thee!
O come and hear what cruel wrongs
    Befel the dark Ladie.

The opening stanza in the present text was the sixth stanza in the *Morning Post* version, and the fifth stanza of the present text was the fifth stanza in the *Morning Post* version.

5–6. O ever in my waking dreams
      I dwell upon [*M.P.*]
  7. lay] sate [*M.P.*]

The Moonshine stealing o'er the scene
Had blended with the Lights of Eve;   10
And she was there, my Hope, my Joy,
    My own dear Genevieve!

She lean'd against the Armed Man,
The Statue of the Armed Knight:
She stood and listen'd to my Harp   15
    Amid the ling'ring Light.

Few Sorrows hath she of her own,
My Hope, my Joy, my Genevieve!
She loves me best, whene'er I sing
    The Songs, that make her grieve.   20

I play'd a soft and doleful Air,
I sang an old and moving Story –
An old rude Song that fitted well
    The Ruin wild and hoary.

She listen'd with a flitting Blush,   25
With downcast Eyes and modest Grace;
For well she knew, I could not choose
    But gaze upon her Face.

I told her of the Knight, that wore
Upon his Shield a burning Brand;   30
And that for ten long Years he woo'd
    The Lady of the Land.

I told her, how he pin'd: and, ah!
The low, the deep, the pleading tone,
With which I sang another's Love,   35
    Interpreted my own.

---

21. soft] sad [*M.P.*]

She listen'd with a flitting Blush,
With downcast Eyes and modest Grace;
And she forgave me, that I gaz'd
    Too fondly on her Face !   40

But when I told the cruel scorn
Which craz'd this bold and lovely Knight,
And that he cross'd the mountain woods
    Nor rested day nor night;

That sometimes from the savage Den,   45
And sometimes from the darksome Shade,
And sometimes starting up at once
    In green and sunny Glade,

There came, and look'd him in the face,
An Angel beautiful and bright;   50
And that he knew, it was a Fiend,
    This miserable Knight !

And that, unknowing what he did,
He leapt amid a murd'rous Band,
And sav'd from Outrage worse than Death   55
    The Lady of the Land;

And how she wept and clasp'd his knees
And how she tended him in vain –
And ever strove to expiate
    The Scorn, that craz'd his Brain.   60

---

43. And that he cross'd] And how he roam'd [*M.P.*]
44–45. And how he cross'd the Woodman's paths
    Tho' briars and swampy mosses beat,
    How boughs rebounding scourg'd his limbs,
    And low stubs gor'd his feet. [*M.P.*]
45. That] How [*M.P.*]
53. And that,] And how, [1802].
54. murd'rous] lawless [*M.P.*]
59. ever] meekly [*M.P.*]

And that she nurs'd him in a Cave;
And how his Madness went away
When on the yellow forest leaves
　　A dying Man he lay;

His dying words – but when I reach'd   65
That tenderest strain of all the Ditty,
My falt'ring Voice and pausing Harp
　　Disturb'd her Soul with Pity!

All Impulses of Soul and Sense
Had thrill'd my guileless Genevieve,   70
The Music, and the doleful Tale,
　　The rich and balmy Eve;

And Hopes, and Fears that kindle Hope,
An undistinguishable Throng!
And gentle Wishes long subdued,   75
　　Subdued and cherish'd long!

She wept with pity and delight,
She blush'd with love and maiden shame;
And, like the murmur of a dream,
　　I heard her breathe my name.   80

Her Bosom heav'd – she stepp'd aside;
As conscious of my Look, she stepp'd –
Then suddenly with timorous eye
　　She fled to me and wept.

80–81. I saw her bosom heave and swell,
　　Heave and swell with inward sighs –
　　I could not choose but love to see
　　Her gentle bosom rise. [*M.P.*]
81. Her Bosom heav'd] Her wet cheek glowed [*M.P.*]
84. fled] flew [*M.P.*]

She half inclosed me with her arms,   85
She press'd me with a meek embrace;
And bending back her head look'd up,
    And gaz'd upon my face.

'Twas partly Love, and partly Fear,
And partly 'twas a bashful Art   90
That I might rather feel than see
    The Swelling of her Heart.

I calm'd her fears; and she was calm,
And told her love with virgin Pride.
And so I won my Genevieve,   95
    My bright and beauteous Bride!

At the end of the text the *Morning Post* version adds three
stanzas: –
    And now once more a tale of woe,
    A woeful tale of love I sing;
    For thee, my Genevieve! it sighs,
    And trembles on the string.

    When last I sang the cruel scorn
    That craz'd this bold and lonely knight,
    And how he roam'd the mountain woods,
    Nor rested day or night;

    I promis'd thee a sister tale
    Of Man's perfidious Cruelty;
    Come, then, and hear what cruel wrong
    Befel the Dark Ladie.

The Latin epigraph opposite was taken by Wordsworth from Selden's foreword to Drayton's *Polyolbion* and is a private joke against the lawyer Sir James Mackintosh. Translated the phrase means 'Something not at all to your taste, Papinianus'.

[Papinianus was a Roman Lawyer.]

LYRICAL BALLADS,

WITH

OTHER POEMS.

IN TWO VOLUMES.

By W. WORDSWORTH.

─────────

Quam nihil ad genium, Papiniane, tuum!

VOL. II.

LONDON:
PRINTED FOR T. N. LONGMAN AND O. REES, PATERNOSTER-ROW,
BY BIGGS AND CO. BRISTOL.
1800.

Hart-Leap Well

Hart-Leap Well is a small spring of water, about five miles from Richmond in Yorkshire, and near the side of the road which leads from Richmond to Askrigg. Its name is derived from a remarkable chace, the memory of which is preserved by the monuments spoken of in the second Part of the following Poem, which monuments do now exist as I have there described them.

The Knight had ridden down from Wensley moor
With the slow motion of a summer's cloud;
He turn'd aside towards a Vassal's door,
And, "Bring another Horse!" he cried aloud.

"Another Horse!" – That shout the Vassal heard,
And saddled his best steed, a comely Grey;
Sir Walter mounted him; he was the third
Which he had mounted on that glorious day.

Joy sparkled in the prancing Courser's eyes;
The horse and horseman are a happy pair;   10
But, though Sir Walter like a falcon flies,
There is a doleful silence in the air.

A rout this morning left Sir Walter's Hall,
That as they gallop'd made the echoes roar;
But horse and man are vanish'd, one and all;
Such race, I think, was never seen before.

Sir Walter, restless as a veering wind,
Calls to the few tired dogs that yet remain:
Brach, Swift and Music, noblest of their kind,
Follow, and up the weary mountain strain.   20

The Knight halloo'd, he chid and cheer'd them on
With suppliant gestures and upbraidings stern;
But breath and eye-sight fail, and, one by one,
The dogs are stretch'd among the mountain fern.

Where is the throng, the tumult of the chace?
The bugles that so joyfully were blown?
– This race it looks not like an earthly race;
Sir Walter and the Hart are left alone.

The poor Hart toils along the mountain side;
I will not stop to tell how far he fled,   30
Nor will I mention by what death he died;
But now the Knight beholds him lying dead.

Dismounting then, he lean'd against a thorn;
He had no follower, dog, nor man, nor boy:
He neither smack'd his whip, nor blew his horn,
But gaz'd upon the spoil with silent joy.

Close to the thorn on which Sir Walter lean'd,
Stood his dumb partner in this glorious act;
Weak as a lamb the hour that it is yean'd,
And foaming like a mountain cataract.   40

Upon his side the Hart was lying stretch'd:
His nose half-touch'd a spring beneath a hill,
And with the last deep groan his breath had fetch'd
The waters of the spring were trembling still.

---

20. And weary up the mountain strain. [can. errat. 1800].
25. chace] race [1802].
27. – This Chase it looks not like an earthly Chase [1802].

And now, too happy for repose or rest,
Was never man in such a joyful case,
Sir Walter walk'd all round, north, south and west,
And gaz'd, and gaz'd upon that darling place.

And turning up the hill, it was at least
Nine roods of sheer ascent, Sir Walter found   50
Three several marks which with his hoofs the beast
Had left imprinted on the verdant ground.

Sir Walter wiped his face, and cried, "Till now
Such sight was never seen by living eyes:
Three leaps have borne him from this lofty brow,
Down to the very fountain where he lies.

I'll build a Pleasure-house upon this spot,
And a small Arbour, made for rural joy;
'Twill be the traveller's shed, the pilgrim's cot,
A place of love for damsels that are coy.   60

A cunning Artist will I have to frame
A bason for that fountain in the dell;
And they, who do make mention of the same,
From this day forth, shall call it Hart-leap Well.

And, gallant brute! to make thy praises known,
Another monument shall here be rais'd;
Three several pillars, each a rough hewn stone,
And planted where thy hoofs the turf have graz'd.

And in the summer-time when days are long,
I will come hither with my paramour,   70
And with the dancers, and the minstrel's song,
We will make merry in that pleasant bower.

---

49. turning] climbing [1802].
51. Three several hoof-marks which the hunted Beast [1802].

Till the foundations of the mountains fail
My mansion with its arbour shall endure,
– The joy of them who till the fields of Swale,
And them who dwell among the woods of Ure."

Then home he went, and left the Hart, stone-dead,
With breathless nostrils stretch'd above the spring.
And soon the Knight perform'd what he had said,
The fame whereof through many a land did ring.   80

Ere thrice the moon into her port had steer'd,
A cup of stone receiv'd the living well;
Three pillars of rude stone Sir Walter rear'd,
And built a house of pleasure in the dell.

And near the fountain, flowers of stature tall
With trailing plants and trees were intertwin'd,
Which soon composed a little sylvan hall,
A leafy shelter from the sun and wind.

And thither, when the summer days were long,
Sir Walter journey'd with his paramour;   90
And with the dancers and the minstrel's song
Made merriment within that pleasant bower.

The Knight, Sir Walter, died in course of time,
And his bones lie in his paternal vale. –
But there is matter for a second rhyme,
And I to this would add another tale.

PART SECOND

The moving accident is not my trade,
To freeze the blood I have no ready arts;
'Tis my delight, alone in summer shade,
To pipe a simple song to thinking hearts.   100

---

98. freeze] curl [1800, corr. to freeze, second errat.]

As I from Hawes to Richmond did repair,
It chanc'd that I saw standing in a dell
Three aspins at three corners of a square,
And one, not four yards distant, near a well.

What this imported I could ill divine,
And, pulling now the rein my horse to stop,
I saw three pillars standing in a line,
The last stone pillar on a dark hill-top.

The trees were grey, with neither arms nor head;
Half-wasted the square mound of tawny green;   110
So that you just might say, as then I said,
"Here in old time the hand of man has been."

I look'd upon the hills both far and near;
More doleful place did never eye survey;
It seem'd as if the spring-time came not here,
And Nature here were willing to decay.

I stood in various thoughts and fancies lost,
When one who was in Shepherd's garb attir'd,
Came up the hollow. Him did I accost,
And what this place might be I then inquir'd.   120

The Shepherd stopp'd, and that same story told
Which in my former rhyme I have rehears'd.
"A jolly place," said he, "in times of old,
But something ails it now; the spot is curs'd.

You see these lifeless stumps of aspin wood,
Some say that they are beeches, others elms,
These were the Bower; and here a Mansion stood,
The finest palace of a hundred realms.

103. aspins] misprinted aspins [1800: 1802 throughout].

The arbour does its own condition tell,
You see the stones, the fountain, and the stream,   130
But as to the great Lodge, you might as well
Hunt half a day for a forgotten dream.

There's neither dog nor heifer, horse nor sheep,
Will wet his lips within that cup of stone;
And, oftentimes, when all are fast asleep,
This water doth send forth a dolorous groan.

Some say that here a murder has been done,
And blood cries out for blood: but, for my part,
I've guess'd, when I've been sitting in the sun,
That it was all for that unhappy Hart.   140

What thoughts must through the creature's brain have
        pass'd!
From the stone on the summit of the steep
Are but three bounds, and look, Sir, at this last!
O Master! it has been a cruel leap.

For thirteen hours he ran a desperate race;
And in my simple mind we cannot tell
What cause the Hart might have to love this place,
And come and make his death-bed near the well.

Here on the grass perhaps asleep he sank,
Lull'd by this fountain in the summer-tide;   150
This water was perhaps the first he drank
When he had wander'd from his mother's side.

In April here beneath the scented thorn
He heard the birds their morning carols sing,
And he, perhaps, for aught we know, was born
Not half a furlong from that self-same spring.

142. To this place from the stone upon the steep [can. errat. 1800].
142. From the stone upon the summit of the steep [1802].

But now here's neither grass nor pleasant shade;
The sun on drearier hollow never shone:
So will it be, as I have often said,
Till trees, and stones, and fountain all are gone." 160

"Grey-headed Shepherd, thou hast spoken well;
Small difference lies between thy creed and mine;
This beast not unobserv'd by Nature fell,
His death was mourn'd by sympathy divine.

The Being, that is in the clouds and air,
That is in the green leaves among the groves,
Maintains a deep and reverential care
For them the quiet creatures whom he loves.

The Pleasure-house is dust: — behind, before,
This is no common waste, no common gloom; 170
But Nature, in due course of time, once more
Shall here put on her beauty and her bloom.

She leaves these objects to a slow decay
That what we are, and have been, may be known;
But, at the coming of the milder day,
These monuments shall all be overgrown.

One lesson, Shepherd, let us two divide,
Taught both by what she shews, and what conceals,
Never to blend our pleasure or our pride
With sorrow of the meanest thing that feels. 180

There was a Boy, ye knew him well, ye Cliffs
And Islands of Winander! many a time,
At evening, when the stars had just begun
To move along the edges of the hills,
Rising or setting, would he stand alone,
Beneath the trees, or by the glimmering lake,
And there, with fingers interwoven, both hands
Press'd closely palm to palm and to his mouth
Uplifted, he, as through an instrument,
Blew mimic hootings to the silent owls   10
That they might answer him. And they would shout
Across the wat'ry vale and shout again
Responsive to his call, with quivering peals,
And long halloos, and screams, and echoes loud
Redoubled and redoubled, a wild scene
Of mirth and jocund din. And, when it chanced
That pauses of deep silence mock'd his skill,
Then, sometimes, in that silence, while he hung
Listening, a gentle shock of mild surprize
Has carried far into his heart the voice   20
Of mountain torrents, or the visible scene
Would enter unawares into his mind
With all its solemn imagery, its rocks,
Its woods, and that uncertain heaven, receiv'd
Into the bosom of the steady lake.

15. a wild scene] concourse wild [1805].
25. Followed by
     This Boy was taken from his Mates, and died
     In childhood, ere he was ten years old. [1805].

Fair are the woods, and beauteous is the spot,
The vale where he was born: the Church-yard hangs
Upon a slope above the village school,
And there along that bank when I have pass'd
At evening, I believe, that near his grave   30
A full half-hour together I have stood,
Mute – for he died when he was ten years old.

*The Brothers**

These Tourists, Heaven preserve us ! needs must live
A profitable life: some glance along,
Rapid and gay, as if the earth were air,
And they were butterflies to wheel about
Long as their summer lasted; some, as wise,
Upon the forehead of a jutting crag
Sit perch'd with book and pencil on their knee,
And look and scribble, scribble on and look,
Until a man might travel twelve stout miles,
Or reap an acre of his neighbour's corn.   10

But, for that moping son of Idleness
Why can he tarry *yonder*? – In our church-yard
Is neither epitaph nor monument,
Tomb-stone nor name, only the turf we tread,

* This Poem was intended to be the concluding poem of a series of pastorals, the scene of which was laid among the mountains of Cumberland and Westmoreland. I mention this to apologise for the abruptness with which the poem begins.

30. that near his grave] that oftentimes [1805].
32. Mute – looking at the grave in which he lies. [1805].

And a few natural graves. To Jane, his Wife,
Thus spake the homely Priest of Ennerdale.
It was a July evening, and he sate
Upon the long stone-seat beneath the eaves
Of his old cottage, as it chanced that day,
Employ'd in winter's work. Upon the stone   20
His Wife sate near him, teasing matted wool,
While, from the twin cards tooth'd with glittering wire,
He fed the spindle of his youngest child,
Who turn'd her large round wheel in the open air
With back and forward steps. Towards the field
In which the parish chapel stood alone,
Girt round with a bare ring of mossy wall,
While half an hour went by, the Priest had sent
Many a long look of wonder, and at last,
Risen from his seat, beside the snow-white ridge   30
Of carded wool which the old Man had piled
He laid his implements with gentle care,
Each in the other lock'd; and, down the path
Which from his cottage to the church-yard led,
He took his way, impatient to accost
The Stranger, whom he saw still lingering there.

'Twas one well known to him in former days,
A Shepherd-lad: who ere his thirteenth year
Had chang'd his calling, with the mariners
A fellow-mariner, and so had fared   40
Through twenty seasons; but he had been rear'd
Among the mountains, and he in his heart
Was half a Shepherd on the stormy seas.
Oft in the piping shrouds had Leonard heard
The tones of waterfalls, and inland sounds
Of caves and trees; and when the regular wind
Between the tropics fill'd the steady sail

---

30. snow-white] snowy [1800 amend. second errat.].

And blew with the same breath through days and weeks,
Lengthening invisibly its weary line
Along the cloudless main, he, in those hours   50
Of tiresome indolence would often hang
Over the vessel's side, and gaze and gaze,
And, while the broad green wave and sparkling foam
Flash'd round him images and hues, that wrought
In union with the employment of his heart,
He, thus by feverish passion overcome,
Even with the organs of his bodily eye,
Below him, in the bosom of the deep
Saw mountains, saw the forms of sheep that graz'd
On verdant hills, with dwellings among trees,   60
And Shepherds clad in the same country grey
Which he himself had worn.*
                              And now at length,
From perils manifold, with some small wealth
Acquir'd by traffic in the Indian Isles,
To his paternal home he is return'd,
With a determin'd purpose to resume
The life which he liv'd there, both for the sake
Of many darling pleasures, and the love
Which to an only brother he has borne   70
In all his hardships, since that happy time
When, whether it blew foul or fair, they two
Were brother Shepherds on their native hills.
– They were the last of all their race; and now,
When Leonard had approach'd his home, his heart
Fail'd in him, and, not venturing to inquire
Tidings of one whom he so dearly lov'd,
Towards the church-yard he had turn'd aside,
That, as he knew in what particular spot
His family were laid, he thence might learn   80

---

* This description of the Calenture is sketched from an imperfect
recollection of an admirable one in prose, by Mr. Gilbert, Author of the
Hurricane.

If still his Brother liv'd, or to the file
Another grave was added. – He had found
Another grave, near which a full half hour
He had remain'd, but, as he gaz'd, there grew
Such a confusion in his memory,
That he began to doubt, and he had hopes
That he had seen this heap of turf before,
That it was not another grave, but one
He had forgotten. He had lost his path,
As up the vale he came that afternoon,   90
Through fields which once had been well known to him.
And Oh! what joy the recollection now
Sent to his heart! he lifted up his eyes,
And looking round he thought that he perceiv'd
Strange alteration wrought on every side
Among the woods and fields, and that the rocks,
And the eternal hills, themselves were chang'd.

By this the Priest who down the field had come
Unseen by Leonard, at the church-yard gate
Stopp'd short, and thence, at leisure, limb by limb   100
He scann'd him with a gay complacency.
Aye, thought the Vicar, smiling to himself,
'Tis one of those who needs must leave the path
Of the world's business, to go wild alone:
His arms have a perpetual holiday,
The happy man will creep about the fields
Following his fancies by the hour, to bring
Tears down his cheek, or solitary smiles
Into his face, until the setting sun
Write Fool upon his forehead. Planted thus   110
Beneath a shed that overarch'd the gate
Of this rude church-yard, till the stars appear'd
The good man might have commun'd with himself
But that the Stranger, who had left the grave,
Approach'd; he recogniz'd the Priest at once,

And after greetings interchang'd, and given
By Leonard to the Vicar as to one
Unknown to him, this dialogue ensued.

LEONARD

You live, Sir, in these dales, a quiet life:
Your years make up one peaceful family;   120
And who would grieve and fret, if, welcome come
And welcome gone, they are so like each other,
They cannot be remember'd. Scarce a funeral
Comes to this church-yard once in eighteen months;
And yet, some changes must take place among you.
And you, who dwell here, even among these rocks
Can trace the finger of mortality,
And see, that with our threescore years and ten
We are not all that perish. – I remember,
For many years ago I pass'd this road,   130
There was a foot-way all along the fields
By the brook-side – 'tis gone – and that dark cleft!
To me it does not seem to wear the face
Which then it had.

PRIEST

        Why, Sir, for aught I know,
That chasm is much the same –

LEONARD

        But, surely, yonder –

PRIEST

Aye, there indeed, your memory is a friend
That does not play you false. – On that tall pike,
(It is the loneliest place of all these hills)   140
There were two Springs which bubbled side by side,
As if they had been made that they might be

Companions for each other: ten years back,
Close to those brother fountains, the huge crag
Was rent with lightning – one is dead and gone,
The other, left behind, is flowing still. –
For accidents and changes such as these,
Why we have store of them! a water-spout
Will bring down half a mountain; what a feast
For folks that wander up and down like you,   150
To see an acre's breadth of that wide cliff
One roaring cataract – a sharp May storm
Will come with loads of January snow,
And in one night send twenty score of sheep
To feed the ravens, or a Shepherd dies
By some untoward death among the rocks:
The ice breaks up and sweeps away a bridge –
A wood is fell'd: – and then for our own homes!
A child is born or christen'd, a field plough'd,
A daughter sent to service, a web spun,   160
The old house-clock is deck'd with a new face;
And hence, so far from wanting facts or dates
To chronicle the time, we all have here
A pair of diaries, one serving, Sir,
For the whole dale, and one for each fire-side,
Your's was a stranger's judgment: for historians
Commend me to these vallies.

LEONARD

                    Yet your church-yard
Seems, if such freedom may be used with you,
To say that you are heedless of the past.   170
Here's neither head nor foot-stone, plate of brass,
An orphan could not find his mother's grave:
Cross-bones or skull, type of our earthly state

---

161. house-clock] misprint house-cloth [1800].
172. Second errat. 1800.

Or emblem of our hopes: the dead man's home
Is but a fellow to that pasture field.

PRIEST

Why there, Sir, is a thought that's new to me.
The Stone-cutters, 'tis true, might beg their bread
If every English church-yard were like ours:
Yet your conclusion wanders from the truth.
We have no need of names and epitaphs,
We talk about the dead by our fire-sides.   180
And then for our immortal part, *we* want
No symbols, Sir, to tell us that plain tale:
The thought of death sits easy on the man
Who has been born and dies among the mountains.

LEONARD

Your dalesmen, then, do in each other's thoughts
Possess a kind of second life: no doubt
You, Sir, could help me to the history
Of half these Graves?

PRIEST

                    For eight-score winters past,
With what I've witness'd, and with what I've heard,
Perhaps I might, and, on a winter's evening,   190
If you were seated at my chimney's nook
By turning o'er these hillocks one by one,
We two could travel, Sir, through a strange round,
Yet all in the broad high-way of the world.
Now there's a grave – your foot is half upon it,
It looks just like the rest, and yet that man
Died broken-hearted.

---

188. For eight-score winters past, [second errat. 1800].

LEONARD

                    'Tis a common case,
We'll take another: who is he that lies
Beneath yon ridge, the last of those three graves; –   200
It touches on that piece of native rock
Left in the church-yard wall.

PRIEST

                    That's Walter Ewbank.
He had as white a head and fresh a cheek
As ever were produc'd by youth and age
Engendering in the blood of hale fourscore.
For five long generations had the heart
Of Walter's forefathers o'erflow'd the bounds
Of their inheritance, that single cottage,
You see it yonder, and those few green fields.   210
They toil'd and wrought, and still, from sire to son,
Each struggled, and each yielded as before
A little – yet a little – and old Walter,
They left to him the family heart, and land
With other burthens than the crop it bore.
Year after year the old man still preserv'd
A chearful mind, and buffeted with bond,
Interest and mortgages; at last he sank,
And went into his grave before his time.
Poor Walter! whether it was care that spurr'd him   220
God only knows, but to the very last
He had the lightest foot in Ennerdale:
His pace was never that of an old man:
I almost see him tripping down the path
With his two Grandsons after him – but you,
Unless our Landlord be your host to-night,
Have far to travel, and in these rough paths
Even in the longest day of midsummer –

---

216. preserv'd] kept up [1802].

LEONARD

But these two Orphans!

PRIEST

Orphans! such they were –   230
Yet not while Walter liv'd – for, though their Parents
Lay buried side by side as now they lie,
The old Man was a father to the boys,
Two fathers in one father: and if tears
Shed, when he talk'd of them where they were not,
And hauntings from the infirmity of love,
Are aught of what makes up a mother's heart,
This old Man in the day of his old age
Was half a mother to them – If you weep, Sir,
To hear a stranger talking about strangers,   240
Heaven bless you when you are among your kindred!
Aye. You may turn that way – it is a grave
Which will bear looking at.

LEONARD

These Boys I hope
They lov'd this good old Man –

PRIEST

They did – and truly,
But that was what we almost overlook'd,
They were such darlings of each other. For
Though from their cradles they had liv'd with Walter,
The only kinsman near them in the house,   250
Yet he being old, they had much love to spare,
And it all went into each other's hearts.
Leonard, the elder by just eighteen months,
Was two years taller: 'twas a joy to see,
To hear, to meet them! from their house the School
Was distant three short miles, and in the time

Of storm and thaw, when every water-course
And unbridg'd stream, such as you may have notic'd
Crossing our roads at every hundred steps,
Was swoln into a noisy rivulet,   260
Would Leonard then, when elder boys perhaps
Remain'd at home, go staggering through the fords
Bearing his Brother on his back. – I've seen him,
On windy days, in one of those stray brooks,
Aye, more than once I've seen him mid-leg deep,
Their two books lying both on a dry stone
Upon the hither side: – and once I said,
As I remember, looking round these rocks
And hills on which we all of us were born,
That God who made the great book of the world   270
Would bless such piety –

LEONARD

                                        It may be then –

PRIEST

Never did worthier lads break English bread:
The finest Sunday that the Autumn saw,
With all its mealy clusters of ripe nuts,
Could never keep these boys away from church,
Or tempt them to an hour of sabbath breach.
Leonard and James! I warrant, every corner
Among these rocks and every hollow place
Where foot could come, to one or both of them   280
Was known as well as to the flowers that grow there.
Like roe-bucks they went bounding o'er the hills:
They play'd like two young ravens on the crags:
Then they could write, aye and speak too, as well
As many of their betters – and for Leonard!
The very night before he went away,

---

281. grow] grew [1800 amend. second errat.].

In my own house I put into his hand
A Bible, and I'd wager twenty pounds,
That, if he is alive, he has it yet.

LEONARD

It seems, these Brothers have not liv'd to be   290
A comfort to each other. –

PRIEST

That they might
Live to that end, is what both old and young
In this our valley all of us have wish'd,
And what, for my part, I have often pray'd:
But Leonard –

LEONARD

Then James still is left among you –

PRIEST

'Tis of the elder Brother I am speaking:
They had an Uncle, he was at that time
A thriving man, and traffick'd on the seas: 300
And, but for this same Uncle, to this hour
Leonard had never handled rope or shroud.
For the Boy lov'd the life which we lead here;
And, though a very Stripling, twelve years old;
His soul was knit to this his native soil.
But, as I said, old Walter was too weak
To strive with such a torrent; when he died,
The estate and house were sold, and all their sheep,
A pretty flock, and which, for aught I know,
Had clothed the Ewbanks for a thousand years.   310
Well – all was gone, and they were destitute.
And Leonard, chiefly for his brother's sake,
Resolv'd to try his fortune on the seas.

'Tis now twelve years since we had tidings from him.
If there was one among us who had heard
That Leonard Ewbank was come home again,
From the great Gavel,* down by Leeza's Banks,
And down the Enna, far as Egremont,
The day would be a very festival,
And those two bells of ours, which there you see   320
Hanging in the open air – but, O good Sir!
This is sad talk – they'll never sound for him
Living or dead – When last we heard of him
He was in slavery among the Moors
Upon the Barbary Coast – 'Twas not a little
That would bring down his spirit, and, no doubt,
Before it ended in his death, the Lad
Was sadly cross'd – Poor Leonard! when we parted,
He took me by the hand and said to me,
If ever the day came when he was rich,   330
He would return, and on his Father's Land
He would grow old among us.

LEONARD

                    If that day
Should come, 'twould needs be a glad day for him;
He would himself, no doubt, be happy then
As any that should meet him –

PRIEST

                    Happy, Sir –

* The great Gavel, so called I imagine, from its resemblance to the
Gable end of a house, is one of the highest of the Cumberland mountains.
It stands at the head of the several vales of Ennerdale, Wastdale, and
Borrowdale.

The Leeza is a River which follows into the Lake of Ennerdale: on
issuing from the Lake, it changes its name, and is called the End, Eyne,
or Enna. It falls into the sea a little below Egremont.

---

335. be happy then] be as happy then [1800 amend. second errat.]

LEONARD

You said his kindred all were in their graves,
And that he had one Brother –

PRIEST

                  That is but   **340**
A fellow tale of sorrow. From his youth
James, though not sickly, yet was delicate,
And Leonard being always by his side
Had done so many offices about him,
That, though he was not of a timid nature,
Yet still the spirit of a mountain boy
In him was somewhat check'd, and when his Brother
Was gone to sea and he was left alone
The little colour that he had was soon
Stolen from his cheek, he droop'd, and pin'd and
      pin'd: **350**

LEONARD

But these are all the graves of full grown men!

PRIEST

Aye, Sir, that pass'd away: we took him to us.
He was the child of all the dale – he liv'd
Three months with one, and six months with another:
And wanted neither food, nor clothes, nor love,
And many, many happy days were his.
But, whether blithe or sad, 'tis my belief
His absent Brother still was at his heart.
And, when he liv'd beneath our roof, we found
(A practice till this time unknown to him)   **360**
That often, rising from his bed at night,
He in his sleep would walk about, and sleeping
He sought his Brother Leonard – You are mov'd!
Forgive me, Sir: before I spoke to you,
I judg'd you most unkindly.

LEONARD

                              But this youth,
How did he die at last?

PRIEST

                              One sweet May morning,
It will be twelve years since, when Spring returns,
He had gone forth among the new-dropp'd lambs,   370
With two or three companions whom it chanc'd
Some further business summon'd to a house
Which stands at the Dale-head. James, tir'd perhaps,
Or from some other cause remain'd behind.
You see yon precipice – it almost looks
Like some vast building made of many crags
And in the midst is one particular rock
That rises like a column from the vale,
Whence by our Shepherds it is call'd, the Pillar.
James pointed to its summit, over which   380
They all had purpos'd to return together,
And told them that he there would wait for them:
They parted, and his comrades pass'd that way
Some two hours after, but they did not find him
At the appointed place, a circumstance
Of which they took no heed: but one of them,
Going by chance, at night, into the house
Which at this time was James's home, there learn'd
That nobody had seen him all that day:
The morning came, and still, he was unheard of: 390
The neighbours were alarm'd, and to the Brook
Some went, and some towards the Lake; ere noon
They found him at the foot of that same Rock
Dead, and with mangled limbs. The third day after
I buried him, poor Lad, and there he lies.

---

380. James pointed] James, pointing [1800 amend. second errat.]
382. And told] Inform'd [1800 amend. second errat.]
385–386. Upon the Pillar – at the appointed place.
        Of this they took no heed: but one of them, [1802].

LEONARD

And that then *is* his grave! – Before his death
You said that he saw many happy years?

PRIEST

Aye, that he did –

LEONARD

And all went well with him –

PRIEST

If he had one, the Lad had twenty homes.   400

LEONARD

And you believe then, that his mind was easy –

PRIEST

Yes, long before he died, he found that time
Is a true friend to sorrow, and unless
His thoughts were turn'd on Leonard's luckless fortune,
He talk'd about him with a chearful love.

LEONARD

He could not come to an unhallow'd end!

PRIEST

Nay, God forbid! You recollect I mention'd
A habit which disquietude and grief
Had brought upon him, and we all conjectur'd
That, as the day was warm, he had lain down   410
Upon the grass, and, waiting for his comrades
He there had fallen asleep, that in his sleep
He to the margin of the precipice
Had walked, and from the summit had fallen head-long,
And so no doubt he perish'd: at the time,
We guess, that in his hands he must have had

His Shepherd's staff; for midway in the cliff
It had been caught, and there for many years
It hung – and moulder'd there.

          The Priest here ended –   420
The Stranger would have thank'd him, but he felt
Tears rushing in; both left the spot in silence,
And Leonard, when they reach'd the church-yard gate,
As the Priest lifted up the latch, turn'd round,
And, looking at the grave, he said, "My Brother."
The Vicar did not hear the words: and now,
Pointing towards the Cottage, he entreated
That Leonard would partake his homely fare:
The other thank'd him with a fervent voice,
But added, that, the evening being calm,   430
He would pursue his journey. So they parted.

It was not long ere Leonard reach'd a grove
That overhung the road: he there stopp'd short,
And, sitting down beneath the trees, review'd
All that the Priest had said: his early years
Were with him in his heart: his cherish'd hopes,
And thoughts which had been his an hour before,
All press'd on him with such a weight, that now,
This vale, where he had been so happy, seem'd
A place in which he could not bear to live: 440
So he relinquish'd all his purposes.
He travell'd on to Egremont; and thence,
That night, address'd a letter to the Priest
Reminding him of what had pass'd between them.
And adding, with a hope to be forgiven,
That it was from the weakness of his heart,
He had not dared to tell him, who he was.

This done, he went on shipboard, and is now
A Seaman, a grey headed Mariner.

---

443. address'd a letter] he wrote [1802].

Ellen Irwin,
OR
*the Braes of Kirtle**

Fair Ellen Irwin, when she sate
Upon the Braes of Kirtle,
Was lovely as a Grecian Maid
Adorn'd with wreaths of myrtle.

Young Adam Bruce beside her lay,
And there did they beguile the day
With love and gentle speeches,
Beneath the budding beeches.

From many Knights and many Squires
The Bruce had been selected,   10
And Gordon, fairest of them all,
By Ellen was rejected.
Sad tidings to that noble Youth!
For it may be proclaim'd with truth,
If Bruce hath lov'd sincerely,
The Gordon loves as dearly.

But what is Gordon's beauteous face?
And what are Gordon's crosses
To them who sit by Kirtle's Braes
Upon the verdant mosses?   20
Alas that ever he was born!
Vhe Gordon, couch'd behind a thorn,
Sees them and their caressing,
Beholds them bless'd and blessing.

---

* The Kirtle is a River in the Southern part of Scotland, on whose
banks the events here related took place.

Proud Gordon cannot bear the thoughts
That through his brain are travelling,
And, starting up, to Bruce's heart
He launch'd a deadly jav'lin!
Fair Ellen saw it when it came,
And, stepping forth to meet the same,   30
Did with her body cover
The Youth her chosen lover.

And, falling into Bruce's arms,
Thus died the beauteous Ellen,
Thus from the heart of her true-love
The mortal spear repelling.
And Bruce, as soon as he had slain
The Gordon, sail'd away to Spain,
And fought with rage incessant
Against the Moorish Crescent.   40

But many days and many months,
And many years ensuing,
This wretched Knight did vainly seek
The death that he was wooing:
So coming back across the wave,
Without a groan on Ellen's grave
His body he extended,
And there his sorrow ended.

Now ye who willingly have heard
The tale I have been telling,   50
May in Kirkonnel church-yard view
The grave of lovely Ellen:
By Ellen's side the Bruce is laid,
And, for the stone upon his head,
May no rude hand deface it,
And its forlorn Hic jacet.

Strange fits of passion I have known,
And I will dare to tell,
But in the lover's ear alone,
What once to me befel.

When she I lov'd, was strong and gay
And like a rose in June,
I to her cottage bent my way,
Beneath the evening moon.

Upon the moon I fix'd my eye,
All over the wide lea;   10
My horse trudg'd on, and we drew nigh
Those paths so dear to me.

And now we reach'd the orchard plot,
And, as we climb'd the hill,
Towards the roof of Lucy's cot
The moon descended still.

In one of those sweet dreams I slept,
Kind Nature's gentlest boon!
And, all the while, my eyes I kept
On the descending moon.   20

My horse mov'd on; hoof after hoof
He rais'd and never stopp'd:
When down behind the cottage roof
At once the planet dropp'd.

What fond and wayward thoughts will slide
Into a Lover's head –
"O mercy!" to myself I cried,
"If Lucy should be dead!"

Song

She dwelt among th' untrodden ways
    Beside the springs of Dove,
A Maid whom there were none to praise
    And very few to love.

A Violet by a mossy stone
    Half-hidden from the Eye!
– Fair, as a star when only one
    Is shining in the sky!
She *liv'd* unknown, and few could know
    When Lucy ceas'd to be;   10
But she is in her Grave, and Oh!
    The difference to me.

A slumber did my spirit seal,
    I had no human fears:
She seem'd a thing that could not feel
    The touch of earthly years.

No motion has she now, no force
    She neither hears nor sees
Roll'd round in earth's diurnal course
    With rocks and stones and trees!

The Waterfall and the Eglantine

"Begone, thou fond presumptuous Elf,
Exclaim'd a thundering Voice,
Nor dare to thrust thy foolish self
Between me and my choice!
A falling Water swoln with snows
Thus spake to a poor Briar-rose,
That all bespatter'd with his foam,
And dancing high, and dancing low,
Was living, as a child might know,
In an unhappy home.   10

"Dost thou presume my course to block?
Off, off! or, puny Thing!
I'll hurl thee headlong with the rock
To which thy fibres cling."
The Flood was tyrannous and strong;
The patient Briar suffer'd long,
Nor did he utter groan or sigh,
Hoping the danger would be pass'd:
But seeing no relief, at last
He ventur'd to reply.   20

"Ah!" said the Briar, "Blame me not!
Why should we dwell in strife?
We who in this, our natal spot,
Once liv'd a happy life!
You stirr'd me on my rocky bed —
What pleasure thro' my veins you spread!
The Summer long from day to day
My leaves you freshen'd and bedew'd;
Nor was it common gratitude
That did your cares repay.   30

When Spring came on with bud and bell,
Among these rocks did I
Before you hang my wreath to tell
That gentle days were nigh!
And in the sultry summer hours
I shelter'd you with leaves and flowers;
And in my leaves now shed and gone
The linnet lodg'd and for us two
Chaunted his pretty songs when you
Had little voice or none.   40

But now proud thoughts are in your breast –
What grief is mine you see.
Ah! would you think, ev'n yet how blest
Together we might be!
Though of both leaf and flower bereft,
Some ornaments to me are left –

Rich store of scarlet hips is mine,
With which I in my humble way
Would deck you many a Winter's day,
A happy Eglantine!"   50

What more he said, I cannot tell.
The stream came thundering down the dell
And gallop'd loud and fast;
I listen'd, nor aught else could hear,
The Briar quak'd and much I fear,
Those accents were his last.

The Oak and the Broom,

A PASTORAL

His simple truths did Andrew glean
Beside the babbling rills;
A careful student he had been
Among the woods and hills.
One winter's night when through the Trees
The wind was thundering, on his knees
His youngest born did Andrew hold:
And while the rest, a ruddy quire
Were seated round their blazing fire,
This Tale the Shepherd told.   10

I saw a crag, a lofty stone
As ever tempest beat!
Out of its head an Oak had grown,
A Broom out of its feet.
The time was March, a chearful noon –
The thaw-wind with the breath of June
Breath'd gently from the warm South-west;
When in a voice sedate with age
This Oak, half giant and half sage,
His neighbour thus address'd.   20

"Eight weary weeks, thro' rock and clay,
Along this mountain's edge
The Frost hath wrought both night and day,
Wedge driving after wedge.
Look up, and think, above your head
What trouble surely will be bred;
Last night I heard a crash – 'tis true,
The splinters took another road –
I see them yonder – what a load
For such a Thing as you!   30

You are preparing as before
To deck your slender shape;
And yet, just three years back – no more –
You had a strange escape.
Down from yon Cliff a fragment broke,
It came, you know, with fire and smoke
And hither did it bend its way.
This pond'rous block was caught by me,
And o'er your head, as you may see,
'Tis hanging to this day.   40

The Thing had better been asleep,
Whatever thing it were,
Or Breeze, or Bird, or fleece of Sheep,
That first did plant you there.
For you and your green twigs decoy
The little witless Shepherd-boy
To come and slumber in your bower;
And trust me, on some sultry noon,
Both you and he, Heaven knows how soon!
Will perish in one hour.   50

From me this friendly warning take" –
– The Broom began to doze,
And thus to keep herself awake
Did gently interpose.
"My thanks for your discourse are due;
That it is true, and more than true,
I know and I have known it long;
Frail is the bond, by which we hold
Our being, be we young or old,
Wise, foolish, weak or strong.   60

---

37. And hitherward it bent its way. [1802].
43. Or Breeze, or Bird, or Dog, or Sheep, [1802].

Disasters, do the best we can,
Will reach both great and small;
And he is oft the wisest man,
Who is not wise at all.
For me, why should I wish to roam?
This spot is my paternal home,
It is my pleasant Heritage;
My Father many a happy year
Here spread his careless blossoms, here
Attain'd a good old age.   70

Even such as his may be my lot.
What cause have I to haunt
My heart with terrors? Am I not
In truth a favor'd plant!
The Spring for me a garland weaves
Of yellow flowers and verdant leaves,
And, when the Frost is in the sky,
My branches are so fresh and gay
That You might look on me and say
This plant can never die.   80

The butterfly, all green and gold,
To me hath often flown,
Here in my Blossoms to behold
Wings lovely as his own.
When grass is chill with rain or dew,
Beneath my shade the mother ewe
Lies with her infant lamb; I see
The love, they to each other make,
And the sweet joy, which they partake,
It is a joy to me.''   90

Her voice was blithe, her heart was light;
The Broom might have pursued

Her speech, until the stars of night
Their journey had renew'd.
But in the branches of the Oak
Two Ravens now began to croak
Their nuptial song, a gladsome air;
And to her own green bower the breeze
That instant brought two stripling Bees
To feed and murmur there.   100

One night the Wind came from the North
And blew a furious blast,
At break of day I ventur'd forth
And near the Cliff I pass'd.
The storm had fall'n upon the Oak
And struck him with a mighty stroke,
And whirl'd and whirl'd him far away;
And in one hospitable Cleft
The little careless Broom was left
To live for many a day.   110

Lucy Gray

Oft I had heard of Lucy Gray,
And when I cross'd the Wild,
I chanc'd to see at break of day
The solitary Child.

No Mate, no comrade Lucy knew;
She dwelt on a wild Moor,
The sweetest Thing that ever grew
Beside a human door !

You yet may spy the Fawn at play,
The Hare upon the Green;   10
But the sweet face of Lucy Gray
Will never more be seen.

"To-night will be a stormy night,
You to the Town must go,
And take a lantern, Child, to light
Your Mother thro' the snow."

"That, Father ! will I gladly do;
'Tis scarcely afternoon –
The Minster-clock has just struck two,
And yonder is the Moon."   20

At this the Father rais'd his hook
And snapp'd a faggot-band;
He plied his work, and Lucy took
The lantern in her hand.

Not blither is the mountain roe,
With many a wanton stroke
Her feet disperse the powd'ry snow
That rises up like smoke.

The storm came on before its time,
She wander'd up and down,   30
And many a hill did Lucy climb
But never reach'd the Town.

The wretched Parents all that night
Went shouting far and wide;
But there was neither sound nor sight
To serve them for a guide.

At day-break on a hill they stood
That overlook'd the Moor;
And thence they saw the Bridge of Wood
A furlong from their door.   40

And now they homeward turn'd, and cry'd
"In Heaven we all shall meet!"
When in the snow the Mother spied
The print of Lucy's feet.

Then downward from the steep hill's edge
They track'd the footmarks small;
And through the broken hawthorn-hedge,
And by the long stone-wall;

And then an open field they cross'd,
The marks were still the same;   50
They track'd them on, nor ever lost,
And to the Bridge they came.

They follow'd from the snowy bank
The footmarks, one by one,
Into the middle of the plank,
And further there were none.

Yet some maintain that to this day
She is a living Child,
That you may see sweet Lucy Gray
Upon the lonesome Wild.   60

O'er rough and smooth she trips along,
And never looks behind;
And sings a solitary song
That whistles in the wind.

The Idle Shepherd-Boys,
or
Dungeon-Gill Force,*

A PASTORAL

I

The valley rings with mirth and joy,
Among the hills the Echoes play
A never, never ending song
To welcome in the May.
The Magpie chatters with delight;
The mountain Raven's youngling Brood
Have left the Mother and the Nest,
And they go rambling east and west

In search of their own food,
Or thro' the glittering Vapors dart   10
In very wantonness of Heart.

II

Beneath a rock, upon the grass,
Two Boys are sitting in the sun;
It seems they have no work to do
Or that their work is done.
On pipes of sycamore they play
The fragments of a Christmas Hymn,
Or with that plant which in our dale
We call Stag-horn, or Fox's Tail
Their rusty Hats they trim: 20
And thus as happy as the Day,
Those Shepherds wear the time away.

* Gill in the dialect of Cumberland and Westmoreland is a short and
for the most part a steep narrow valley, with a stream running through
it. Force is the word universally employed in these dialects for Waterfall.

III

Along the river's stony marge
The sand-lark chaunts a joyous song;
The thrush is busy in the Wood,
And carols loud and strong.
A thousand lambs are on the rocks,
All newly born! both earth and sky
Keep jubilee, and more than all,
Those Boys with their green Coronal,   30
They never hear the cry,
That plaintive cry! which up the hill
Comes from the depth of Dungeon-Gill.

IV

Said Walter, leaping from the ground,
"Down to the stump of yon old yew
I'll run with you a race." – No more –
Away the Shepherds flew.
They leapt, they ran, and when they came
Right opposite to Dungeon-Gill,
Seeing, that he should lose the prize,   40
"Stop!" to his comrade Walter cries –
James stopp'd with no good will:
Said Walter then, "Your task is here,
'Twill keep you working half a year.

V

Till you have cross'd where I shall cross,
Say that you'll neither sleep nor eat."
James proudly took him at his word,
But did not like the feat.

---

36. We'll for this Whistle run a race". [1802].
    We'll for our Whistles run a race". [1805].
45–48. "Now cross where I shall cross – come on,
    And follow me where I shall lead" –
    James proudly took him at his word,
    But did not like the deed. [1802].
  (47). James proudly] The other [1805].

It was a spot, which you may see
If ever you to Langdale go: 50
Into a chasm a mighty Block
Hath fallen, and made a bridge of rock;
The gulph is deep below,
And in a bason black and small
Receives a lofty Waterfall.

VI

With staff in hand across the cleft
The Challenger began his march;
And now, all eyes and feet, hath gain'd
The middle of the arch.
When list ! he hears a piteous moan –   60
Again ! his heart within him dies –
His pulse is stopp'd, his breath is lost,
He totters, pale as any ghost,
And, looking down, he spies
A Lamb, that in the pool is pent
Within that black and frightful rent.

VII

The Lamb had slipp'd into the stream,
And safe without a bruise or wound
The Cataract had borne him down
Into the gulph profound.   70
His dam had seen him when he fell,
She saw him down the torrent borne;
And while with all a mother's love
She from the lofty rocks above
Sent forth a cry forlorn,
The Lamb, still swimming round and round
Made answer to that plaintive sound.

VIII

When he had learnt, what thing it was,
That sent this rueful cry; I ween,
The Boy recover'd heart, and told   80
The sight which he had seen.
Both gladly now deferr'd their task;
Nor was there wanting other aid –
A Poet, one who loves the brooks
Far better than the sages' books,
By chance had thither stray'd;
And there the helpless Lamb he found
By those huge rocks encompass'd round.

IX

He drew it gently from the pool,
And brought it forth into the light: 90
The Shepherds met him with his charge
An unexpected sight !
Into their arms the Lamb they took,
Said they, "He's neither maim'd nor scarr'd" –
Then up the steep ascent they hied
And placed him at his Mother's side;
And gently did the Bard
Those idle Shepherd-boys upbraid,
And bade them better mind their trade.

'Tis said, that some have died for love:
And here and there a church-yard grave is found
In the cold North's unhallow'd ground,
Because the wretched man himself had slain,
His love was such a grievous pain.
And there is one whom I five years have known;
He dwells alone
Upon Helvellyn's side.
He loved – The pretty Barbara died,
And thus he makes his moan: 10
Three years had Barbara in her grave been laid
When thus his moan he made.

Oh ! move thou Cottage from behind that oak
Or let the aged tree uprooted lie,
That in some other way yon smoke
May mount into the sky !
The clouds pass on; they from the Heavens depart:
I look – the sky is empty space;
I know not what I trace;
But when I cease to look, my hand is on my heart.   20

O ! what a weight is in these shades ! Ye leaves,
When will that dying murmur be suppress'd?
Your sound my heart of peace bereaves,
It robs my heart of rest.
Thou Thrush, that singest loud and loud and free,
Into yon row of willows flit,
Upon that alder sit;
Or sing another song, or chuse another tree.

Roll back, sweet rill! back to thy mountain bounds,
And there for ever be thy waters chain'd!   30
For thou dost haunt the air with sounds
That cannot be sustain'd;
If still beneath that pine-tree's ragged bough
Headlong yon waterfall must come,
Oh let it then be dumb! –
Be any thing, sweet rill, but that which thou art now.

Thou Eglantine whose arch so proudly towers
(Even like a rainbow spanning half the vale)
Thou one fair shrub, oh! shed thy flowers,
And stir not in the gale.   40
For thus to see thee nodding in the air,
To see thy arch thus stretch and bend,
Thus rise and thus descend,
Disturbs me, till the sight is more than I can bear.

The man who makes this feverish complaint
Is one of giant stature, who could dance
Equipp'd from head to foot in iron mail.
Ah gentle Love! if ever thought was thine
To store up kindred hours for me, thy face
Turn from me, gentle Love, nor let me walk   50
Within the sound of Emma's voice, or know
Such happiness as I have known to-day.

Poor Susan

At the corner of Wood-Street, when day-light appears,
There's a Thrush that sings loud, it has sung for three years:
Poor Susan has pass'd by the spot and has heard
In the silence of morning the song of the bird.

'Tis a note of enchantment; what ails her? She sees
A mountain ascending, a vision of trees;
Bright volumes of vapour through Lothbury glide,
And a river flows on through the vale of Cheapside.

Green pastures she views in the midst of the dale,
Down which she so often has tripp'd with her pail,   10
And a single small cottage, a nest like a dove's,
The only one dwelling on earth that she loves.

She looks, and her heart is in Heaven, but they fade,
The mist and the river, the hill and the shade;
The stream will not flow, and the hill will not rise,
And the colours have all pass'd away from her eyes.

Poor Outcast ! return – to receive thee once more
The house of thy Father will open its door,
And thou once again, in thy plain russet gown,
May'st hear the thrush sing from a tree of its own.   20

---

2. There's a Thrush] Hang's a thrush [1820].

12. only one] one only [1802].
16–20. St. om. [1802].

Inscription

For the Spot where the HERMITAGE *stood on St. Herbert's Island, Derwent-Water*

═══════

If thou in the dear love of some one friend
Hast been so happy, that thou know'st what thoughts
Will, sometimes, in the happiness of love
Make the heart sink, then wilt thou reverence
This quiet spot. – St. Herbert hither came
And here, for many seasons, from the world
Remov'd, and the affections of the world
He dwelt in solitude. He living here,
This island's sole inhabitant ! had left
A Fellow-labourer, whom the good Man lov'd   10
As his own soul; and when within his cave
Alone he knelt before the crucifix
While o'er the lake the cataract of Lodore
Peal'd to his orisons, and when he pac'd
Along the beach of this small isle and thought
Of his Companion, he had pray'd that both
Might die in the same moment. Nor in vain
So pray'd he: – as our Chronicles report,
Though here the Hermit number'd his last days,
Far from St. Cuthbert his beloved friend,   20
Those holy men both died in the same hour.

─────────────────────────────────

4. sink,] sick, [1802].
8-10. He dwelt in solitude. – But he had left
       A Fellow-labourer, whom the good Man loved [1802].
16. had pray'd] would pray [1802].

Inscription

For the House (an Outhouse) on the Island at Grasmere

Rude is this Edifice, and Thou hast seen
Buildings, albeit rude, that have maintain'd
Proportions more harmonious, and approach'd
To somewhat of a closer fellowship
With the ideal grace. Yet as it is
Do take it in good part; for he, the poor
Vitruvius of our village, had no help
From the great city; never on the leaves
Of red Morocco folio saw display'd
The skeletons and pre-existing ghosts   10
Of Beauties yet unborn, the rustic Box,
Snug Cot, with Coach-house, Shed and Hermitage.
It is a homely pile, yet to these walls
The heifer comes in the snow-storm, and here
The new-dropp'd lamb finds shelter from the wind.
And hither does one Poet sometimes row
His pinnace, a small vagrant barge, up-piled
With plenteous store of heath and wither'd fern,
A lading which he with his sickle cuts
Among the mountains, and beneath this roof   20
He makes his summer couch, and here at noon
Spreads out his limbs, while, yet unshorn, the sheep
Panting beneath the burthen of their wool
Lie round him, even as if they were a part
Of his own household: nor, while from his bed
He through that door-place looks toward the lake
And to the stirring breezes, does he want
Creations lovely as the work of sleep,
Fair sights, and visions of romantic joy.

---

22. unshorn] unborn [1800: amend. second errat.].

To a Sexton

Let thy wheel-barrow alone.
Wherefore, Sexton, piling still
In thy bone-house bone on bone?
'Tis already like a hill
In a field of battle made,
Where three thousand skulls are laid.
– These died in peace each with the other,
Father, Sister, Friend, and Brother.

Mark the spot to which I point!
From this platform eight feet square   10
Take not even a finger-joint:
Andrew's whole fire-side is there.
Here, alone, before thine eyes,
Simon's sickly Daughter lies
From weakness, now, and pain defended,
Whom he twenty winters tended.

Look but at the gardener's pride,
How he glories, when he sees
Roses, lilies, side by side,
Violets in families.   20
By the heart of Man, his tears,
By his hopes and by his fears,
Thou, old Grey-beard! art the Warden
Of a far superior garden.

Thus then, each to other dear,
Let them all in quiet lie,
Andrew there and Susan here,
Neighbours in mortality.
And should I live through sun and rain
Seven widow'd years without my Jane,   30
O Sexton, do not then remove her,
Let one grave hold the Lov'd and Lover!

Andrew Jones

I hate that Andrew Jones: he'll breed
His children up to waste and pillage.
I wish the press-gang or the drum
With its tantara sound would come,
And sweep him from the village!

I said not this, because he loves
Through the long day to swear and tipple;
But for the poor dear sake of one
To whom a foul deed he had done,
A friendless Man, a travelling Cripple!   10

For this poor crawling helpless wretch
Some Horseman who was passing by,
A penny on the ground had thrown;
But the poor Cripple was alone
And could not stoop – no help was nigh.

Inch-thick the dust lay on the ground
For it had long been droughty weather:
So with his staff the Cripple wrought
Among the dust till he had brought
The halfpennies together.   20

It chanc'd that Andrew pass'd that way
Just at the time; and there he found
The Cripple in the mid-day heat
Standing alone, and at his feet
He saw the penny on the ground.

He stooped and took the penny up:
And when the Cripple nearer drew,

---

26. stooped] stopp'd [1800 amend. second errat.].

Quoth Andrew, "Under half-a-crown,
What a man finds is all his own,
And so, my Friend, good day to you." 30

And *hence* I said, that Andrew's boys
Will all be train'd to waste and pillage;
And wish'd the press-gang, or the drum
With its tantara sound, would come
And sweep him from the village!

The Two Thieves,

or

The last Stage of Avarice

Oh now that the genius of Bewick were mine
And the skill which He learn'd on the Banks of the Tyne;
When the Muses might deal with me just as they chose
For I'd take my last leave both of verse and of prose.

What feats would I work with my magical hand!
Book-learning and books should be banish'd the land
And for hunger and thirst and such troublesome calls
Every ale-house should then have a feast on its walls.

The Traveller would hang his wet clothes on a chair
Let them smoke, let them burn, not a straw would he care, 10
For the Prodigal Son, Joseph's Dream and his Sheaves,
Oh what would they be to my tale of two Thieves!

Little Dan is unbreech'd, he is three birth-days old,
His Grandsire that age more than thirty times old,
There are ninety good seasons of fair and foul weather
Between them, and both go a stealing together.

15. There are] There's [1800 amend. second errat.].

With chips is the Carpenter strewing his floor?
Is a cart-load of peats at an old Woman's door?
Old Daniel his hand to the treasure will slide,
And his Grandson's as busy at work by his side.   20

Old Daniel begins, he stops short and his eye
Through the lost look of dotage is cunning and sly.
'Tis a look which at this time is hardly his own,
But tells a plain tale of the days that are flown.

Dan once had a heart which was mov'd by the wires
Of manifold pleasures and many desires:
And what if he cherish'd his purse? 'Twas no more
Than treading a path trod by thousands before.

'Twas a path trod by thousands, but Daniel is one
Who went something farther than others have gone;   30
And now with old Daniel you see how it fares
You see to what end he has brought his grey hairs.

The pair sally forth hand in hand; ere the sun
Has peer'd o'er the beeches their work is begun:
And yet into whatever sin they may fall,
This Child but half knows it and that not at all.

They hunt through the street with deliberate tread,
And each in his turn is both leader and led;
And wherever they carry their plots and their wiles,
Every face in the village is dimpled with smiles.   40

Neither check'd by the rich nor the needy they roam,
For grey-headed Dan has a daughter at home;
Who will gladly repair all the damage that's done,
And three, were it ask'd, would be render'd for one.

---

22. lost] last [1805].
30. farther] further [1805].

Old Man! whom so oft I with pity have ey'd,
I love thee and love the sweet boy at thy side;
Long yet may'st thou live, for a teacher we see
That lifts up the veil of our nature in thee.

———

A whirl-blast from behind the hill
Rush'd o'er the wood with startling sound:
Then all at once the air was still,
And showers of hail-stones patter'd round.
Where leafless Oaks tower'd high above,
I sate within an undergrove
Of tallest hollies, tall and green,
A fairer bower was never seen.
From year to year the spacious floor
With wither'd leaves is cover'd o'er,   10
You could not lay a hair between:
And all the year the bower is green.
But see! where'er the hailstones drop
The wither'd leaves all skip and hop,
There's not a breeze – no breath of air –
Yet here, and there, and every where
Along the floor, beneath the shade
By those embowering hollies made,
The leaves in myriads jump and spring,
As if with pipes and music rare   20
Some Robin Good-fellow were there,
And all those leaves, that jump and spring,
Were each a joyous, living thing.

Oh! grant me Heaven a heart at ease
That I may never cease to find,
Even in appearances like these
Enough to nourish and to stir my mind!

Song

For the Wandering Jew

Though the torrents from their fountains
Roar down many a craggy steep,
Yet they find among the mountains
Resting-places calm and deep.

Though almost with eagle pinion
O'er the rocks the Chamois roam,
Yet he has some small dominion
Which no doubt he calls his home.

If on windy days the Raven
Gambol like a dancing skiff,   10
Not the less he loves his haven
On the bosom of the cliff.

Though the Sea-horse in the ocean
Own no dear domestic cave;
Yet he slumbers without motion
On the calm and silent wave.

Day and night my toils redouble!
Never nearer to the goal,
Night and day, I feel the trouble,
Of the Wanderer in my soul.   20

Ruth

When Ruth was left half desolate,
Her Father took another Mate;
And so, not seven years old,
The slighted Child at her own will
Went wandering over dale and hill
In thoughtless freedom bold.

And she had made a pipe of straw
And from that oaten pipe could draw
All sounds of winds and floods;
Had built a bower upon the green,   10
As if she from her birth had been
An Infant of the woods.

There came a Youth from Georgia's shore,
A military Casque he wore
With splendid feathers drest;
He brought them from the Cherokees;
The feathers nodded in the breeze
And made a gallant crest.

From Indian blood you deem him sprung:
Ah no! he spake the English tongue   20
And bare a Soldier's name;
And when America was free

3–4. And Ruth, not seven years old,
    A slighted Child, at her own will [1802].
12–13. Beneath her Father's roof, alone
    She seem'd to live; her thoughts her own;
    Herself her own delight:
    Pleas'd with herself, nor sad nor gay,
    She pass'd her time; and in this way
    Grew up to Woman's height. [1802].
    21. bare] bore [1805].

From battle and from jeopardy
He cross the ocean came.

With hues of genius on his cheek
In finest tones the Youth could speak.
– While he was yet a Boy
The moon, the glory of the sun,
And streams that murmur as they run
Had been his dearest joy.   30

He was a lovely Youth! I guess
The panther in the wilderness
Was not so fair as he;
And when he chose to sport and play,
No dolphin ever was so gay
Upon the tropic sea.

Among the Indians he had fought,
And with him many tales he brought
Of pleasure and of fear,
Such tales as told to any Maid   40
By such a Youth in the green shade
Were perilous to hear.

He told of Girls, a happy rout,
Who quit their fold with dance and shout
Their pleasant Indian Town
To gather strawberries all day long,
Returning with a choral song
When day-light is gone down.

He spake of plants divine and strange
That ev'ry day their blossoms change,   50
Ten thousand lovely hues!
With budding, fading, faded flowers
They stand the wonder of the bowers
From morn to evening dews.

---

50. ev'ry day] every hour [1802].

He told of the Magnolia,* spread
High as a cloud, high over head !
The Cypress and her spire,
Of† flowers that with one scarlet gleam
Cover a hundred leagues and seem
To set the hills on fire.   60

* Magnolia grandiflora.
† The splendid appearance of these scarlet flowers, which are
scattered with such profusion over the Hills in the Southern parts of
North America is frequently mentioned by Bartram in his Travels.

54–55. In 1802 7 stanzas were inserted:

(1)
Of march and ambush, siege and fight,
Then did he tell; and with delight
The heart of Ruth would ache;
Wild histories they were, and dear:
But 'twas a thing of heaven to hear
When of himself he spake!

(2)
Sometimes most earnestly he said;
"O Ruth! I have been worse than dead:
False thoughts, thoughts bold and vain,
Encompass'd me on every side
When I, in thoughtlessness and pride,
    (in confidence and pride [1805])
Had cross'd the Atlantic Main.

(3)
"Whatever in those Climes I found
Irregular in sight or sound
Did to my mind impart
A kindred impulse, seem'd allied
To my own powers, and justified
The workings of my heart.

(4)
Nor less to feed unhallow'd thought
The beauteous forms of nature wrought,
Fair trees and lovely flowers;
The breezes their own languor lent;
The stars had feelings which they sent
Into those magic bowers.

The Youth of green Savannahs spake,
And many an endless endless lake
With all its fairy crowds
Of islands that together lie
As quietly as spots of sky
Among the evening clouds:

---

(5)

Yet, in my worst pursuits, I ween,
That often there did intervene
Pure hopes of high intent;
My passions, amid forms so fair
And stately, wanted not their share
Of noble sentiment.

(6)

So was it then, and so is now
For, Ruth! with thee I know not how
I feel my spirit burn
Even as the east when day comes forth;
And to the west, and south, and north,
The morning doth return.

(7)

It is a purer, better mind:
O Maiden innocent and kind,
What sights I might have seen!"
Even now upon my eyes they break!
– And he again began to speak
Of Lands where he had been.

In 1805 only the first 2 (1) and (2) and the last (7) of these
additional stanzas were retained here. Following stanzas (1)
and (2) and inserted before stanza (7) were the following 2
stanzas:

"It was a fresh and glorious world,
A banner bright that was unfurled
Before me suddenly:
I looked upon those hills and plains,
And seemed as if let loose from chains
To live at liberty.

"But wherefore speak of this? for now,
Sweet Ruth! with thee, I know not how,
I feel my spirit burn –
Even as the east when day comes forth;
And to the west, and south, and north,
The morning doth return.

And then he said "How sweet it were
A fisher or a hunter there,
A gardener in the shade,
Still wandering with an easy mind   70
To build a household fire and find
A home in every glade.

What days and what sweet years! Ah me!
Our life were life indeed, with thee
So pass'd in quiet bliss,
And all the while" said he "to know
That we were in a world of woe,
On such an earth as this!

And then he sometimes interwove
Dear thoughts about a Father's love,   80
"For there," said he, "are spun
Around the heart such tender ties
That our own children to our eyes
Are dearer than the sun.

Sweet Ruth! and could you go with me
My helpmate in the woods to be,
Our shed at night to rear;
Or run, my own adopted bride,
A sylvan huntress at my side
And drive the flying deer!   90

Beloved Ruth!" No more he said
Sweet Ruth alone at midnight shed
A solitary tear,
She thought again – and did agree
With him to sail across the sea,
And drive the flying deer.

"And now, as fitting is and right,
We in the Church our faith will plight,
A Husband and a Wife."

Even so they did; and I may say   100
That to sweet Ruth that happy day
Was more than human life.

Through dream and vision did she sink,
Delighted all the while to think
That on those lonesome floods
And green Savannahs she should share
His board with lawful joy, and bear
His name in the wild woods.

But, as you have before been told,
This Stripling, sportive gay and bold,   110
And, with his dancing crest,
So beautiful, through savage lands
Had roam'd about with vagrant bands
Of Indians in the West.

The wind, the tempest roaring high,
The tumult of a tropic sky
Might well be dangerous food
For him, a Youth to whom was given
So much of earth so much of Heaven,
And such impetuous blood.   120

Whatever in those climes he found
Irregular in sight or sound
Did to his mind impart
A kindred impulse, seem'd allied
To his own powers, and justified
The workings of his heart.

Nor less to feed voluptuous thought
The beauteous forms of Nature wrought,
Fair trees and lovely flowers;
The breezes their own languor lent,   130
The stars had feelings which they sent
Into those magic bowers.

Yet, in his worst pursuits, I ween,
That sometimes there did intervene
Pure hopes of high intent:
For passions link'd to forms so fair
And stately, needs must have their share
Of noble sentiment.

But ill he liv'd, much evil saw
With men to whom no better law   140
Nor better life was known;
Deliberately and undeceiv'd
Those wild men's vices he receiv'd,
And gave them back his own.

His genius and his moral frame
Were thus impair'd, and he became
The slave of low desires;
A man who without self-controul
Would seek what the degraded soul
Unworthily admires.   150

And yet he with no feign'd delight
Had woo'd the Maiden, day and night
Had lov'd her, night and morn;
What could he less than love a Maid
Whose heart with so much nature play'd
So kind and so forlorn?

But now the pleasant dream was gone,
No hope, no wish remain'd, not one,
They stirr'd him now no more,

---

139. But ill he liv'd,] Ill did he live, [1802].
121-38. stan 20.s (3), (4), (5) p. 181 [1802].

New objects did new pleasure give,　　　160
And once again he wish'd to live
As lawless as before.

Meanwhile as thus with him it fared,
They for the voyage were prepared
And went to the sea-shore,
But, when they thither came, the Youth
Deserted his poor Bride, and Ruth
Could never find him more.

"God help thee Ruth!" – Such pains she had
That she in half a year was mad　　　170
And in a prison hous'd,
And there, exulting in her wrongs,
Among the music of her songs
She fearfully carouz'd.

Yet sometimes milder hours she knew,
Nor wanted sun, nor rain, nor dew,
Nor pastimes of the May,
They all were with her in her cell,
And a wild brook with chearful knell
Did o'er the pebbles play.　　　180

When Ruth three seasons thus had lain
There came a respite to her pain,
She from her prison fled;
But of the Vagrant none took thought,
And where it liked her best she sought
Her shelter and her bread.

Among the fields she breath'd again:
The master-current of her brain
Ran permanent and free,

And to the pleasant Banks of Tone*   190
She took her way, to dwell alone
Under the greenwood tree.

The engines of her grief, the tools
That shap'd her sorrow, rocks and pools,
And airs that gently stir
The vernal leaves, she loved them still,
Nor ever tax'd them with the ill
Which had been done to her.

A Barn her *winter* bed supplies,
But till the warmth of summer skies   200
And summer days is gone,
(And in this tale we all agree)
She sleeps beneath the greenwood tree,
And other home hath none.

If she is press'd by want of food
She from her dwelling in the wood
Repairs to a road side,

* The Tone is a River of Somersetshire at no great distance from the
Quantock Hills. These Hills, which are alluded to a few stanzas below,
are extremely beautiful, and in most places richly covered with Coppice
woods.

190–191. And, coming to the banks of Tone,
            There did she rest; and dwell alone [1802].
      193. grief] pain [1802].
  202. (And all do in this tale agree) [1805].
204–205. In 1802 the following stanza inserted;

            The neighbours grieve for her, and say   1
            That she will, long before her day,
            Be broken down and old.
            Sore aches she needs must have ! but less
            Of mind, than body's wretchedness,   5
            From damp, and rain, and cold.

      (1–2) The neighbours . . . her day]
            An innocent life, yet far astray!
            And Ruth will, long before her day, [1805].

And there she begs at one steep place,
Where up and down with easy pace
The horsemen-travellers ride.   210

That oaten pipe of hers is mute
Or thrown away, but with a flute
Her loneliness she cheers;
This flute made of a hemlock stalk
At evening in his homeward walk
The Quantock Woodman hears.

I, too, have pass'd her on the hills
Setting her little water-mills
By spouts and fountains wild,
Such small machinery as she turn'd   220
Ere she had wept, ere she had mourn'd
A young and happy Child!

Farewell! and when thy days are told
Ill-fated Ruth! in hallow'd mold
Thy corpse shall buried be,
For thee a funeral bell shall ring,
And all the congregation sing
A Christian psalm for thee.

Lines

Written with a Slate-pencil upon a Stone,
the largest of a heap lying near a deserted Quarry,
upon one of the Islands at Rydale

Stranger! this hillock of misshapen stones
Is not a ruin of the ancient time,
Nor, as perchance thou rashly deem'st, the Cairn
Of some old British Chief: 'tis nothing more
Than the rude embryo of a little dome
Or pleasure-house, which was to have been built
Among the birch-trees of this rocky isle.
But, as it chanc'd, Sir William having learn'd
That from the shore a full-grown man might wade,
And make himself a freeman of this spot   10
At any hour he chose, the Knight forthwith
Desisted, and the quarry and the mound
Are monuments of his unfinish'd task. –
The block on which these lines are trac'd, perhaps,
Was once selected as the corner-stone
Of the intended pile, which would have been
Some quaint odd play-thing of elaborate skill,
So that, I guess, the linnet and the thrush,
And other little builders who dwell here,
Had wonder'd at the work. But blame him not,   20
For old Sir William was a gentle Knight
Bred in this vale to which he appertain'd
With all his ancestry. Then peace to him
And for the outrage which he had devis'd
Entire forgiveness. – But if thou art one
On fire with thy impatience to become
An Inmate of these mountains, if disturb'd

6. which was to have been built] once destin'd to be built [1802].

By beautiful conceptions, thou hast hewn
Out of the quiet rock the elements
Of thy trim mansion destin'd soon to blaze   30
In snow-white splendour, think again, and taught
By old Sir William and his quarry, leave
Thy fragments to the bramble and the rose,
There let the vernal slow-worm sun himself,
And let the red-breast hop from stone to stone.

In the School of ———— *is a tablet on which are inscribed, in
gilt letters, the names of the several persons who have been School-
masters there since the foundation of the School, with the time at
which they entered upon and quitted their office. Opposite one of
those names the Author wrote the following lines*

If Nature, for a favorite Child
In thee hath temper'd so her clay,
That every hour thy heart runs wild
Yet never once doth go astray,

Read o'er these lines; and then review
This tablet, that thus humbly rears   10
In such diversity of hue
Its history of two hundred years.

– When through this little wreck of fame,
Cypher and syllable, thine eye
Has travell'd down to Matthew's name,
Pause with no common sympathy.

And if a sleeping tear should wake
Then be it neither check'd nor stay'd:
For Matthew a request I make
Which for himself he had not made.   20

31. splendour] glory [1802].

Poor Matthew, all his frolics o'er,
Is silent as a standing pool,
Far from the chimney's merry roar,
And murmur of the village school.

The sighs which Matthew heav'd were sighs
Of one tir'd out with fun and madness;
The tears which came to Matthew's eyes
Were tears of light, the oil of gladness.

Yet sometimes when the secret cup
Of still and serious thought went round   30
It seem'd as if he drank it up,
He felt with spirit so profound.

— Thou soul of God's best earthly mould,
Thou happy soul, and can it be
That these two words of glittering gold
Are all that must remain of thee?

The Two April Mornings

We walk'd along, while bright and red
Uprose the morning sun,
And Matthew stopp'd, he look'd, and said,
"The will of God be done!"

A village Schoolmaster was he,
With hair of glittering grey;
As blithe a man as you could see
On a spring holiday.

36. of thee] to thee [1805].

And on that morning, through the grass,
And by the steaming rills,　　　　　　　　　　10
We travell'd merrily to pass
A day among the hills.

"Our work," said I, "was well begun;
Then, from thy breast what thought,
Beneath so beautiful a sun,
So sad a sigh has brought?

A second time did Matthew stop,
And fixing still his eye
Upon the eastern mountain-top
To me he made reply.　　　　　　　　　　　20

Yon cloud with that long purple cleft
Brings fresh into my mind
A day like this which I have left
Full thirty years behind.

And on that slope of springing corn
The self-same crimson hue
Fell from the sky that April morn,
The same which now I view!

With rod and line my silent sport
I plied by Derwent's wave,　　　　　　　　　30
And, coming to the church, stopp'd short
Beside my Daughter's grave.

Nine summers had she scarcely seen
The pride of all the vale;
And then she sang! – she would have been
A very nightingale.

25-29. And just above yon slope of corn
　　　　　Such colours, and no other
　　　　　Were in the sky, that April morn,
　　　　　Of this the very brother. [1802].
35. sang!] sung; – [1802].

Six feet in earth my Emma lay,
And yet I lov'd her more,
For so it seem'd, than till that day
I e'er had lov'd before.   40

And, turning from her grave, I met
Beside the church-yard Yew
A blooming Girl, whose hair was wet
With points of morning dew.

A basket on her head she bare,
Her brow was smooth and white,
To see a Child so very fair,
It was a pure delight!

No fountain from its rocky cave
E'er tripp'd with foot so free,   50
She seem'd as happy as a wave
That dances on the sea.

There came from me a sigh of pain
Which I could ill confine;
I look'd at her and look'd again;
– And did not wish her mine.

Matthew is in his grave, yet now
Methinks I see him stand,
As at that moment, with his bough
Of wilding in his hand.   60

The Fountain,

A CONVERSATION

We talk'd with open heart, and tongue
Affectionate and true,
A pair of Friends, though I was young,
And Matthew seventy-two.

We lay beneath a spreading oak,
Beside a mossy seat,
And from the turf a fountain broke,
And gurgled at our feet.

Now, Matthew, let us try to match
This water's pleasant tune   10
With some old Border-song, or catch
That suits a summer's noon.

Or of the Church-clock and the chimes
Sing here beneath the shade,
That half-mad thing of witty rhymes
Which you last April made!

In silence Matthew lay, and eyed
The spring beneath the tree;
And thus the dear old Man replied,
The grey-hair'd Man of glee.   20

"Down to the vale this water steers,
How merrily it goes!
'Twill murmur on a thousand years,
And flow as now it flows.

17. In silence] On silence [1800 amend. second errat.].

And here, on this delightful day,
I cannot chuse but think
How oft, a vigorous Man, I lay
Beside this Fountain's brink.

My eyes are dim with childish tears,
My heart is idly stirr'd,   30
For the same sound is in my ears,
Which in those days I heard.

Thus fares it still in our decay:
And yet the wiser mind
Mourns less for what age takes away
Than what it leaves behind.

The blackbird in the summer trees,
The lark upon the hill,
Let loose their carols when they please,
Are quiet when they will.   40

With Nature never do *they* wage
A foolish strife; they see
A happy youth, and their old age
Is beautiful and free:

But we are press'd by heavy laws,
And often, glad no more,
We wear a face of joy, because
We have been glad of yore.

If there is one who need bemoan
His kindred laid in earth,   50
The household hearts that were his own,
It is the man of mirth.

My days, my Friend, are almost gone,
My life has been approv'd,
And many love me, but by none
Am I enough belov'd."

"Now both himself and me he wrongs,
The man who thus complains!
I live and sing my idle songs
Upon these happy plains,   60

And, Matthew, for thy Children dead
I'll be a son to thee!"
At this he grasp'd his hands, and said,
"Alas! that cannot be."

We rose up from the fountain-side,
And down the smooth descent
Of the green sheep-track did we glide,
And through the wood we went,

And, ere we came to Leonard's Rock,
He sang those witty rhymes   70
About the crazy old church-clock
And the bewilder'd chimes.

Nutting

It seems a day,
(I speak of one from many singled out)
One of those heavenly days which cannot die,
When forth I sallied from our cottage-door,*
And with a wallet o'er my shoulder slung,
A nutting crook in hand, I turn'd my steps
Towards the distant woods, a Figure quaint,
Trick'd out in proud disguise of Beggar's weeds
Put on for the occasion, by advice
And exhortation of my frugal Dame.   10
Motley accoutrement! of power to smile

* The house at which I was boarded during the time I was at School.

2. Added second errat. 1800.
11. accoutrement!] accoutrements! [1800 amend. second errat.].

At thorns, and brakes, and brambles, and, in **truth,**
More ragged than need was. Among the woods,
And o'er the pathless rocks, I forc'd my way
Until, at length, I came to one dear nook
Unvisited, where not a broken bough
Droop'd with its wither'd leaves, ungracious sign
Of devastation, but the hazels rose
Tall and erect, with milk-white clusters hung,
A virgin scene ! – A little while I stood,   20
Breathing with such suppression of the heart
As joy delights in; and with wise restraint
Voluptuous, fearless of a rival, eyed
The banquet, or beneath the trees I sate
Among the flowers, and with the flowers I play'd;
A temper known to those, who, after long
And weary expectation, have been bless'd
With sudden happiness beyond all hope. –
– Perhaps it was a bower beneath whose leaves
The violets of five seasons re-appear   30
And fade, unseen by any human eye,
Where fairy water-breaks do murmur on
For ever, and I saw the sparkling foam,
And with my cheek on one of those green stones
That, fleec'd with moss, beneath the shady trees,
Lay round me scatter'd like a flock of sheep,
I heard the murmur and the murmuring sound,
In that sweet mood when pleasure loves to pay
Tribute to ease, and, of its joy secure
The heart luxuriates with indifferent things,   40
Wasting its kindliness on stocks and stones,
And on the vacant air. Then up I rose,
And dragg'd to earth both branch and bough, with crash
And merciless ravage; and the shady nook
Of hazels, and the green and mossy bower
Deform'd and sullied, patiently gave up
Their quiet being: and unless I now

Confound my present feelings with the past,
Even then, when from the bower I turn'd away,
Exulting, rich beyond the wealth of kings   50
I felt a sense of pain when I beheld
The silent trees and the intruding sky. –

Then, dearest Maiden! move along these shades
In gentleness of heart with gentle hand
Touch, – for there is a Spirit in the woods.

———

Three years she grew in sun and shower,
Then Nature said, "A lovelier flower
On earth was never sown;
This Child I to myself will take,
She shall be mine, and I will make
A Lady of my own.

Myself will to my darling be
Both law and impulse, and with me
The Girl in rock and plain,
In earth and heaven, in glade and bower,   10
Shall feel an overseeing power
To kindle or restrain.

She shall be sportive as the fawn
That wild with glee across the lawn
Or up the mountain springs,
And hers shall be the breathing balm,
And hers the silence and the calm
Of mute insensate things.

The floating clouds their state shall lend
To her, for her the willow bend,   20

7–8. Her Teacher I myself will be,
      She is my darling; and with me [1802 only].

Nor shall she fail to see
Even in the motions of the storm
Grace that shall mould the Maiden's form
By silent sympathy.

The stars of midnight shall be dear
To her, and she shall lean her ear
In many a secret place
Where rivulets dance their wayward round,
And beauty born of murmuring sound
Shall pass into her face.   30

And vital feelings of delight
Shall rear her form to stately height,
Her virgin bosom swell,
Such thoughts to Lucy I will give
While she and I together live
Here in this happy dell.

Thus Nature spake – The work was done –
How soon my Lucy's race was run!
She died and left to me
This heath, this calm and quiet scene,   40
The memory of what has been,
And never more will be.

The Pet-Lamb,

A PASTORAL

The dew was falling fast, the stars began to blink;
I heard a voice, it said, Drink, pretty Creature, drink!
And, looking o'er the hedge, before me I espied,
A snow-white mountain Lamb with a Maiden at its side.

No other sheep were near, the Lamb was all alone,
And by a slender cord was tether'd to a stone;
With one knee on the grass did the little Maiden kneel,
While to that Mountain Lamb she gave its evening meal.

The Lamb while from her hand he thus his supper took
Seem'd to feast with head and ears, and his tail with pleasure
    shook.   10
"Drink, pretty Creature, drink," she said in such a tone
That I almost receiv'd her heart into my own.

'Twas little Barbara Lewthwaite, a Child of beauty rare,
I watch'd them with delight, they were a lovely pair.
Now with her empty Can the Maiden turn'd away,
But ere ten yards were gone her footsteps did she stay.

Towards the Lamb she look'd, and from that shady place
I unobserv'd could see the workings of her face:
If Nature to her tongue could measur'd numbers bring
Thus, thought I, to her Lamb that little Maid might sing. 20

"What ails thee, Young One? What? Why pull so at thy cord?
Is it not well with thee? Well both for bed and board?
Thy plot of grass is soft, and green as grass can be,
Rest little Young One, rest; what is't that aileth thee?

---

23. A beauty that shall mould her form [1800 amend. second
    errat.].

15. Now with her empty Can] And now with empty Can [1800
    amend. second errat.].

20. might] would [1800 amend. second errat.].

What is it thou would'st seek? What is wanting to thy heart?
Thy limbs are they not strong? And beautiful thou art:
This grass is tender grass, these flowers they have no peers,
And that green corn all day is rustling in thy ears.

If the Sun is shining hot, do but stretch thy woollen chain,
This beech is standing by, its covert thou can'st gain,   30
For rain and mountain storms the like thou need'st not fear,
The rain and storm are things which scarcely can come here.

Rest, little Young One, rest; thou hast forgot the day
When my Father found thee first in places far away:
Many flocks are on the hills, but thou wert own'd by none,
And thy Mother from thy side for evermore was gone.

He took thee in his arms, and in pity brought thee home,
A blessed day for thee! then whither would'st thou roam?
A faithful nurse thou hast, the dam that did thee yean
Upon the mountain tops no kinder could have been.   40

Thou know'st that twice a day I have brought thee in this
     Can
Fresh water from the brook as clear as ever ran;
And twice in the day when the ground is wet with dew
I bring thee draughts of milk, warm milk it is and new.

Thy limbs will shortly be twice as stout as they are now,
Then I'll yoke thee to my cart like a pony in the plough,
My playmate thou shalt be, and when the wind is cold
Our hearth shall be thy bed, our house shall be thy fold.

It will not, will not rest! – poor Creature can it be
That 'tis thy Mother's heart which is working so in thee?   50
Things that I know not of belike to thee are dear,
And dreams of things which thou can'st neither see nor hear.

---

29. is] be [1802].

Alas, the mountain tops that look so green and fair!
I've heard of fearful winds and darkness that come there,
The little brooks, that seem all pastime and all play,
When they are angry, roar like lions for their prey.

Here thou need'st not dread the raven in the sky,
He will not come to thee, our Cottage is hard by,
Night and day thou art safe as living thing can be,
Be happy then and rest, what is't that aileth thee?   60

As homeward through the lane I went with lazy feet,
This song to myself did I oftentimes repeat,
And it seem'd as I retrac'd the ballad line by line
That but half of it was hers, and one half of it was mine.

Again, and once again did I repeat the song,
"Nay" said I, "more than half to the Damsel must belong,
For she look'd with such a look, and she spake with such a
      tone,
That I almost receiv'd her heart into my own."

58-60. Night and day thou art safe, – our Cottage is hard by.
        Why bleat so after me? Why pull so at thy chain?
        Sleep – and at break of day I will come to thee again!
                                                    [1802]

Written in Germany, on one of the coldest days of the Century

I must apprize the Reader that the stoves in North Germany generally have the impression of a galloping Horse upon them, this being part of the Brunswick Arms.

━━━━━

A fig for your languages, German and Norse,
Let me have the song of the Kettle,
And the tongs and the poker, instead of that horse
That gallops away with such fury and force
On this dreary dull plate of black metal.

Our earth is no doubt made of excellent stuff,
But her pulses beat slower and slower,
The weather in Forty was cutting and rough,
And then, as Heaven knows, the glass stood low enough,
And *now* it is four degrees lower.   10

Here's a Fly, a disconsolate creature, perhaps
A child of the field, or the grove,
And sorrow for him! this dull treacherous heat
Has seduc'd the poor fool from his winter retreat,
And he creeps to the edge of my stove.

Alas! how he fumbles about the domains
Which this comfortless oven environ,
He cannot find out in what track he must crawl,
Now back to the tiles, and now back to the wall,
And now on the brink of the iron.   20

Stock-still there he stands like a traveller bemaz'd,
The best of his skill he has tried;
His feelers methinks I can see him put forth
To the East and the West, and the South and the North,
But he finds neither guide-post nor guide.

See! his spindles sink under him, foot, leg and thigh,
His eyesight and hearing are lost,

Between life and death his blood freezes and thaws,
And his two pretty pinions of blue dusky gauze
Are glued to his sides by the frost.   30

No Brother, no Friend has he near him, while I
Can draw warmth from the cheek of my Love,
As blest and as glad in this desolate gloom,
As if green summer grass were the floor of my room,
And woodbines were hanging above.

Yet, God is my witness, thou small helpless Thing,
Thy life I would gladly sustain
Till summer comes up from the South, and with crowds
Of thy brethren a march thou should'st sound through the
    clouds,
And back to the forests again.   40

The Childless Father

Up, Timothy, up with your Staff and away !
Not a soul in the village this morning will stay;
The Hare has just started from Hamilton's grounds,
And Skiddaw is glad with the cry of the hounds.

– Of coats and of jackets grey, scarlet, and green,
On the slopes of the pastures all colours were seen,
With their comely blue aprons and caps white as snow,
The girls on the hills made a holiday show.

The bason of box-wood,* just six months before,
Had stood on the table at Timothy's door,   10

* In several parts of the North of England, when a funeral takes place, a bason full of Sprigs of Box-wood is placed at the door of the house from which the Coffin is taken up, and each person who attends the funeral ordinarily takes a Sprig of this Box-wood, and throws it into the grave of the deceased.

---

5. grey, scarlet, and green] both grey, red and green [1800 amend. errat.].

A Coffin through Timothy's threshold had pass'd,
One Child did it bear and that Child was his last.

Now fast up the dell came the noise and the fray,
The horse and the horn, and the hark ! hark away !
Old Timothy took up his Staff, and he shut
With a leisurely motion the door of his hut.

Perhaps to himself at that moment he said,
"The key I must take, for my Ellen is dead"
But of this in my ears not a word did he speak,
And he went to the chase with a tear on his cheek.   20

The Old Cumberland Beggar,

A DESCRIPTION

*The class of Beggars to which the old man here described belongs,
will probably soon be extinct. It consisted of poor, and, mostly,
old and infirm persons, who confined themselves to a stated round
in their neighbourhood, and had certain fixed days, on which, at
different houses, they regularly received charity; sometimes in
money, but mostly in provisions.*

I saw an aged Beggar in my walk,
And he was seated by the highway side
On a low structure of rude masonry
Built at the foot of a huge hill, that they
Who lead their horses down the steep rough road
May thence remount at ease. The aged man
Had placed his staff across the broad smooth stone
That overlays the pile, and from a bag
All white with flour, the dole of village dames,

He drew his scraps and fragments, one by one,   10
And scann'd them with a fix'd and serious look
Of idle computation. In the sun,
Upon the second step of that small pile,
Surrounded by those wild unpeopled hills,
He sate, and eat his food in solitude;
And ever, scatter'd from his palsied hand,
That still attempting to prevent the waste,
Was baffled still, the crumbs in little showers
Fell on the ground, and the small mountain birds,
Not venturing yet to peck their destin'd meal,   20
Approached within the length of half his staff.

Him from my childhood have I known, and then
He was so old, he seems not older now;
He travels on, a solitary man,
So helpless in appearance, that for him
The sauntering horseman-traveller does not throw
With careless hand his alms upon the ground,
But stops, that he may safely lodge the coin
Within the old Man's hat; nor quits him so,
But still when he has given his horse the rein   30
Towards the aged Beggar turns a look,
Sidelong and half-reverted. She who tends
The toll-gate, when in summer at her door
She turns her wheel, if on the road she sees
The aged Beggar coming, quits her work,
And lifts the latch for him that he may pass.
The Post-boy when his rattling wheels o'ertake
The aged Beggar, in the woody lane,
Shouts to him from behind, and, if perchance
The old Man does not change his course, the Boy   40
Turns with less noisy wheels to the road-side,
And passes gently by, without a curse

---

15. He sat, and ate his food in solitude [1805].

Upon his lips, or anger at his heart.
He travels on, a solitary Man,
His age has no companion. On the ground
His eyes are turn'd, and, as he moves along,
They move along the ground; and evermore,
Instead of common and habitual sight
Of fields with rural works, of hill and dale,
And the blue sky, one little span of earth   50
Is all his prospect. Thus, from day to day,
Bowbent, his eyes for ever on the ground,
He plies his weary journey, seeing still,
And never knowing that he sees, some straw,
Some scatter'd leaf, or marks which, in one track,
The nails of cart or chariot wheel have left
Impress'd on the white road, in the same line,
At distance still the same. Poor Traveller!
His staff trails with him, scarcely do his feet
Disturb the summer dust, he is so still   60
In look and motion that the cottage curs,
Ere he have pass'd the door, will turn away
Weary of barking at him. Boys and girls,
The vacant and the busy, maids and youths,
And urchins newly breech'd all pass him by:
Him even the slow-pac'd waggon leaves behind.

But deem not this man useless. – Statesmen! ye
Who are so restless in your wisdom, ye
Who have a broom still ready in your hands
To rid the world of nuisances; ye proud,   70
Heart-swoln, while in your pride ye contemplate
Your talents, power, and wisdom, deem him not
A burthen of the earth. 'Tis Nature's law
That none, the meanest of created things,
Of forms created the most vile and brute,
The dullest or most noxious, should exist
Divorced from good, a spirit and pulse of good,

A life and soul to every mode of being
Inseparably link'd. While thus he creeps
From door to door, the Villagers in him   80
Behold a record which together binds
Past deeds and offices of charity
Else unremember'd, and so keeps alive
The kindly mood in hearts which lapse of years,
And that half-wisdom half-experience gives
Make slow to feel, and by sure steps resign
To selfishness and cold oblivious cares.
Among the farms and solitary huts
Hamlets, and thinly-scattered villages,
Where'er the aged Beggar takes his rounds,   90
The mild necessity of use compels
To acts of love; and habit does the work
Of reason, yet prepares that after joy
Which reason cherishes. And thus the soul,
By that sweet taste of pleasure unpursu'd
Doth find itself insensibly dispos'd
To virtue and true goodness. Some there are,
By their good works exalted, lofty minds
And meditative, authors of delight
And happiness, which to the end of time   100
Will live, and spread, and kindle; minds like these,
In childhood, from this solitary being,
This helpless wanderer, have perchance receiv'd,
(A thing more precious far than all that books
Or the solicitudes of love can do !)
That first mild touch of sympathy and thought,
In which they found their kindred with a world
Where want and sorrow were. The easy man
Who sits at his own door, and like the pear
Which overhangs his head from the green wall,   110
Feeds in the sunshine; the robust and young,
The prosperous and unthinking, they who live
Shelter'd, and flourish in a little grove

Of their own kindred, all behold in him
A silent monitor, which on their minds
Must needs impress a transitory thought
Of self-congratulation, to the heart
Of each recalling his peculiar boons,
His charters and exemptions; and perchance,
Though he to no one give the fortitude   120
And circumspection needful to preserve
His present blessings, and to husband up
The respite of the season, he, at least,
And 'tis no vulgar service, makes them felt.

Yet further. – Many, I believe, there are
Who live a life of virtuous decency,
Men who can hear the Decalogue and feel
No self-reproach, who of the moral law
Establish'd in the land where they abide
Are strict observers, and not negligent,   130
Meanwhile, in any tenderness of heart
Or act of love to those with whom they dwell,
Their kindred, and the children of their blood.
Praise be to such, and to their slumbers peace !
– But of the poor man ask, the abject poor,
Go and demand of him, if there be here,
In this cold abstinence from evil deeds,
And these inevitable charities,
Wherewith to satisfy the human soul.
No – man is dear to man: the poorest poor   140
Long for some moments in a weary life
When they can know and feel that they have been
Themselves the fathers and the dealers out
Of some small blessings, have been kind to such
As needed kindness, for this single cause,
That we have all of us one human heart.
– Such pleasure is to one kind Being known
My Neighbour, when with punctual care, each week

Duly as Friday comes, though press'd herself
By her own wants, she from her chest of meal   150
Takes one unsparing handful for the scrip
Of this old Mendicant, and, from her door
Returning with exhilarated heart,
Sits by her fire and builds her hope in heav'n.

Then let him pass, a blessing on his head !
And while, in that vast solitude to which
The tide of things has led him, he appears
To breathe and live but for himself alone,
Unblam'd, uninjur'd, let him bear about
The good which the benignant law of heaven   160
Has hung around him, and, while life is his,
Still let him prompt the unletter'd Villagers
To tender offices and pensive thoughts.
Then let him pass, a blessing on his head !
And, long as he can wander, let him breathe
The freshness of the vallies, let his blood
Struggle with frosty air and winter snows,
And let the charter'd wind that sweeps the heath
Beat his grey locks against his wither'd face.
Reverence the hope whose vital anxiousness   170
Gives the last human interest to his heart.
May never House, misnamed of industry,
Make him a captive; for that pent-up din,
Those life-consuming sounds that clog the air,
Be his the natural silence of old age.
Let him be free of mountain solitudes,
And have around him, whether heard or not,
The pleasant melody of woodland birds.
Few are his pleasures; if his eyes, which now
Have been so long familiar with the earth,   180
No more behold the horizontal sun
Rising or setting, let the light at least
Find a free entrance to their languid orbs.

And let him, *where* and *when* he will, sit down
Beneath the trees, or by the grassy bank
Of high-way side, and with the little birds
Share his chance-gather'd meal, and, finally,
As in the eye of Nature he has liv'd,
So in the eye of Nature let him die.

Rural Architecture

There's George Fisher, Charles Fleming, and Reginald Shore,
Three rosy-cheek'd School-boys, the highest not more
Than the height of a Counsellor's bag;
To the top of Great How* did it please them to climb,
And there they built up without mortar or lime
A Man on the peak of the crag.

They built him of stones gather'd up as they lay,
They built him and christen'd him all in one day,
An Urchin both vigorous and hale;
And so without scruple they call'd him Ralph Jones.   10
Now Ralph is renown'd for the length of his bones;
The Magog of Legberthwaite dale.

Just half a week after the Wind sallied forth,
And, in anger or merriment, out of the North
Coming on with a terrible pother,
From the peak of the crag blew the Giant away.
And what did these School-boys? – The very next day
They went and they built up another.

---

* Great How is a single and conspicuous hill, which rises towards
the foot of Thirl-mere, on the western side of the beautiful dale of
Legberthwaite, along the high road between Keswick and Ambleside.

– Some little I've seen of blind boisterous works
In Paris and London, 'mong Christians or Turks,   20
Spirits busy to do and undo:
At remembrance whereof my blood sometimes will flag.
– Then, light-hearted Boys, to the top of the Crag!
And I'll build up a Giant with you.

A Poet's Epitaph

Art thou a Statesman, in the van
Of public business train'd and bred,
– First learn to love one living man;
Then may'st thou think upon the dead.

A Lawyer art thou? – draw not nigh;
Go, carry to some other place
The hardness of thy coward eye,
The falsehood of thy sallow face.

Art thou a man of purple cheer?
A rosy man, right plump to see?   10
Approach; yet Doctor, not too near:
This grave no cushion is for thee.

Art thou a man of gallant pride,
A Soldier, and no man of chaff?
Welcome! – but lay thy sword aside,
And lean upon a Peasant's staff.

Physician art thou? One, all eyes,
Philosopher! a fingering slave,
One that would peep and botanize
Upon his mother's grave?   20

Wrapp'd closely in thy sensual fleece
O turn aside, and take, I pray,
That he below may rest in peace,
Thy pin-point of a soul away!

19–24. St. om. [1805].

– A Moralist perchance appears;
Led, Heaven knows how ! to this poor sod:
And He has neither eyes nor ears;
Himself his world, and his own God;

One to whose smooth-rubb'd soul can cling
Nor form nor feeling great nor small,   30
A reasoning, self-sufficing thing,
An intellectual All in All !

Shut close the door ! press down the latch:
Sleep in thy intellectual crust,
Nor lose ten tickings of thy watch,
Near this unprofitable dust.

But who is He with modest looks,
And clad in homely russet brown?
He murmurs near the running brooks
A music sweeter than their own.   40

He is retired as noontide dew,
Or fountain in a noonday grove;
And you must love him, ere to you
He will seem worthy of your love.

The outward shews of sky and earth,
Of hill and valley he has view'd;
And impulses of deeper birth
Have come to him in solitude.

In common things that round us lie
Some random truths he can impart   50
The harvest of a quiet eye
That broods and sleeps on his own heart.

31. self-sufficing] self-sufficient [1802].

But he is weak, both man and boy,
Hath been an idler in the land;
Contented if he might enjoy
The things which others understand.

– Come hither in thy hour of strength,
Come, weak as is a breaking wave !
Here stretch thy body at full length;
Or build thy house upon this grave. –   60

A Character,

in the antithetical Manner

I marvel how Nature could ever find space
For the weight and the levity seen in his face:
There's thought and no thought, and there's paleness and
    bloom,
And bustle and sluggishness, pleasure and gloom.

There's weakness, and strength both redundant and vain;
Such strength, as if ever affliction and pain
Could pierce through a temper that's soft to disease,
Would be rational peace – a philosopher's ease.

There's indifference, alike when he fails and succeeds,
And attention full ten times as much as there needs,   10
Pride where there's no envy, there's so much of joy;
And mildness, and spirit both forward and coy.

There's freedom, and sometimes a diffident stare
Of shame scarcely seeming to know that she's there.
There's virtue, the title it surely may claim,
Yet wants, heaven knows what, to be worthy the name.

What a picture ! 'tis drawn without nature or art,
– Yet the Man would at once run away with your heart,
And I for five centuries right gladly would be
Such an odd, such a kind happy creature as he.   20

A Fragment

Between two sister moorland rills
There is a spot that seems to lie
Sacred to flowrets of the hills,
And sacred to the sky.
And in this smooth and open dell
There is a tempest-stricken tree;
A corner-stone by lightning cut,
The last stone of a cottage hut;
And in this dell you see
A thing no storm can e'er destroy,   10
The shadow of a Danish Boy.

In clouds above, the lark is heard,
He sings his blithest and his best;
But in this lonesome nook the bird
Did never build his nest.
No beast, no bird hath here his home;
The bees borne on the breezy air
Pass high above those fragrant bells
To other flowers, to other dells,
Nor ever linger there.   20
The Danish Boy walks here alone:
The lovely dell is all his own.

A spirit of noon day is he,
He seems a Form of flesh and blood;
A piping Shepherd he might be,
A Herd-boy of the wood.
A regal vest of fur he wears,

In colour like a raven's wing;
It fears nor rain, nor wind, nor dew,
But in the storm 'tis fresh and blue   30
As budding pines in Spring;
His helmet has a vernal grace,
Fresh as the bloom upon his face.

A harp is from his shoulder slung;
He rests the harp upon his knee,
And there in a forgotten tongue
He warbles melody.
Of flocks and herds both far and near
He is the darling and the joy,
And often, when no cause appears,   40
The mountain ponies prick their ears,
They hear the Danish Boy,
While in the dell he sits alone
Beside the tree and corner-stone.

When near this blasted tree you pass,
Two sods are plainly to be seen
Close at its root, and each with grass
Is cover'd fresh and green.
Like turf upon a new-made grave
These two green sods together lie,   50
Nor heat, nor cold, nor rain, nor wind
Can these two sods together bind,
Nor sun, nor earth, nor sky,
But side by side the two are laid,
As if just sever'd by the spade.

There sits he: in his face you spy
No trace of a ferocious air,
Nor ever was a cloudless sky
So steady or so fair.

---

38. Of flocks upon the neighbouring hills [1802].
45–55. St. om. [1802].

The lovely Danish Boy is blest   60
And happy in his flowery cove;
From bloody deeds his thoughts are far;
And yet he warbles songs of war;
They seem like songs of love,
For calm and gentle is his mien;
Like a dead Boy he is serene.

* * * * * * * * * * *

Poems on the Naming of Places

Advertisement

By Persons resident in the country and attached to rural
objects, many places will be found unnamed or of unknown
names, where little Incidents will have occurred, or
feelings been experienced, which will have given to such
places a private and peculiar interest. From a wish to give
some sort of record to such Incidents or renew the gratifi-
cation of such Feelings, Names have been given to Places
by the Author and some of his Friends, and the following
Poems written in consequence.

Poems on the Naming of Places

I

It was an April Morning: fresh and clear
The Rivulet, delighting in its strength,
Ran with a young man's speed, and yet the voice
Of waters which the winter had supplied
Was soften'd down into a vernal tone.
The spirit of enjoyment and desire,
And hopes and wishes, from all living things
Went circling, like a multitude of sounds.
The budding groves appear'd as if in haste
To spur the steps of June; as if their shades   10
Of *various* green were hindrances that stood
Between them and their object: yet, meanwhile,
There was such deep contentment in the air
That every naked ash, and tardy tree
Yet leafless, seem'd as though the countenance
With which it look'd on this delightful day
Were native to the summer. – Up the brook
I roam'd in the confusion of my heart,
Alive to all things and forgetting all.
At length I to a sudden turning came   20
In this continuous glen, where down a rock
The stream, so ardent in its course before,
Sent forth such sallies of glad sound, that all
Which I till then had heard, appear'd the voice
Of common pleasure: beast and bird, the lamb,
The Shepherd's dog, the linnet and the thrush
Vied with this waterfall, and made a song
Which, while I listen'd, seem'd like the wild growth

Or like some natural produce of the air
That could not cease to be. Green leaves were here,   30
But 'twas the foliage of the rocks, the birch,
The yew, the holly, and the bright green thorn,
With hanging islands of resplendent furze:
And on a summit, distant a short space,
By any who should look beyond the dell,
A single mountain Cottage might be seen.
I gaz'd and gaz'd, and to myself I said,
"Our thoughts at least are ours; and this wild nook,
My EMMA, I will dedicate to thee."
— Soon did the spot become my other home,   40
My dwelling, and my out-of-doors abode.
And, of the Shepherds who have seen me there,
To whom I sometimes in our idle talk
Have told this fancy, two or three, perhaps,
Years after we are gone and in our graves,
When they have cause to speak of this wild place,
May call it by the name of EMMA'S DELL.

II

To Joanna

Amid the smoke of cities did you pass
Your time of early youth, and there you learn'd,
From years of quiet industry, to love
The living Beings by your own fire-side,
With such a strong devotion, that your heart
Is slow towards the sympathies of them
Who look upon the hills with tenderness,
And make dear friendships with the streams and groves.
Yet we who are transgressors in this kind,
Dwelling retired in our simplicity   10
Among the woods and fields, we love you well,

Joanna! and I guess, since you have been
So distant from us now for two long years,
That you will gladly listen to discourse
However trivial, if you thence are taught
That they, with whom you once were happy, talk
Familiarly of you and of old times.

While I was seated, now some ten days past,
Beneath those lofty firs, that overtop
Their ancient neighbour, the old Steeple tower,   20
The Vicar from his gloomy house hard by
Came forth to greet me, and when he had ask'd,
"How fares Joanna, that wild-hearted Maid!
And when will she return to us?" he paus'd,
And after short exchange of village news,
He with grave looks demanded, for what cause,
Reviving obsolete Idolatry,
I like a Runic Priest, in characters
Of formidable size, had chisel'd out
Some uncouth name upon the native rock,   30
Above the Rotha, by the forest side.
– Now, by those dear immunities of heart
Engender'd betwixt malice and true love,
I was not loth to be so catechiz'd,
And this was my reply. – "As it befel,
One summer morning we had walk'd abroad
At break of day, Joanna and myself.
– 'Twas that delightful season, when the broom,
Full flower'd, and visible on every steep,
Along the copses runs in veins of gold.   40
Our pathway led us on to Rotha's banks,
And when we came in front of that tall rock
Which looks towards the East, I there stopp'd short,
And trac'd the lofty barrier with my eye
From base to summit; such delight I found
To note in shrub and tree, in stone and flower,

That intermixture of delicious hues,
Along so vast a surface, all at once,
In one impression, by connecting force
Of their own beauty, imag'd in the heart.   50
– When I had gaz'd perhaps two minutes' space,
Joanna, looking in my eyes, beheld
That ravishment of mine, and laugh'd aloud.
The rock, like something starting from a sleep,
Took up the Lady's voice, and laugh'd again:
That ancient Woman seated on Helm-crag
Was ready with her cavern; Hammar-Scar,
And the tall Steep of Silver-How sent forth
A noise of laughter; southern Loughrigg heard,
And Fairfield answer'd with a mountain tone: 60
Helvellyn far into the clear blue sky
Carried the Lady's voice, – old Skiddaw blew
His speaking trumpet; – back out of the clouds
Of Glaramara southward came the voice;
And Kirkstone toss'd it from his misty head.
Now whether, (said I to our cordial Friend
Who in the hey-day of astonishment
Smil'd in my face) this were in simple truth
A work accomplish'd by the brotherhood
Of ancient mountains, or my ear was touch'd   70
With dreams and visionary impulses,
Is not for me to tell; but sure I am
That there was a loud uproar in the hills.
And, while we both were listening, to my side
The fair Joanna drew, as if she wish'd
To shelter from some object of her fear.
– And hence, long afterwards, when eighteen moons
Were wasted, as I chanc'd to walk alone
Beneath this rock, at sun-rise, on a calm
And silent morning, I sate down, and there,   80
In memory of affections old and true,
I chissel'd out in those rude characters

Joanna's name upon the living stone.
And I, and all who dwell by my fire-side
Have call'd the lovely rock, Joanna's Rock."

NOTE

In Cumberland and Westmoreland are several Inscriptions upon the native rock which from the wasting of Time and the rudeness of the Workmanship had been mistaken for Runic. They are without doubt Roman.

The Rotha, mentioned in this poem, is the River which flowing through the Lakes of Grasmere and Rydale falls into Wyndermere. On Helm-Crag, that impressive single Mountain at the head of the Vale of Grasmere, is a Rock which from most points of view bears a striking resemblance to an Old Woman cowering. Close by this rock is one of those Fissures or Caverns, which in the language of the Country are called Dungeons. The other Mountains either immediately surround the Vale of Grasmere, or belong to the same Cluster.

III

There is an Eminence, – of these our hills
The last that parleys with the setting sun.
We can behold it from our Orchard-seat,
And, when at evening we pursue our walk
Along the public way, this Cliff, so high
Above us, and so distant in its height,
Is visible, and often seems to send
Its own deep quiet to restore our hearts.
The meteors make of it a favorite haunt:
The star of Jove, so beautiful and large   10
In the mid heav'ns, is never half so fair
As when he shines above it. 'Tis in truth
The loneliest place we have among the clouds.
And She who dwells with me, whom I have lov'd
With such communion, that no place on earth
Can ever be a solitude to me,
Hath said, this lonesome Peak shall bear my Name.

IV

A narrow girdle of rough stones and crags,
A rude and natural causeway, interpos'd
Between the water and a winding slope
Of copse and thicket, leaves the eastern shore
Of Grasmere safe in its own privacy.
And there, myself and two beloved Friends,
One calm September morning, ere the mist
Had altogether yielded to the sun,
Saunter'd on this retir'd and difficult way.
– Ill suits the road with one in haste, but we   10
Play'd with our time; and, as we stroll'd along,
It was our occupation to observe
Such objects as the waves had toss'd ashore,
Feather, or leaf, or weed, or wither'd bough,
Each on the other heap'd along the line
Of the dry wreck. And in our vacant mood,
Not seldom did we stop to watch some tuft
Of dandelion seed or thistle's beard,
Which, seeming lifeless half, and half impell'd
By some internal feeling, skimm'd along   20
Close to the surface of the lake that lay
Asleep in a dead calm, ran closely on
Along the dead calm lake, now here, now there,
In all its sportive wanderings all the while
Making report of an invisible breeze
That was its wings, its chariot, and its horse,
Its very playmate, and its moving soul.
– And often, trifling with a privilege
Alike indulg'd to all, we paus'd, one now,
And now the other, to point out, perchance   30
To pluck, some flower or water-weed, too fair
Either to be divided from the place
On which it grew, or to be left alone
To its own beauty. Many such there are,

Fair ferns and flowers, and chiefly that tall plant
So stately, of the Queen Osmunda nam'd,
Plant lovelier in its own retir'd abode
On Grasmere's beach, than Naid by the side
Of Grecian brook, or Lady of the Mere
Sole-sitting by the shores of old Romance.   40
– So fared we that sweet morning: from the fields
Meanwhile, a noise was heard, the busy mirth
Of Reapers, Men and Women, Boys and Girls.
Delighted much to listen to those sounds,
And in the fashion which I have describ'd,
Feeding unthinking fancies, we advanc'd
Along the indented shore; when suddenly,
Through a thin veil of glittering haze, we saw
Before us on a point of jutting land
The tall and upright figure of a Man   50
Attir'd in peasant's garb, who stood alone
Angling beside the margin of the lake.
That way we turn'd our steps; nor was it long,
Ere making ready comments on the sight
Which then we saw, with one and the same voice
We all cried out, that he must be indeed
An idle man, who thus could lose a day
Of the mid harvest, when the labourer's hire
Is ample, and some little might be stor'd
Wherewith to chear him in the winter time.   60
Thus talking of that Peasant we approach'd
Close to the spot where with his rod and line
He stood alone; whereat he turn'd his head
To greet us – and we saw a man worn down
By sickness, gaunt and lean, with sunken cheeks
And wasted limbs, his legs so long and lean
That for my single self I look'd at them,
Forgetful of the body they sustain'd. –

---

35. plant] Fern [1802].

Too weak to labour in the harvest field,
The man was using his best skill to gain   70
A pittance from the dead unfeeling lake
That knew not of his wants. I will not say
What thoughts immediately were ours, nor how
The happy idleness of that sweet morn,
With all its lovely images, was chang'd
To serious musing and to self-reproach.
Nor did we fail to see within ourselves
What need there is to be reserv'd in speech,
And temper all our thoughts with charity.
– Therefore, unwilling to forget that day,   80
My Friend, Myself, and She who then receiv'd
The same admonishment, have call'd the place
By a memorial name, uncouth indeed
As e'er by Mariner was giv'n to Bay
Or Foreland on a new-discover'd coast,
And, POINT RASH-JUDGMENT is the Name it bears.

V

To M. H.

Our walk was far among the ancient trees:
There was no road, nor any woodman's path,
But the thick umbrage, checking the wild growth
Of weed and sapling, on the soft green turf
Beneath the branches of itself had made
A track which brought us to a slip of lawn,
And a small bed of water in the woods.
All round this pool both flocks and herds might drink
On its firm margin, even as from a well
Or some stone-bason which the Herdsman's hand   10
Had shap'd for their refreshment, nor did sun
Or wind from any quarter ever come
But as a blessing to this calm recess,

This glade of water and this one green field.
The spot was made by Nature for herself:
The travellers know it not, and 'twill remain
Unknown to them; but it is beautiful,
And if a man should plant his cottage near,
Should sleep beneath the shelter of its trees,
And blend its waters with his daily meal,   20
He would so love it that in his death-hour
Its image would survive among his thoughts,
And, therefore, my sweet MARY, this still nook
With all its beeches we have named from You.

Michael,

A PASTORAL POEM

If from the public way you turn your steps
Up the tumultuous brook of Green-head Gill,
You will suppose that with an upright path
Your feet must struggle; in such bold ascent
The pastoral Mountains front you, face to face.
But, courage! for beside that boisterous Brook
The mountains have all open'd out themselves,
And made a hidden valley of their own.
No habitation there is seen; but such
As journey thither find themselves alone   10
With a few sheep, with rocks and stones, and kites
That overhead are sailing in the sky.

It is in truth an utter solitude,
Nor should I have made mention of this Dell
But for one object which you might pass by,
Might see and notice not. Beside the brook
There is a straggling heap of unhewn stones!
And to that place a story appertains,

Which, though it be ungarnish'd with events,
Is not unfit, I deem, for the fire-side,   20
Or for the summer shade. It was the first,
The earliest of those tales that spake to me
Of Shepherds, dwellers in the vallies, men
Whom I already lov'd, not verily
For their own sakes, but for the fields and hills
Where was their occupation and abode.
And hence this Tale, while I was yet a boy
Careless of books, yet having felt the power
Of Nature, by the gentle agency
Of natural objects led me on to feel   30
For passions that were not my own, and think
At random and imperfectly indeed
On man; the heart of man and human life.
Therefore, although it be a history
Homely and rude, I will relate the same
For the delight of a few natural hearts,
And with yet fonder feeling, for the sake
Of youthful Poets, who among these Hills
Will be my second self when I am gone.

Upon the Forest-side in Grasmere Vale   40
There dwelt a Shepherd, Michael was his name,
An old man, stout of heart, and strong of limb.
His bodily frame had been from youth to age
Of an unusual strength; his mind was keen
Intense and frugal, apt for all affairs,
And in his Shepherd's calling he was prompt
And watchful more than ordinary men.
Hence he had learn'd the meaning of all winds,
Of blasts of every tone, and often-times
When others heeded not, He heard the South   50
Make subterraneous music, like the noise
Of Bagpipers on distant Highland hills;
The Shepherd, at such warning, of his flock

Bethought him, and he to himself would say
The winds are now devising work for me!
And truly at all times the storm, that drives
The Traveller to a shelter, summon'd him
Up to the mountains: he had been alone
Amid the heart of many thousand mists
That came to him and left him on the heights.   60
So liv'd he till his eightieth year was pass'd.

And grossly that man errs, who should suppose
That the green Valleys, and the Streams and Rocks
Were things indifferent to the Shepherd's thoughts.
Fields, where with chearful spirits he had breath'd
The common air; the hills, which he so oft
Had climb'd with vigorous steps; which had impress'd
So many incidents upon his mind
Of hardship, skill or courage, joy or fear;
Which like a book preserv'd the memory   70
Of the dumb animals, whom he had sav'd,
Had fed or shelter'd, linking to such acts,
So grateful in themselves, the certainty
Of honorable gains; these fields, these hills
Which were his living Being, even more
Than his own Blood – what could they less? had laid
Strong hold on his affections, were to him
A pleasurable feeling of blind love,
The pleasure which there is in life itself.

He had not passed his days in singleness.   80
He had a Wife, a comely Matron, old
Though younger than himself full twenty years.
She was a woman of a stirring life
Whose heart was in her house: two wheels she had
Of antique form, this large for spinning wool,

---

74. honorable gains] honourable gain [1805].

That small for flax, and if one wheel had rest,
It was because the other was at work.
The Pair had but one Inmate in their house,
An only Child, who had been born to them
When Michael telling o'er his years began   90
To deem that he was old, in Shepherd's phrase,
With one foot in the grave. This only son,
With two brave sheep dogs tried in many a storm,
The one of an inestimable worth,
Made all their Household. I may truly say,
That they were as a proverb in the vale
For endless industry. When day was gone,
And from their occupations out of doors
The Son and Father were come home, even then
Their labour did not cease, unless when all   100
Turn'd to their cleanly supper-board, and there
Each with a mess of pottage and skimm'd milk,
Sate round their basket pil'd with oaten cakes,
And their plain home-made cheese. Yet when their meal
Was ended, LUKE (for so the Son was nam'd)
And his old Father, both betook themselves
To such convenient work, as might employ
Their hands by the fire-side; perhaps to card
Wool for the House-wife's spindle, or repair
Some injury done to sickle, flail, or scythe,   110
Or other implement of house or field.

Down from the ceiling by the chimney's edge,
Which in our ancient uncouth country style
Did with a huge projection overbrow
Large space beneath, as duly as the light
Of day grew dim, the House-wife hung a lamp;
An aged utensil, which had perform'd
Service beyond all others of its kind.
Early at evening did it burn and late,
Surviving Comrade of uncounted Hours   120

Which going by from year to year had found
And left the Couple neither gay perhaps
Nor chearful, yet with objects and with hopes
Living a life of eager industry.
And now, when LUKE was in his eighteenth year,
There by the light of this old lamp they sate,
Father and Son, while late into the night
The House-wife plied her own peculiar work,
Making the cottage thro' the silent hours
Murmur as with the sound of summer flies.   130
Not with a waste of words, but for the sake
Of pleasure, which I know that I shall give
To many living now, I of this Lamp
Speak thus minutely: for there are no few
Whose memories will bear witness to my tale.
The Light was famous in its neighbourhood,
And was a public Symbol of the life,
The thrifty Pair had liv'd. For, as it chanc'd,
Their Cottage on a plot of rising ground
Stood single, with large prospect North and South,   140
High into Easedale, up to Dunmal-Raise,
And Westward to the village near the Lake.
And from this constant light so regular
And so far seen, the House itself by all
Who dwelt within the limits of the vale,
Both old and young, was nam'd The Evening Star.

Thus living on through such a length of years,
The Shepherd, if he lov'd himself, must needs
Have lov'd his Help-mate; but to Michael's heart
This Son of his old age was yet more dear –   150
Effect which might perhaps have been produc'd
By that instinctive tenderness, the same
Blind Spirit, which is in the blood of all,

131–135. Om. [1805].

Or that a child, more than all other gifts,
Brings hope with it, and forward-looking thoughts,
And stirrings of inquietude, when they
By tendency of nature needs must fail.
From such, and other causes, to the thoughts
Of the old Man his only Son was now
The dearest object that he knew on earth.   160
Exceeding was the love he bare to him,
His Heart and his Heart's joy! For oftentimes
Old Michael, while he was a babe in arms,
Had done him female service, not alone
For dalliance and delight, as is the use
Of Fathers, but with patient mind enforc'd
To acts of tenderness; and he had rock'd
His cradle with a woman's gentle hand.

And in a later time, ere yet the Boy
Had put on Boy's attire, did Michael love,   170
Albeit of a stern unbending mind,
To have the young one in his sight, when he
Had work by his own door, or when he sate
With sheep before him on his Shepherd's stool,
Beneath that large old Oak, which near their door
Stood, and from its enormous breadth of shade
Chosen for the Shearer's covert from the sun,
Thence in our rustic dialect was call'd
The CLIPPING TREE,* a name which yet it bears.
There, while they two were sitting in the shade,   180
With others round them, earnest all and blithe,
Would Michael exercise his heart with looks
Of fond correction and reproof bestow'd
Upon the child, if he disturb'd the sheep
By catching at their legs, or with his shouts
Scar'd them, while they lay still beneath the shears.

* Clipping is the word used in the North of England for shearing.

And when by Heaven's good grace the Boy grew up
A healthy Lad, and carried in his cheek
Two steady roses that were five years old,
Then Michael from a winter coppice cut   190
With his own hand a sapling, which he hoop'd
With iron, making it throughout in all
Due requisites a perfect Shepherd's Staff,
And gave it to the Boy; wherewith equipp'd
He as a Watchman oftentimes was plac'd
At gate or gap, to stem or turn the flock,
And to his office prematurely call'd
There stood the urchin, as you will divine,
Something between a hindrance and a help,
And for this cause not always, I believe,   200
Receiving from his Father hire of praise.
Though nought was left undone which staff or voice,
Or looks, or threatening gestures could perform.
But soon as Luke, full ten years old, could stand
Against the mountain blasts, and to the heights,
Not fearing toil, nor length of weary ways,
He with his Father daily went, and they
Were as companions, why should I relate
That objects which the Shepherd loved before
Were dearer now? that from the Boy there came   210
Feelings and emanations, things which were
Light to the sun and music to the wind;
And that the Old Man's heart seemed born again.
Thus in his Father's sight the Boy grew up:
And now when he had reached his eighteenth year,
He was his comfort and his daily hope.

While this good household thus were living on
From day to day, to Michael's ear there came

217. While in the fashion which I have described
   This simple Household thus were living on [1802].

Distressful tidings. Long before the time
Of which I speak, the Shepherd had been bound   220
In surety for his Brother's Son, a man
Of an industrious life, and ample means,
But unforeseen misfortunes suddenly
Had press'd upon him, and old Michael now
Was summon'd to discharge the forfeiture,
A grievous penalty, but little less
Than half his substance. This un-look'd for claim
At the first hearing, for a moment took
More hope out of his life than he supposed
That any old man ever could have lost.   230
As soon as he had gather'd so much strength
That he could look his trouble in the face,
It seem'd that his sole refuge was to sell
A portion of his patrimonial fields.
Such was his first resolve; he thought again,
And his heart fail'd him. "Isabel," said he,
Two evenings after he had heard the news,
"I have been toiling more than seventy years,
And in the open sun-shine of God's love
Have we all liv'd, yet if these fields of ours   240
Should pass into a Stranger's hand, I think
That I could not lie quiet in my grave.
Our lot is a hard lot; the Sun itself
Has scarcely been more diligent than I,
And I have liv'd to be a fool at last
To my own family. An evil Man
That was, and made an evil choice, if he
Were false to us; and if he were not false,
There are ten thousand to whom loss like this
Had been no sorrow. I forgive him – but   250
'Twere better to be dumb than to talk thus.
When I began, my purpose was to speak
Of remedies and of a chearful hope.
Our Luke shall leave us, Isabel; the land

Shall not go from us, and it shall be free,
He shall possess it, free as is the wind
That passes over it. We have, thou knowest,
Another Kinsman, he will be our friend
In this distress. He is a prosperous man,
Thriving in trade, and Luke to him shall go,   260
And with his Kinsman's help and his own thrift,
He quickly will repair this loss, and then
May come again to us. If here he stay,
What can be done? Where every one is poor
What can be gain'd?" At this, the old man paus'd,
And Isabel sate silent, for her mind
Was busy, looking back into past times.
There's Richard Bateman, thought she to herself,
He was a parish-boy – at the church-door
They made a gathering for him, shillings, pence,   270
And halfpennies, wherewith the Neighbours bought
A Basket, which they fill'd with Pedlar's wares,
And with this Basket on his arm, the Lad
Went up to London, found a Master there,
Who out of many chose the trusty Boy
To go and overlook his merchandise
Beyond the seas, where he grew wond'rous rich,
And left estates and monies to the poor,
And at his birth-place built a Chapel, floor'd
With Marble, which he sent from foreign lands.   280
These thoughts, and many others of like sort,
Pass'd quickly thro' the mind of Isabel,
And her face brighten'd. The Old Man was glad,
And thus resum'd. "Well! Isabel, this scheme
These two days has been meat and drink to me.
Far more than we have lost is left us yet.
– We have enough – I wish indeed that I
Were younger, but this hope is a good hope.
– Make ready Luke's best garments, of the best
Buy for him more, and let us send him forth   290

To-morrow, or the next day, or to-night:
– If he could go, the Boy should go to-night."

Here Michael ceas'd, and to the fields went forth
With a light heart. The House-wife for five days
Was restless morn and night, and all day long
Wrought on with her best fingers to prepare
Things needful for the journey of her Son.
But Isabel was glad when Sunday came
To stop her in her work; for, when she lay
By Michael's side, she for the two last nights   300
Heard him, how he was troubled in his sleep:
And when they rose at morning she could see
That all his hopes were gone. That day at noon
She said to Luke, while they two by themselves
Were sitting at the door, "Thou must not go,
We have no other Child but thee to lose,
None to remember – do not go away,
For if thou leave thy Father he will die."
The Lad made answer with a jocund voice,
And Isabel, when she had told her fears,   310
Recover'd heart. That evening her best fare
Did she bring forth, and all together sate
Like happy people round a Christmas fire.

Next morning Isabel resum'd her work,
And all the ensuing week the house appear'd
As cheerful as a grove in Spring: at length
The expected letter from their Kinsman came,
With kind assurances that he would do
His utmost for the welfare of the Boy,
To which requests were added that forthwith   320
He might be sent to him. Ten times or more
The letter was read over; Isabel
Went forth to shew it to the neighbours round:
Nor was there at that time on English Land

A prouder heart than Luke's. When Isabel
Had to her house return'd, the Old Man said,
"He shall depart to-morrow." To this word
The House-wife answered, talking much of things
Which, if at such short notice he should go,
Would surely be forgotten. But at length   330
She gave consent, and Michael was at ease.

Near the tumultous brook of Green-head Gill,
In that deep Valley, Michael had design'd
To build a Sheep-fold, and, before he heard
The tidings of his melancholy loss,
For this same purpose he had gathered up
A heap of stones, which close to the brook side
Lay thrown together, ready for the work.
With Luke that evening thitherward he walk'd;
And soon as they had reach'd the place he stopp'd,   340
And thus the Old Man spake to him. "My Son,
To-morrow thou wilt leave me; with full heart
I look upon thee, for thou art the same
That wert a promise to me ere thy birth,
And all thy life hast been my daily joy.
I will relate to thee some little part
Of our two histories; 'twill do thee good
When thou art from me, even if I should speak
Of things thou canst not know of. – After thou
First cam'st into the world, as it befalls   350
To new-born infants, thou didst sleep away
Two days, and blessings from thy Father's tongue
Then fell upon thee. Day by day pass'd on,
And still I lov'd thee with encreasing love.
Never to living ear came sweeter sounds
Than when I heard thee by our own fire-side
First uttering without words a natural tune,
When thou, a feeding babe, didst in thy joy
Sing at thy Mother's breast. Month follow'd month,

And in the open fields my life was pass'd   360
And in the mountains, else I think that thou
Hadst been brought up upon thy father's knees.
– But we were playmates, Luke; among these hills,
As well thou know'st, in us the old and young
Have play'd together, nor with me didst thou
Lack any pleasure which a boy can know."

Luke had a manly heart; but at these words
He sobb'd aloud; the Old Man grasp'd his hand,
And said, "Nay do not take it so – I see
That these are things of which I need not speak.   370
– Even to the utmost I have been to thee
A kind and a good Father: and herein
I but repay a gift which I myself
Receiv'd at others hands, for, though now old
Beyond the common life of man, I still
Remember them who lov'd me in my youth.
Both of them sleep together: here they liv'd
As all their Forefathers had done, and when
At length their time was come, they were not loth
To give their bodies to the family mold.   380
I wish'd that thou should'st live the life they liv'd.
But 'tis a long time to look back, my Son,
And see so little gain from sixty years.
These fields were burthen'd when they came to me;
'Till I was forty years of age, not more
Than half of my inheritance was mine.
I toil'd and toil'd; God bless'd me in my work,
And 'till these three weeks past the land was free.
– It looks as if it never could endure
Another Master. Heaven forgive me, Luke,   390
If I judge ill for thee, but it seems good
That thou should'st go." At this the Old Man paus'd,
Then, pointing to the Stones near which they stood,
Thus, after a short silence, he resum'd:

"This was a work for us, and now, my Son,
It is a work for me. But, lay one Stone –
Here, lay it for me, Luke, with thine own hands.
I for the purpose brought thee to this place.
Nay, Boy, be of good hope: – we both may live
To see a better day. At eighty-four   400
I still am strong and stout; – do thou thy part,
I will do mine. – I will begin again
With many tasks that were resign'd to thee;
Up to the heights, and in among the storms,
Will I without thee go again, and do
All works which I was wont to do alone,
Before I knew thy face. – Heaven bless thee, Boy!
Thy heart these two weeks has been beating fast
With many hopes – it should be so – yes – yes –
I knew that thou could'st never have a wish   410
To leave me, Luke, thou hast been bound to me
Only by links of love, when thou art gone
What will be left to us! – But, I forget
My purposes. Lay now the corner-stone,
As I requested, and hereafter, Luke,
When thou art gone away, should evil men
Be thy companions, let this Sheep-fold be
Thy anchor and thy shield; amid all fear
And all temptation, let it be to thee
An emblem of the life thy Fathers liv'd,   420
Who, being innocent, did for that cause
Bestir them in good deeds. Now, fare thee well –
When thou return'st, thou in this place wilt see
A work which is not here, a covenant
'Twill be between us – but whatever fate

---

398. Om. [1802].
417–420. Be thy companions, think of me, my Son,
              And of this moment; hither turn thy thoughts,
              And God will strengthen thee: amid all fear
              And all temptation, Luke, I pray that thou
              Mayst bear in mind the life thy Fathers liv'd, [1802].

Befall thee, I shall love thee to the last,
And bear thy memory with me to the grave.''

The Shepherd ended here; and Luke stoop'd down,
And as his Father had requested, laid
The first stone of the Sheep-fold; at the sight   430
The Old Man's grief broke from him, to his heart
He press'd his Son, he kissed him and wept;
And to the House together they return'd.

Next morning, as had been resolv'd, the Boy
Began his journey, and when he had reach'd
The public Way, he put on a bold face;
And all the Neighbours as he pass'd their doors
Came forth, with wishes and with farewell pray'rs,
That follow'd him 'till he was out of sight.

A good report did from their Kinsman come,   440
Of Luke and his well-doing; and the Boy
Wrote loving letters, full of wond'rous news,
Which, as the House-wife phrased it, were throughout
The prettiest letters that were ever seen.
Both parents read them with rejoicing hearts.
So, many months pass'd on: and once again
The Shepherd went about his daily work
With confident and cheerful thoughts; and now
Sometimes when he could find a leisure hour
He to that valley took his way, and there   450
Wrought at the Sheep-fold. Meantime Luke began
To slacken in his duty, and at length
He in the dissolute city gave himself
To evil courses: ignominy and shame
Fell on him, so that he was driven at last
To seek a hiding-place beyond the seas.

There is a comfort in the strength of love;
'Twill make a thing endurable, which else

Would break the heart: – Old Michael found it so.
I have convers'd with more than one who well   460
Remember the Old Man, and what he was
Years after he had heard this heavy news.
His bodily frame had been from youth to age
Of an unusual strength. Among the rocks
He went, and still look'd up upon the sun,
And listen'd to the wind; and as before
Perform'd all kinds of labour for his Sheep,
And for the land his small inheritance.
And to that hollow Dell from time to time
Did he repair, to build the Fold of which   470
His flock had need. 'Tis not forgotten yet
The pity which was then in every heart
For the Old Man – and 'tis believ'd by all
That many and many a day he thither went,
And never lifted up a single stone.

There, by the Sheep-fold, sometimes was he seen
Sitting alone, with that his faithful Dog,
Then old, beside him, lying at his feet.
The length of full seven years from time to time
He at the building of this Sheep-fold wrought,   480
And left the work unfinished when he died.

Three years, or little more, did Isabel,
Survive her Husband: at her death the estate
Was sold, and went into a Stranger's hand.
The Cottage which was nam'd The Evening Star
Is gone, the ploughshare has been through the ground
On which it stood; great changes have been wrought
In all the neighbourhood, yet the Oak is left
That grew beside their Door; and the remains
Of the unfinished Sheep-fold may be seen   490
Beside the boisterous brook of Green-head Gill.

Wordsworth's Prefaces of 1800 and 1802

There are two main versions of the Preface to *Lyrical Ballads*. The first is that of 1800 (the 1798 edition of the poems had been prefaced simply by an *Advertisement, v.* p. 7) and the second that of 1802, which is the basis of Wordsworth's final version of 1850. The main difference between the two versions is the addition in the 1802 text of the passage which discusses the question, 'What is a Poet?' (*v.* p. 254). The 1800 text is reproduced here with the 1802 variants in italics. Footnotes marked by a * are Wordsworth's, those by a † are our own. The text of the 1805 reprint of the Preface is identical with that of 1802, except for one or two slight typographical differences. Also, in the 1802 edition Wordsworth included an Appendix on poetic diction which is reprinted in the present volume as Appendix B (*v.* p. 314).

PREFACE

THE First Volume of these Poems has already been submitted to general perusal. It was published, as an experiment[1] which, I hoped, might be of some use to ascertain, how far, by fitting to metrical arrangement a selection of the real language of men in a state of vivid sensation, that sort of pleasure and that quantity of pleasure may be imparted, which a Poet may rationally endeavour to impart.

I had formed no very inaccurate estimate of the probable effect of those Poems: I flattered myself that they who should be pleased with them would read them with more than common

---

[1] *experiment, . . . hand, . . . aware, . . . variety, . . . weakness,*

pleasure: and on the other hand[1] I was well aware[1] that by those who should dislike them they would be read with more than common dislike. The result has differed from my expectation in this only, that I have pleased a greater number, than I ventured to hope I should please.

For the sake of variety[1] and from a consciousness of my own weakness[1] I was induced to request the assistance of a Friend, who furnished me with the Poems of the ANCIENT MARINER, the FOSTER-MOTHER'S TALE, the NIGHTINGALE, the DUNGEON, and the Poem entitled LOVE. I should not, however, have requested this assistance, had I not believed that the poems[2] of my Friend would in a great measure have the same tendency as my own, and that, though there would be found a difference, there would be found no discordance in the colours of our style; as our opinions on the subject of poetry do almost entirely coincide.

Several of my Friends are anxious for the success of these Poems from a belief, that[3] if the views, with which they were composed, were indeed realized, a class of Poetry would be produced, well adapted to interest mankind permanently, and not unimportant in the multiplicity[3] and in the quality of its moral relations: and on this account they have advised me to prefix a systematic defence of the theory, upon which the poems were written. But I was unwilling to undertake the task, because[4] I knew that on this occasion the Reader would look coldly upon my arguments, since I might be suspected of having been principally influenced by the selfish and foolish hope of *reasoning* him into an approbation of these particular

---

[2] *Poems*

[3] *that, if the views with which they were composed were . . . multiplicity, and*

[4] *because, . . . opinions,*

Poems: and I was still more unwilling to undertake the task, because adequately to display my opinions[4] and fully to enforce my arguments would require a space wholly disproportionate to the nature of a preface. For to treat the subject with the clearness and coherence, of which I believe it susceptible, it would be necessary to give a full account of the present state of the public taste in this country, and to determine how far this taste is healthy or depraved; which[5] again could not be determined, without pointing out, in what manner language and the human mind act and react on each other, and without retracing the revolutions not of literature alone[5] but likewise of society itself. I have therefore altogether declined to enter regularly upon this defence; yet I am sensible, that there would be some impropriety in abruptly obtruding upon the Public, without a few words of introduction, Poems so materially different from those, upon which general approbation is at present bestowed.

It is supposed, that by the act of writing in verse an Author makes a formal engagement that he will gratify certain known habits of association,[6] that he not only thus apprizes the Reader that certain classes of ideas and expressions will be found in his book, but that others will be carefully excluded. This exponent or symbol held forth by metrical language must in different æras of literature have excited very different expectations: for example, in the age of Catullus Terence and Lucretius, and that of Statius or Claudian,[7] and in our own country, in the age of Shakespeare and Beaumont and Fletcher, and that of Donne and Cowley, or Dryden, or Pope. I will not take upon me to determine the exact import of the promise which by the act of writing in verse an Author in the present

---

[5] *which, again, . . . re-act . . . revolutions, . . . alone,*

[6] *association;*

[7] *Catullus, Terence, and Lucretius . . . Claudian;*

day[8] makes to his Reader; but I am certain it will appear to many persons that I have not fulfilled the terms of an engagement thus voluntarily contracted.[9] I hope therefore the Reader will not censure me, if I attempt to state what I have proposed to myself to perform,[9] and also, (as far as the limits of a preface will permit) to explain some of the chief reasons which have determined me in the choice of my purpose: that at least he may be spared any unpleasant feeling of disappointment, and that I myself may be protected from the most dishonorable accusation which can be brought against an Author, namely, that of an indolence which prevents him from endeavouring to ascertain what is his duty, or, when his duty is ascertained[10] prevents him from performing it.

The principal object then[10] which I proposed to myself in these Poems was to make the incidents of common life interesting[11] by tracing in them, truly though not ostentatiously, the

---

[8] *Author, . . . day,*

[9] after "contracted" inserts the following (*v.* the 1798 Advertisement *v.* p. 7): *They who have been accustomed to the gaudiness and inane phraseology of many modern writers, if they persist in reading this book to its conclusion, will, no doubt, frequently have to struggle with feelings of strangeness and aukwardness: they will look round for poetry, and will be induced to inquire by what species of courtesy these attempts can be permitted to assume that title. . . . perform;*

[10] *ascertained, . . . object, then,*

[11] "to make the incidents . . . interesting" becomes *to chuse incidents and situations from common life, and to relate or describe them, throughout, as far as was possible, in a selection of language really used by men; and, at the same time, to throw over them a certain colouring of imagination, whereby ordinary things should be presented to the mind in an unusual way; and further, and above all, to make these incidents and situations interesting by*

primary laws of our nature: chiefly as far as regards the manner in which we associate ideas in a state of excitement. Low and rustic life was generally chosen because in that situation[12] the essential passions of the heart find a better soil in which they can attain their maturity, are less under restraint, and speak a plainer and more emphatic language; because in that situation[13] our elementary feelings exist[13] in a state of greater simplicity and consequently may be more accurately contemplated and more forcibly communicated; because the manners of rural life germinate from those elementary feelings; and from the necessary character of rural occupations[13] are more easily comprehended; and are more durable; and lastly, because in that situation[14] the passions of men are incorporated with the beautiful and permanent forms of nature. The language too[14] of these men is adopted (purified indeed from what appear to be its real defects, from all lasting and rational causes of dislike or disgust) because such men hourly communicate with the best objects from which the best part of language is originally derived; and because, from their rank in society and the sameness and narrow circle of their intercourse, being less under the action[15] of social vanity they convey their feelings and notions in simple and unelaborated expressions. Accordingly[16] such a language arising out of repeated experience and regular feelings is a more permanent and a far more philosophical language than that which is frequently substituted for it by Poets, who think that they are conferring honour upon themselves and their art in proportion as they separate them-

---

[12] *chosen, because in that condition, the*

[13] *because in that condition of life . . . co-exist . . . simplicity, . . . contemplated, . . . occupations,*

[14] *condition . . . language, too,*

[15] *influence*

[16] *Accordingly, such a language, . . . feelings, . . . permanent, . . . language, . . . and their art, . . . expression, . . . tastes, and fickleappetites,*

selves from the sympathies of men, and indulge in arbitrary and capricious habits of expression in order to furnish food for fickle tastes and fickle appetites of their own creation.*

I cannot[17] be insensible of the present outcry against the triviality and meanness both of thought and language, which some of my contemporaries have occasionally introduced into their metrical compositions; and I acknowledge[17] that this defect where it exists, is more dishonorable to the Writer's own character than false refinement or arbitrary innovation, though I should contend at the same time that it is far less pernicious in the sum of its consequences. From such verses the Poems in these volumes will be found distinguished at least by one mark of difference, that each of them has a worthy *purpose*. Not that I mean to say, that I always began to write with a distinct purpose formally conceived; but I believe that my habits of meditation have so formed my feelings, as that my descriptions of such objects as strongly excite those feelings, will be found to carry along with them a *purpose*. If in this opinion I am mistaken[18] I can have little right to the name of a Poet. For all good poetry is the spontaneous overflow of powerful feelings; but though this be true, Poems to which any value can be attached, were never produced on any variety of subjects but by a man who[19] being possessed of more than usual organic sensibility had also thought long and deeply. For our continued influxes of feeling are modified and directed by our thoughts, which are indeed the representatives of all our past feelings; and as by contemplating the relation of these general representatives[20] to each other, we discover what is really important to men, so by the repetition and continuance of this

* It is worth while here to observe that the affecting parts of Chaucer are almost always expressed in language pure and universally intelligible even to this day.

---

[17] *I cannot, however, . . . acknowledge, that this defect,*

[18] *mistaken,*

[19] *a man, who . . . sensibility, had*   [20] See opposite page.

act feelings connected with important subjects[20] will be nourished, till at length, if we be originally possessed of much organic sensibility, such habits of mind will be produced that by obeying blindly and mechanically the impulses of those habits we shall describe objects and utter sentiments of such a nature and in such connection with each other, that the understanding of the being to whom we address ourselves, if he be in a healthful state of association, must necessarily be in some degree enlightened, his taste exalted, and his affections ameliorated.[20]

I have said that each of these poems has a purpose. I have also informed my Reader what this purpose will be found principally to be: namely to illustrate[21] the manner in which our feelings and ideas are associated in a state of excitement. But speaking in less general language,[22] it is to follow the fluxes and refluxes of the mind when agitated by the great and simple affections of our nature. This object I have endeavoured in these short essays to attain by various means; by tracing the maternal passion through many of its more subtle windings, as in the poems of the IDIOT BOY and the MAD MOTHER; by accompanying the last struggles of a human being[23] at the approach of death, cleaving in solitude to life and society, as in the Poem of the FORSAKEN INDIAN; by shewing, as in the Stanzas entitled WE ARE SEVEN, the perplexity and obscurity which in childhood attend our notion of death, or

---

[20] and, . . . representatives to each other we discover what is really important to men, so, . . . this act, our feelings will be connected . . . subjects, till at length, if we be possessed of much sensibility, . . . produced, that, by . . . habits, . . . objects, and utter sentiments, . . . in some degree enlightened, and his affections ameliorated.

[21] namely to illustrate

[22] But, speaking in language somewhat more appropriate,

[23] human being, at the

K*

rather our utter inability to admit that notion; or by displaying the strength of fraternal, or to speak more philosophically, of moral attachment when early associated with the great and beautiful objects of nature, as in THE BROTHERS; or, as in the Incident of SIMON LEE, by placing my Reader in the way of receiving from ordinary moral sensations another and more salutary impression than we are accustomed to receive from them. It has also been part of my general purpose to attempt to sketch characters under the influence of less impassioned feelings, as in[24] the OLD MAN TRAVELLING, THE TWO THIEVES, &c. characters of which the elements are simple, belonging rather to nature than to manners, such as exist now[25] and will probably always exist, and which from their constitution may be distinctly and profitably contemplated. I will not abuse the indulgence of my Reader by dwelling longer upon this subject; but it is proper that I should mention one other circumstance which distinguishes these Poems from the popular Poetry of the day; it is this, that the feeling therein developed gives importance to the action and situation[26] and not the action and situation to the feeling. My meaning will be rendered perfectly intelligible by referring my Reader to the Poems entitled POOR SUSAN and the CHILDLESS FATHER, particularly to the last Stanza of the latter Poem.

I will not suffer a sense of false modesty to prevent me from asserting, that I point my Reader's attention to this mark of distinction far[26] less for the sake of these particular Poems than from the general importance of the subject. The subject is indeed important ! For the human mind is capable of excitement[27] without the application of gross and violent stimulants; and he must have a very faint perception of its beauty and

---

[24] *feelings, as in the* two April mornings, the Fountain, the
[25] *exist now, and*
[26] *situation, . . . distinction, far*
[27] *of being excited*

dignity who does not know this, and who does not further know that[28] one being is elevated above another in proportion as he possesses this capability. It has therefore appeared to me[29] that to endeavour to produce or enlarge this capability is one of the best services in which, at any period, a Writer can be engaged; but this service, excellent at all times, is especially so at the present day. For a multitude of causes unknown to former times[30] are now acting with a combined force to blunt the discriminating powers of the mind, and unfitting it for all voluntary exertion to reduce it to a state of almost savage torpor. The most effective of these causes are the great national events which are daily taking place, and the encreasing accumulation of men in cities, where the uniformity of their occupations produces a craving for extraordinary incident[31] which the rapid communication of intelligence hourly gratifies. To this tendency of life and manners the literature and theatrical exhibitions of the country have conformed themselves. The invaluable works of our elder writers, I had almost said the works of Shakespear and Milton, are driven into neglect by frantic novels, sickly and stupid German Tragedies, and deluges of idle and extravagant stories in verse. – When I think upon this degrading thirst after outrageous stimulation[32] I am almost ashamed to have spoken of the feeble effort with which I have endeavoured to counteract it; and[33] reflecting upon the magnitude of the general evil, I should be oppressed with no dishonorable melancholy, had I not a deep impression of certain inherent and indestructible qualities of the human mind, and likewise of certain powers in the great and permanent objects that act upon it which are equally inherent and

---

[28] *know, that . . . another, in*

[29] *appeared to me, that*

[30] *causes, . . . times, are*

[31] *incident, which*

[32] *stimulation, I*

[33] *and,*

indestructible; and did I not further add to this impression a belief[34] that the time is approaching when the evil will be systematically opposed by men of greater powers[35] and with far more distinguished success.

Having dwelt thus long on the subjects and aim of these Poems, I shall request the Reader's permission to apprize him of a few circumstances relating to their *style*, in order, among other reasons, that I may not be censured for not having performed what I never attempted. Except[36] in a very few instances the Reader will find no personifications of abstract ideas in these volumes, not that I mean to censure such personifications: they may be well fitted for certain sorts of composition, but in these Poems I propose to myself to imitate, and, as far as possible, to adopt the very language of men, and I do not find that such personifications make any regular or natural part of that language. I wish to keep my Reader in the company of flesh and blood, persuaded that by

---

[34] *belief, that*

[35] *opposed, by men of greater powers,*

[36] changes "Except in a very few . . . interest him likewise:" to: *The Reader will find that personifications of abstract ideas rarely occur in these volumes; and, I hope, are utterly rejected as an ordinary device to elevate the style, and raise it above prose. I have proposed to myself to imitate, and, as far as is possible, to adopt the very language of men; and assuredly such personifications do not make any natural or regular part of that language. They are, indeed, a figure of speech occasionally prompted by passion, and I have made use of them as such; but I have endeavoured utterly to reject them as a mechanical device of style, or as a family language which Writers in metre seem to lay claim to by prescription. I have wished to keep my Reader in the company of flesh and blood, persuaded that by so doing I shall interest him. I am, however, well aware that others who pursue a different track may interest him likewise;*

so doing I shall interest him. Not but that I believe that others who pursue a different track may interest him likewise: I do not interfere with their claim, I only wish to prefer a different claim of my own. There will also be found in these volumes little of what is usually called poetic diction; I have taken as much pains to avoid it as others ordinarily take to produce it; this I have done for the reason already alleged, to bring my language near to the language of men, and further, because the pleasure which I have proposed to myself to impart is of a kind very different from that which is supposed by many persons to be the proper object of poetry. I do not know how without being culpably particular I can give my Reader a more exact notion of the style in which I wished these poems to be written than by informing him that I have at all times endeavoured to look steadily at my subject, consequently[37] I hope it will be found that there is[38] in these Poems little falsehood of description, and that my ideas are expressed in language fitted to their respective importance. Something I must have gained by this practice, as it is friendly to one property of all good poetry, namely[39] good sense; but it has necessarily cut me off from a large portion of phrases and figures of speech which from father to son have long been regarded as the common inheritance of Poets. I have also thought it expedient to restrict myself still further, having abstained from the use of many expressions, in themselves proper and beautiful, but which have been foolishly repeated by bad Poets[40] till such feelings of disgust are connected with them as it is scarcely possible by any art of association to overpower.

If in a Poem there should be found a series of lines, or even a single line, in which the language, though naturally arranged

---

[37] *consequently,*

[38] *consequently, I hope that there is*

[39] *namely, good*

[40] *Poets, till*

and according to the strict laws of metre, does not differ from that of prose, there is a numerous class of critics[41] who, when they stumble upon these prosaisms as they call them, imagine that they have made a notable discovery, and exult over the Poet as over a man ignorant of his own profession. Now these men would establish a canon of criticism which the Reader will conclude he must utterly reject[42] if he wishes to be pleased with these volumes. And it would be a most easy task to prove to him[43] that not only the language of a large portion of every good poem, even of the most elevated character, must necessarily, except with reference to the metre, in no respect differ from that of good prose, but likewise that some of the most interesting parts of the best poems will be found to be strictly the language of prose[43] when prose is well written. The truth of this assertion might be demonstrated by innumerable passages from almost all the poetical writings, even of Milton himself. I have not space for much quotation; but, to illustrate the subject in a general manner, I will here adduce a short composition of Gray, who was at the head of those who by their reasonings have attempted to widen the space of separation betwixt Prose and Metrical composition, and was more than any other man curiously elaborate in the structure of his own poetic diction.

> In vain to me the smiling mornings shine,
> And reddening Phoebus lifts his golden fire:
> The birds in vain their amorous descant join,
> Or chearful fields resume their green attire:
> These ears alas ! for other notes repine;
> *A different object do these eyes require;*
> *My lonely anguish melts no heart but mine;*
> *And in my breast the imperfect joys expire;*

---

[41] *critics,*

[42] *reject, if*

[43] *prove to him, . . . of prose,*

> Yet Morning smiles the busy race to cheer,
> And new-born pleasure brings to happier men;
> The fields to all their wonted tribute bear;
> To warm their little loves the birds complain.
> *I fruitless mourn to him that cannot hear*
> *And weep the more because I weep in vain.*†

It will easily be perceived that the only part of this Sonnet which is of any value is the lines printed in Italics: it is equally obvious[44] that[45] except in the rhyme, and in the use of the single word "fruitless" for fruitlessly, which is so far a defect, the language of these lines does in no respect differ from that of prose.

Is there then,[46] it will be asked, no essential difference between the language of prose and metrical composition? I answer that there neither is nor can be any essential difference.[46] We are fond of tracing the resemblance between Poetry and Painting, and, accordingly, we call them Sisters: but where shall we find bonds of connection sufficiently strict to typify the affinity betwixt metrical and prose composition? They both speak by and to the same organs; the bodies in which both of them are clothed may be said to be of the same substance, their affections are kindred and almost identical, not necessarily

---

† Sonnet on the Death of Richard West.

[44] *obvious,*

[45] *that,*

[46] From "Is there then" to "essential difference." becomes: *By the foregoing quotation I have shewn that the language of Prose may yet be well adapted to Poetry; and I have previously asserted that a large portion of the language of every good poem can in no respect differ from that of good Prose. I will go further. I do not doubt that it may be safely affirmed, that there neither is, nor can be, any essential difference between the language of prose and metrical composition.*

differing even in degree; *Poetry sheds no tears "such as Angels weep," but natural and human tears; she can boast of no celestial Ichor that distinguishes her vital juices from those of prose; the same human blood circulates through the veins of them both.

If it be affirmed that rhyme and metrical arrangement of themselves constitute a distinction which overturns what I have been saying on the strict affinity of metrical language with that of prose, and paves the way for other distinctions[49] which the mind voluntarily admits, I answer that[50] the distinction of

* I here use the word "Poetry" (though against my own judgment) as opposed to the word Prose, and synonomous with metrical composition. But much confusion has been introduced into criticism by this contra-distinction of Poetry and Prose, instead of the more philosophical one of Poetry and[47] Science. The only strict antithesis to Prose is Metre.[48]

[47] *of Poetry and Matter of fact, or Science.*

[48] *is Metre; nor is this, in truth, a strict antithesis; because lines and passages of metre so naturally occur in writing prose, that it would be scarcely possible to avoid them, even were it desirable.*

[49] *for other artificial distinctions*

[50] after "I answer that" inserts a passage of over 350 lines ending it as part of the sentence ("the distinction of" etc.) continued on p. 262.

I answer that the language of such Poetry as I am recommending is, as far as is possible, a selection of the language really spoken by men; that this selection, wherever it is made with true taste and feeling, will of itself form a distinction far greater than would at first be imagined, and will entirely separate the composition from the vulgarity and meanness of ordinary life; and, if metre be superadded thereto, I believe that a dissimilitude will be produced altogether sufficient for the gratification of a rational mind. What other distinction would we have? Whence is it to come? And where is it to exist? Not, surely, where the Poet speaks through the mouths of his characters: it cannot be necessary here, either for elevation of style, or any of its supposed ornaments: for, if the Poet's subject be judiciously chosen, it will naturally, and upon fit occasion, lead him to passions the language of which, if selected truly and judiciously, must necessarily be dignified and variegated, and alive with metaphors and figures. I forbear to speak of an incongruity which would shock the intelligent Reader, should the Poet interweave any foreign splendour of his own with that which the passion naturally suggests: it is sufficient to say that such addition is unnecessary. And, surely, it is more probable that those passages, which with propriety abound with metaphors and figures, will have their due effect, if, upon other occasions where the passions are of a milder character, the style also be subdued and temperate.

But, as the pleasure which I hope to give by the Poems I now present to the Reader must depend entirely on just notions upon this subject, and, as it is in itself of the highest importance to our taste and moral feelings, I cannot content myself with these detached remarks. And if, in what I am about to say, it shall appear to some that my labour is unnecessary, and that I am like a man fighting a battle without enemies, I would remind such persons, that, whatever may be the language outwardly holden by men, a practical faith in the opinions which I am wishing to establish is almost unknown. If my conclusions are admitted, and carried as far as they must be carried if admitted at all, our judgments concerning the works of the greatest Poets both ancient and modern will be far different from what they are at present, both when we praise, and when we censure: and our moral feelings influencing, and influenced by these judgments will, I believe, be corrected and purified.

Taking up the subject, then, upon general grounds, I ask what is meant by the word Poet? What is a Poet? To whom does he address himself? And what language is to be expected from him? He is a man speaking to men: a man, it is true, endued with more lively sensibility, more enthusiasm and tenderness, who has a greater knowledge of human nature, and a more comprehensive soul, than are supposed to be common among mankind; a man pleased with his own passions and volitions, and who rejoices more than other men in the spirit of life that is in him; delighting to contemplate similar volitions and passions as manifested in the goings-on of the Universe, and habitually impelled to create them where he does not find them. To these qualities he has added a disposition to be affected more than other men by absent things as if they were present; an ability of conjuring up in himself passions, which are indeed far from being the same as those produced by real events, yet (especially in those parts of the general sympathy which are pleasing and delightful) do more nearly resemble the passions produced by real events, than anything which, from the motions of their own minds merely, other men are accustomed to feel in themselves; whence, and from practice, he has acquired a greater readiness and power in expressing what he thinks and feels, and especially those thoughts and feelings which, by his own choice, or from the structure of his own mind, arise in him without immediate external excitement.

But, whatever portion of this faculty we may suppose even the greatest Poet to possess, there cannot be a doubt but that the language which it will suggest to him, must, in liveliness and truth, fall far short of that which is uttered by men in real life, under the actual pressure of those passions, certain shadows of which the Poet thus produces, or feels to be produced, in himself. However exalted a notion we would wish to cherish of the character of a Poet it is obvious, that, while he describes and imitates passions, his situation is altogether slavish and mechanical, compared with the freedom and power of real and substantial action and suffering. So that it will be the wish of the Poet to bring his feelings near to those of the persons whose feelings he describes, nay, for short spaces of time perhaps, to let himself slip into an entire delusion, and even confound and identify his own feelings with theirs; modifying only the language which is thus suggested to him, by a consideration that he describes for a particular purpose, that of giving pleasure. Here, then, he will apply the principle on which I have so much insisted, namely, that of selection; on this he will depend for removing what would otherwise be painful or disgusting in the passion; he will feel that there is no necessity to trick out or to elevate nature: and, the more industriously he applies this principle, the deeper will be his faith that no words, which his fancy or imagination can suggest, will be to be compared with those which are the emanations of reality and truth.

But it may be said by those who do not object to the general spirit of these remarks, that, as it is impossible for the Poet to produce upon all occasions language as exquisitely fitted for the passion as that which the real passion itself suggests, it is proper that he should consider himself as in the situation of a translator, who deems himself justified when he substitutes excellences of another kind for those which are unattainable by him; and endeavours occasionally to surpass his original, in order to make some amends for the general inferiority to which he feels that he must submit. But this would be to encourage idleness and unmanly despair. Further, it is the language of men who speak of what they do not understand; who talk of Poetry as of a matter of amusement and idle pleasure; who will converse with us as gravely about a taste for Poetry, as they express it, as if it were a thing as indifferent as a taste for Rope-dancing, or Frontiniac or Sherry. Aristotle, I have been told, hath said, that Poetry is the most philosophic of all writing: it is so: its object is truth, not individual and local, but general, and operative; not standing upon external testimony, but carried alive into the heart by passion; truth which is its own testimony, which gives strength and divinity to the tribunal to which it appeals, and receives them from the same tribunal. Poetry is the image of man and nature. The obstacles which stand in the way of the fidelity of the Biographer and Historian, and of their consequent utility, are incalculably greater than those which are to be encountered by the Poet who has an adequate notion of the dignity of his art. The Poet writes under one restriction only, namely, that of the necessity of giving immediate pleasure to a human Being possessed of that information which may be expected from him, not as a lawyer, a physician, a mariner, an

*astronomer or a natural philosopher, but as a Man. Except this
one restriction, there is no object standing between the Poet and the
image of things; between this, and the Biographer and Historian
there are a thousand.*

*Nor let this necessity of producing immediate pleasure be con-
sidered as a degradation of the Poet's art. It is far otherwise. It is
an acknowledgment of the beauty of the universe, an acknowledg-
ment the more sincere, because it is not formal, but indirect; it is
a task light and easy to him who looks at the world in the spirit of
love: further, it is a homage paid to the native and naked dignity
of man, to the grand elementary principle of pleasure, by which he
knows, and feels, and lives, and moves. We have no sympathy but
what is propagated by pleasure: I would not be misunderstood; but
wherever we sympathize with pain it will be found that the sym-
pathy is produced and carried on by subtle combinations with
pleasure. We have no knowledge, that is, no general principles
drawn from the contemplation of particular facts, but what has
been built up by pleasure, and exists in us by pleasure alone. The
Man of Science, the Chemist and Mathematician, whatever
difficulties and disgusts they may have had to struggle with, know
and feel this. However painful may be the objects with which the
Anatomist's knowledge is connected, he feels that his knowledge is
pleasure; and where he has no pleasure he has no knowledge. What
then does the Poet? He considers man and the objects that surround
him as acting and re-acting upon each other, so as to produce an
infinite complexity of pain and pleasure; he considers man in his
own nature and in his ordinary life as contemplating this with a
certain quantity of immediate knowledge, with certain convictions,
intuitions, and deductions which by habit become of the nature of
intuitions; he considers him as looking upon this complex scene of
ideas and sensations, and finding every where objects that immedi-
ately excite in him sympathies which, from the necessities of his
nature, are accompanied by an overbalance of enjoyment.*

*To this knowledge which all men carry about with them, and to
these sympathies in which without any other discipline than that of*

our daily life we are fitted to take delight, the Poet principally directs his attention. He considers man and nature as essentially adapted to each other, and the mind of man as naturally the mirror of the fairest and most interesting qualities of nature. And thus the Poet, prompted by this feeling of pleasure which accompanies him through the whole course of his studies, converses with general nature with affections akin to those, which, through labour and length of time, the Man of Science has raised up in himself, by conversing with those particular parts of nature which are the objects of his studies. The knowledge both of the Poet and the Man of Science is pleasure; but the knowledge of the one cleaves to us as a necessary part of our existence, our natural and unalienable inheritance; the other is a personal and individual acquisition, slow to come to us, and by no habitual and direct sympathy connecting us with our fellow-beings. The Man of Science seeks truth as a remote and unknown benefactor; he cherishes and loves it in his solitude: the Poet, singing a song in which all human beings join with him, rejoices in the presence of truth as our visible friend and hourly companion. Poetry is the breath and finer spirit of all knowledge: it is the impassioned expression which is in the countenance of all Science. Emphatically may it be said of the Poet, as Shakespeare hath said of man, "that he looks before and after." He is the rock of defence of human nature; an upholder and preserver, carrying every where with him relationship and love. In spite of difference of soil and climate, of language and manners, of laws and customs, in spite of things silently gone out of mind and things violently destroyed, the Poet binds together by passion and knowledge the vast empire of human society, as it is spread over the whole earth, and over all time. The objects of the Poet's thoughts are every where; though the eyes and senses of man are, it is true, his favorite guides, yet he will follow wheresoever he can find an atmosphere of sensation in which to move his wings. Poetry is the first and last of all knowledge – it is as immortal as the heart of man. If the labours of men of Science should ever create any material revolution, direct or indirect, in our condition, and in the impressions which we habitually receive, the Poet will sleep then

*no more than at present, but he will be ready to follow the steps of
the Man of Science, not only in those general indirect effects, but he
will be at his side, carrying sensation into the midst of the objects
of the Science itself. The remotest discoveries of the Chemist, the
Botanist, or Mineralogist, will be as proper objects of the Poet's
art as any upon which it can be employed, if the time should ever
come when these things shall be familiar to us, and the relations
under which they are contemplated by the followers of these
respective Sciences shall be manifestly and palpably material to us
as enjoying and suffering beings. If the time should ever come
when what is now called Science, thus familiarized to men, shall
be ready to put on, as it were, a form of flesh and blood, the Poet
will lend his divine spirit to aid the transfiguration, and will
welcome the Being thus produced, as a dear and genuine inmate of
the household of man. – It is not, then, to be supposed that any one,
who holds that sublime notion of Poetry which I have attempted to
convey, will break in upon the sanctity and truth of his pictures by
transitory and accidental ornaments, and endeavour to excite
admiration of himself by arts, the necessity of which must
manifestly depend upon the assumed meanness of his subject.*

*What I have thus far said applies to Poetry in general; but
especially to those parts of composition where the Poet speaks
through the mouths of his characters; and upon this point it
appears to have such weight that I will conclude, there are few
persons of good sense, who would not allow that the dramatic parts
of composition are defective, in proportion as they deviate from the
real language of nature, and are coloured by a diction of the Poet's
own, either peculiar to him as an individual Poet, or belonging
simply to Poets in general, to a body of men who, from the circum-
stance of their compositions being in metre, it is expected will
employ a particular language.*

*It is not, then, in the dramatic parts of composition that we
look for this distinction of language; but still it may be proper and
necessary where the Poet speaks to us in his own person and*

character. To this I answer by referring my Reader to the
description which I have before given of a Poet. Among the
qualities which I have enumerated as principally conducing to
form a Poet, is implied nothing differing in kind from other men,
but only in degree. The sum of what I have there said is, that the
Poet is chiefly distinguished from other men by a greater prompt-
ness to think and feel without immediate external excitement, and
a greater power in expressing such thoughts and feelings as are
produced in him in that manner. But these passions and thoughts
and feelings are the general passions and thoughts and feelings of
men. And with what are they connected? Undoubtedly with our
moral sentiments and animal sensations, and with the causes
which excite these; with the operations of the elements and the
appearances of the visible universe; with storm and sun-shine,
with the revolutions of the seasons, with cold and heat, with loss of
friends and kindred, with injuries and resentments, gratitude and
hope, with fear and sorrow. These, and the like, are the sensations
and objects which the Poet describes, as they are the sensations of
other men, and the objects which interest them. The Poet thinks
and feels in the spirit of the passions of men. How, then, can his
language differ in any material degree from that of all other men
who feel vividly and see clearly? It might be proved *that it is*
impossible. But supposing that this were not the case, the Poet
might then be allowed to use a peculiar language when expressing
his feelings for his own gratification, or that of men like himself.
But Poets do not write for Poets alone, but for men. Unless there-
fore we are advocates for that admiration which depends upon
ignorance, and that pleasure which arises from hearing what we do
not understand, the Poet must descend from this supposed height,
and, in order to excite rational sympathy, he must express himself
as other men express themselves. To this it may be added, that
while he is only selecting from the real language of men, or, which
amounts to the same thing, composing accurately in the spirit of
such selection, he is treading upon safe ground, and we know what
we are to expect from him. Our feelings are the same with respect
to metre; for, as it may be proper to inform the Reader,

rhyme and metre[51] is regular and uniform, and not,[52] like that which is produced by what is usually called poetic diction, arbitrary[53] and subject to infinite caprices upon which no calculation whatever can be made. In the one case[54] the Reader is utterly at the mercy of the Poet respecting what imagery or diction he may choose to connect with the passion, whereas in the other the metre[54] obeys certain laws, to which the Poet and Reader both willingly submit because they are certain, and because no interference is made by them with the passion but such as the concurring testimony of ages has shewn to heighten and improve the pleasure which co-exists with it.

It will now be proper to answer an obvious question, namely, why, professing these opinions have I written in verse? To this in the first place I reply[55], because, however I may have restricted myself, there is still left open to me what confessedly constitutes the most valuable object of all writing whether in prose or verse, the great and universal passions of men, the most general and interesting of their occupations, and the entire world of nature, from which I am at liberty to supply myself with endless combinations of forms and imagery. Now, granting[56] for a moment that whatever is interesting in these objects may be as vividly described in prose, why am I to be condemned[56] if to such description I have endeavoured to superadd the charm which by the consent of all nations is acknowledged to exist in metrical language? To this[57] it will be

---

[51] *the distinction of metre is regular*

[52] *and not like that*

[53] *arbitrary,*

[54] *case, the . . . whereas, in the other, the metre*

[55] *To this, in addition to such answer as is included in what I have already said, I reply in the first place, because,*

[56] *Now, supposing . . . condemned, if . . . charm, which, by . . . nations, is*

[57] *To this, by such as are unconvinced by what I have already said, it may be answered,*

answered, that a very small part of the pleasure given by
Poetry depends upon the metre, and that it is injudicious
to write in metre[58] unless it be accompanied with the other
artificial distinctions of style with which metre is usually
accompanied, and that by such deviation more will be lost
from the shock which will be thereby given to the Reader's
associations[58] than will be counterbalanced by any pleasure
which he can derive from the general power of numbers. In
answer to those who thus[59] contend for the necessity of
accompanying metre with certain appropriate colours of style
in order to the accomplishment of its appropriate end, and who
also, in my opinion, greatly under-rate the power of metre in
itself, it might perhaps[60] be almost sufficient to observe that
poems are extant, written upon more humble subjects, and in
a more naked and simple style than[60] what I have aimed at,
which poems have continued to give pleasure from generation
to generation. Now, if nakedness and simplicity be a defect,
the fact here mentioned affords a strong presumption that
poems somewhat less naked and simple are capable of affording
pleasure at the present day; and[61] all that I am now attempting
is[61] to justify myself for having written under the impression of
this belief.

But I might point out various causes why, when the style is
manly, and the subject of some importance, words metrically
arranged will long continue to impart such a pleasure to man-
kind as he who is sensible of the extent of that pleasure will be
desirous to impart. The end of Poetry is to produce excitement

---

[58] *metre, unless . . . associations,*

[59] *those who still contend*

[60] *it might perhaps, as far as relates to these Poems, have
been almost sufficient to observe, that poems are . . . than I have
aimed at,*

[61] *and, what I wished* chiefly *to attempt, at present, was to
justify*

in coexistence with an overbalance of pleasure. Now, by the supposition, excitement is an unusual and irregular state of the mind; ideas and feelings do not in that state succeed each other in accustomed order. But[62] if the words by which this excitement is produced are in themselves powerful, or the images and feelings have an undue proportion of pain connected with them, there is some danger that the excitement may be carried beyond its proper bounds. Now the co-presence of something regular, something to which the mind has been accustomed when in an unexcited or[63] a less excited state, cannot but have great efficacy in tempering and restraining the passion by an intertexture[64] of ordinary feeling. This[65] may be illustrated by appealing to the Reader's own experience of the reluctance with which he comes to the re-perusal of the distressful parts of Clarissa Harlowe, or the Gamester.† While Shakespeare's writings, in the most pathetic scenes, never act upon us as

---

† Probably refers to the play by Edward Moore, first published in 1753.

[62] *But, if*

[63] *accustomed in various moods and in a less excited state,*

[64] *intertexture of ordinary feeling, and of feeling not strictly and necessarily connected with the passion. This is unquestionably true, and hence, though the opinion will at first appear paradoxical, from the tendency of metre to divest language in a certain degree of its reality, and thus to throw a sort of half consciousness of unsubstantial existence over the whole composition, there can be little doubt but that more pathetic situations and sentiments, that is, those which have a greater proportion of pain connected with them, may be endured in metrical composition, especially in rhyme, than in prose. The metre of the old ballads is very artless; yet they contain many passages which would illustrate this opinion, and, I hope, if the following Poems be attentively perused, similar instances will be found in them.*

[65] *This opinion may be further illustrated by appealing*

pathetic beyond the bounds of pleasure – an effect which[66] is
in a great degree to be ascribed to small, but continual and
regular impulses of pleasurable surprise from the metrical
arrangement. – On the other hand (what it must be allowed
will much more frequently happen) if the Poet's words should
be incommensurate with the passion, and inadequate to raise
the Reader to a height of desirable excitement, then, (unless
the Poet's choice of his metre has been grossly injudicious) in
the feelings of pleasure which the Reader has been accustomed
to connect with metre in general, and in the feeling, whether
chearful or melancholy, which he has been accustomed to
connect with that particular movement of metre, there will
be found something which will greatly contribute to impart
passion to the words, and to effect the complex end which the
Poet proposes to himself.

If I had undertaken a systematic defence of the theory upon
which these poems are written, it would have been my duty to
develope the various causes upon which the pleasure received
from metrical language depends. Among the chief of these
causes is to be reckoned a principle which must be well known
to those who have made any of the Arts the object of accurate
reflection; I mean the pleasure which the mind derives from
the perception of similitude in dissimilitude. This principle is
the great spring of the activity of our minds[67] and their chief
feeder. From this principle the direction of the sexual appetite,
and all the passions connected with it take their origin: It is
the life of our ordinary conversation; and upon the accuracy
with which similitude in dissimilitude, and dissimilitude in
similitude are perceived, depend our taste and our moral
feelings. It would not have been a useless employment to have
applied this principle to the consideration of metre, and to

[66] *an effect which, in a much greater degree than might at first
be imagined, is to be ascribed*
[67] *minds,*

have shown that metre is hence enabled to afford much
pleasure, and to have pointed out in what manner that
pleasure is produced. But my limits will not permit me to
enter upon this subject, and I must content myself with a
general summary.

I have said that Poetry is the spontaneous overflow of
powerful feelings: it takes its origin from emotion recollected
in tranquillity: the emotion is contemplated till by a species
of reaction the tranquillity gradually disappears, and an
emotion,[68] similar to that which was before the subject of
contemplation, is gradually produced, and does itself actually
exist in the mind. In this mood successful composition generally
begins, and in a mood similar to this it is carried on; but the
emotion, of whatever kind and in whatever degree, from
various causes is qualified by various pleasures, so that in
describing any passions whatsoever, which are voluntarily
described, the mind will upon the whole be in a state of enjoy-
ment. Now[69] if Nature be thus cautious in preserving in a state
of enjoyment a being thus employed, the Poet ought to profit
by the lesson thus held forth to him, and ought especially to
take care, that whatever passions he communicates to his
Reader, those passions, if his Reader's mind be sound and
vigorous, should always be accompanied with an overbalance
of pleasure. Now the music of harmonious metrical language,
the sense of difficulty overcome, and the blind association of
pleasure which has been previously received from works of
rhyme or metre of the same or similar construction,[70] all these
imperceptibly make up a complex feeling of delight, which is
of the most important use in tempering the painful feeling

---

[68] *an emotion, kindred to that which*

[69] *Now, if*

[70] *similar construction, an indistinct perception perpetually
renewed of language closely resembling that of real life, and yet,
in the circumstance of metre, differing from it so widely, all these*

which will always be found intermingled with powerful descriptions of the deeper passions. This effect is always produced in pathetic and impassioned poetry; while in lighter compositions[71] the ease and gracefulness with which the Poet manages his numbers are themselves confessedly a principal source of the gratification of the Reader. I might perhaps include all which it is *necessary* to say upon this subject by affirming what few persons will deny, that of two descriptions[72] either of passions, manners, or characters, each of them equally well executed, the one in prose and the other in verse, the verse will be read a hundred times where the prose is read once. We see that Pope by the power of verse alone, has contrived to render the plainest common sense interesting, and even frequently to invest it with the appearance of passion. In consequence of these convictions I related in metre the Tale of GOODY BLAKE and HARRY GILL, which is one of the rudest of this collection. I wished to draw attention to the truth that the power of the human imagination is sufficient to produce such changes even in our physical nature as might almost appear miraculous. The truth is an important one; the fact (for it is a *fact*) is a valuable illustration of it. And I have the satisfaction of knowing that it has been communicated to many hundreds of people who would never have heard of it, had it not been narrated as a Ballad, and in a more impressive metre than is usual in Ballads.

Having thus[73] adverted to a few of the reasons why I have written in verse, and why I have chosen subjects from common life, and endeavoured to bring my language near to the real language of men, if I have been too minute in pleading my own cause, I have at the same time been treating a subject of

---

[71] *while, in lighter compositions, the ease*

[72] *that, of two descriptions, either*

[73] *Having thus explained a few*

general interest; and it is for this reason that I request the Reader's permission to add a few words with reference solely to these particular poems, and to some defects which will probably be found in them. I am sensible that my associations must have sometimes been particular instead of general, and that, consequently, giving to things a false importance, sometimes from diseased impulses I may have written upon unworthy subjects; but I am less apprehensive on this account, than that my language may frequently have suffered from those arbitrary connections of feelings and ideas with particular[74] words, from which no man can altogether protect himself. Hence I have no doubt[75] that in some instances feelings even of the ludicrous may be given to my Readers by expressions which appeared to me tender and pathetic. Such faulty expressions, were I convinced they were faulty at present, and that they must necessarily continue to be so, I would willingly take all reasonable pains to correct. But it is dangerous to make these alterations on the simple authority of a few individuals, or even of certain classes of men; for where the understanding of an Author is not convinced, or his feelings altered, this cannot be done without great injury to himself: for his own feelings are his stay and support, and if he sets them aside in one instance, he may be induced to repeat this act till his mind loses all confidence in itself[76] and becomes utterly debilitated. To this it may be added, that the Reader ought never to forget that he is himself exposed to the same errors as the Poet, and perhaps in a much greater degree: for there can be no presumption in saying[77] that it is not probable he will be so well acquainted with the various stages of meaning through which words have passed, or with the fickleness or stability of the relations of particular ideas to each other; and

---

[74] *particular words and phrases, from which*

[75] *Hence I have no doubt, that,*

[76] *itself,*

[77] *in saying, that*

above all, since he is so much less interested in the subject, he may decide lightly and carelessly.

Long as I have detained my Reader, I hope he will permit me to caution him against a mode of false criticism which has been applied to Poetry in which the language closely resembles that of life and nature. Such verses have been triumphed over in parodies of which Dr. Johnson's Stanza is a fair specimen.

> "I put my hat upon my head,
> And walk'd into the Strand,
> And there I met another man
> Whose hat was in his hand."†

Immediately under these lines I will place one of the most justly admired stanzas of the "*Babes* in the Wood."

> "These pretty Babes with hand in hand
> Went wandering up and down;
> But never more they saw the Man
> Approaching from the Town."

In both[78] of these stanzas the words, and the order of the words, in no respect differ from the most unimpassioned conversation. There are words in both, for example, "the Strand," and "the Town," connected with none but the most familiar ideas; yet the one stanza we admit as admirable, and the other as a fair example of the superlatively contemptible. Whence

---

† Boswell first heard this parody from Garrick on 9 May 1772, but Johnson improved on Garrick's version. Boswell never published the parody because of Percy's sensitiveness. Wordsworth's quotation gives the version as Boswell had it from Johnson, but it is not known where he discovered it. (*v. Poems of Johnson*, ed. Nichol Smith and McAdam, Oxford, 1941, pp. 157-8.)

Percy's version of the second of these stanzas has as its third line, "But never more could see the man," and his title is "The children in the Wood". (*v. Wordsworth's Preface to Lyrical Ballads*, ed. W. J. B. Owen, p. 191.)

[78] *In both these stanzas*

arises this difference? Not from the metre, not from the language, not from the order of the words; but the *matter* expressed in Dr. Johnson's stanza is contemptible. The proper method of treating trivial and simple verses to which Dr. Johnson's stanza would be a fair parallelism is not to say[79] this is a bad kind of poetry, or this is not poetry,[80] but this wants sense; it is neither interesting in itself, nor can *lead* to any thing interesting; the images neither originate in that sane state of feeling which arises out of thought, nor can excite thought or feeling in the Reader. This is the only sensible manner of dealing with such verses: Why trouble yourself about the species till you have previously decided upon the genus? Why take pains to prove that an Ape is not a Newton when it is self-evident that he is not a man.[80]

I have one request to make of my Reader, which is, that in judging these Poems he would decide by his own feelings genuinely, and not by reflection upon what will probably be the judgment of others. How common is it to hear a person say, "I myself do not object to this style of composition or this or that expression, but to such and such classes of people it will appear mean or ludicrous." This mode of criticism[81] so destructive of all sound unadulterated judgment[82] is almost universal: I have therefore to request[83] that the Reader would abide independently by his own feelings, and that if he finds himself affected he would not suffer such conjectures to interfere with his pleasure.

If an Author by any single composition has impressed us with respect for his talents, it is useful to consider this as affording a presumption, that, on other occasions where we

---

[79] *not to say, this is*
[80] *poetry; but this wants . . . man?*
[81] *criticism, so*
[82] *judgment, is*
[83] *request,*

have been displeased, he nevertheless may not have written ill or absurdly; and, further, to give him so much credit for this one composition as may induce us to review what has displeased us with more care than we should otherwise have bestowed upon it. This is not only an act of justice, but in our decisions upon poetry especially, may conduce in a high degree to the improvement of our own taste: for an *accurate* taste in Poetry[84] and in all the other arts, as Sir Joshua Reynolds has observed, is an *acquired* talent, which can only be produced by thought and a long continued intercourse with the best models of composition. This is mentioned[85] not with so ridiculous a purpose as to prevent the most inexperienced Reader from judging for himself, (I have already said that I wish him to judge for himself;) but merely to temper the rashness of decision, and to suggest[85] that if Poetry be a subject on which much time has not been bestowed, the judgment may be erroneous,[85] and that in many cases it necessarily will be so.

I know nothing would have so effectually contributed to further the end which I have in view as to have shewn of what kind the pleasure is, and how the pleasure is produced[86] which is confessedly produced by metrical composition essentially different from what I have here endeavoured to recommend;[86] for the Reader will say that he has been pleased by such composition[86] and what can I do more for him? The power of any art is limited[87] and he will suspect that if I propose to furnish him with new friends it is only upon condition of his abandoning his old friends. Besides, as I have said, the Reader is himself conscious of the pleasure which he has received from such composition, composition to which he has peculiarly

---

[84] *poetry, and*

[85] *mentioned, . . . suggest, that, if . . . erroneous; and that*

[86] *how that pleasure is produced, which is confessedly . . . recommend: for . . . composition; and what*

[87] *limited; and he will suspect, that . . . new friends, it is*

attached the endearing name of Poetry; and all men feel an habitual gratitude, and something of an honorable bigotry for the objects which have long continued to please them: we not only wish to be pleased, but to be pleased in that particular way in which we have been accustomed to be pleased. There is a host of arguments in these feelings; and I should be the less able to combat them successfully, as I am willing to allow, that, in order entirely to enjoy the Poetry which I am recommending, it would be necessary to give up much of what is ordinarily enjoyed. But[88] would my limits have permitted me to point out how this pleasure is produced, I might have removed many obstacles, and assisted my Reader in perceiving that the powers of language are not so limited as he may suppose; and that it is possible that poetry may give other enjoyments, of a purer, more lasting, and more exquisite nature. But this[89] part of my subject I have been obliged altogether to omit: as it has been less my present aim to prove that the interest excited by some other kinds of poetry is less vivid, and less worthy of the nobler powers of the mind, than to offer reasons for presuming, that, if the object which I have proposed to myself were adequately attained, a species of poetry would be produced, which is genuine poetry; in its nature well adapted to interest mankind permanently, and likewise important in the multiplicity and quality of its moral relations.

From what has been said, and from a perusal of the Poems, the Reader will be able clearly to perceive the object which I have proposed to myself: he will determine how far I have attained this object; and, what is a much more important question, whether it be worth attaining; and upon the decision of these two questions will rest my claim to the approbation of the public.

---

[88] *But, would*

[89] *This part of my subject I have not altogether neglected; but it has been less my present aim to prove, that*

Notes to the Poems

The Rime of the Ancyent Marinere (p. 9)

The text of this poem underwent considerable changes between the date of its first publication in 1798 and its publication in *Sibylline Leaves* in 1817. This first version should be compared with the final one which is that given in most modern editions. The main alterations between the first and the last versions are given in footnotes to the text which refer the reader to *The Poetical Works of S. T. Coleridge* ed. E. H. Coleridge, Oxford, 1912, who adopts the text of 1834. The poem was reprinted in *Lyrical Ballads* in 1800, 1802 and 1805. The text in 1802 and 1805 follows that of 1800. It was first published under Coleridge's name in *Sibylline Leaves* in 1817 and in the editions of 1828, 1829 and 1834. The marginal glosses first appeared in 1817 but may have been written much earlier.

In 1800 the poem and the prose *Argument* which precedes it were both changed considerably and the title became: 'The Ancient Mariner. A Poet's Reverie'. No doubt these changes were made at the instigation of Wordsworth, who felt that the *Ancient Mariner* had been a stumbling-block to an appreciation of the 1798 volume. In a letter to Cottle on the 24th June 1799, Wordsworth wrote: 'From what I can gather it seems that The Ancyent Marinere has upon the whole been an injury to the volume, I mean that the old words and the strangeness of it have deterred readers from going on.'[1] In the revised copy of 1800, from which the printer worked for the 1802 edition, 'A Poet's Reverie' is erased on p. 5, but was left on the half-title on p. 1 and remained there in the editions of 1802 and 1805. It may well have been erased in answer to the protest of Charles Lamb who also objected to the Note (afterwards omitted) appended to the poem by Wordsworth in 1800, in which Wordsworth censured Coleridge for not giving

[1] But Coleridge afterwards (perhaps jocularly) defended his poem against this allegation. 'I was told by Longmans that the greater part of the *Lyrical Ballads* had been sold to seafaring men, who having heard of the *Ancient Mariner*, concluded that it was a naval song-book, or, at all event that its, had some relation to nautical matters.' [*T.T.*, 448.]

the Mariner any 'distinct character, either in his profession of
Mariner, or as a human being'. (A copy of Wordsworth's Note and
an extract from Lamb's letter to Wordsworth are given at the end
of this Note to the poem.)

The changes that Coleridge made in his poem for the 1800 edition
were mainly towards the removal of archaisms of vocabulary[1],
spelling, and of quaintness of style. But he also omitted some of the
homelier images appropriate to ballad poetry, e.g. lines such as
'Like chaff we drove along' and 'Or my staff shall make thee skip',
and some of the iteration common to such poetry. The later
versions are in fact more literary, and, although the alterations are
on the whole improvements, the first version has a simple, dramatic
quality that recaptures something of the ballad proper.

The *Ancient Mariner* was planned by Coleridge and Wordsworth
during a walking tour to Linton which started on the 13th
November 1797 and on which they were accompanied by Dorothy
Wordsworth. It was finished in March 1798, and Dorothy recorded
in her *Journal*: 'Coleridge dined with us. He brought his ballad
finished.' [*D.W.*, i. 13.] The central action of the poem came from
Wordsworth who had been reading Shelvocke's *A Voyage round the
World by the Way of the Great South Sea* (1726). During Shelvocke's
voyage one of his crew had shot a black albatross which had
followed the ship in bad weather. Wordsworth also suggested the
navigation of the ship by the dead men and a few of the lines such
as 17-20 and 218-9. But Wordsworth soon withdrew from the
composition of the poem for he wrote, 'our respective manners
proved so widely different that it would have been quite pre-
sumptuous in me to do anything but separate from an undertaking
upon which I could only have been a clog'. [*I.F.*]

A further piece of information about the genesis of the poem was
given by a friend of Wordsworth, the Rev. Alexander Dyce, to
H. N. Coleridge who incorporated it in the form of the following
Note in his 1852 edition of Coleridge's *Poems*. 'When my truly-
honoured friend Mr. Wordsworth was last in London, he . . . made
the following statement which I am quite sure, I give you correctly:
The Ancient Mariner was founded on a strange dream which a
friend of Coleridge [John Cruikshank, Lord Egmont's agent at
Stowey] had, who fancied he saw a skeleton ship with figures in it.
We had both determined to write some poetry for a monthly
magazine, the profits of which were to defray the expenses of a
little excursion we were to make together. *The Ancient Mariner*

---

[1] *e.g.* l. 80 where Coleridge changed 'Pheere' (*i.e.* companion) to 'Mate'.

was intended for this periodical, but was too long. I had very little share in the composition of it, for I soon found that the style of Coleridge and myself would not assimilate. . . .' Coleridge's own account of how he came to write the poem, in Chapter XIV of *Biographia Literaria*, should not be overlooked.

The most detailed account of the sources of the poem is given in J. L. Lowes, *The Road to Xanadu* (1927). Lowes points out that the *Ancient Mariner* was written in place of *The Wanderings of Cain* and tells us that Coleridge's Notebooks refer to a romance on the Wandering Jew which Coleridge was also contemplating at this time. *The Wandering Jew* is the title of a poem in Percy's *Reliques* which were a great influence upon the *Lyrical Ballads*. Another influence upon the poem was Bürger's *Lenore*, the translation of which had had a great vogue in England at this period. *Lenore* had been translated by William Taylor and also [*v*. J. B. Beer's *Coleridge The Visionary*, p. 147] by Sir Walter Scott. Coleridge probably owed something to both of these,[1] but (as Beer suggests) there is an obvious indebtedness to Scott for some of the metrical effects of the *Ancient Mariner* although Percy's *Reliques* played a part here.

A vast literature has grown up around the poem in recent times and it is possible only to summarize some of the main features of this. Some critics have attacked the notion that one can read symbolic meanings into this and Coleridge's other poems. The most distinguished of these are E. E. Stoll [*Symbolism in Coleridge*, P.M.L.A., 1948, lxiii. 214-33] and Elizabeth Schneider [*Coleridge, Opium and Kubla Khan*, Chicago, 1953] both of whom had in mind especially G. Wilson Knight's *The Starlit Dome*, 1941; Miss Maud Bodkin's *Archetypal Patterns in Poetry*, 1934; Kenneth Burke's *The Philosophy of Literary Form*, 1941; and R. Penn Warren's 'A Poem of Pure Imagination,' *Kenyon Review*, 1946, viii, 391-427. None of these last-named is interested in the poet's intentions, but is concerned with meanings of which Coleridge himself may have been unaware. G. Wilson Knight (whose book deals at greater length with *Kubla Khan* than the *Ancient Mariner*) emphasizes the importance of the sexual symbolism in the poem and speaks of it as 'an embracing of *agapé* with a definitely lower place, if not a rejection, accorded to *eros*'. 'The final lesson', he writes, 'is a total

[1] Writing later to his wife from Germany on the 8th November 1798, Coleridge was to say, 'Bürger of all the German Poets pleases me the most, as yet – the Lenore is greatly superior to any of the Translations,' – an indication that he knew more than one translation.

[*C. Letters*, i. 438]

acceptance of God and his universe through humility, with general love to man and beast. But the specifically sexual is left unplaced.' Miss Maud Bodkin discerns in the poem the archetypal pattern of death and rebirth very much in terms of Jungian psychology. She finds in the poem racial memories of the kind laid bare by a study of primitive religions and declares that 'the design itself [of the poem] is determined by forces which do not lie open directly to thought, nor to the control of the will'. Kenneth Burke is perhaps more Freudian than Jungian and interprets the poem in terms of the poet's unconscious tensions (e.g. he sees the 'Albatross as a synecdochic representative of Sara' [the poet's wife]). R. Penn Warren approves generally of Kenneth Burke's approach but views the poem as a symbolical representation of Coleridge's beliefs about the poetic imagination.

E. M. W. Tillyard's *Five Poems, 1470-1870*, 1948, discusses the poem in relation to its political, historical and biographical background. Other recent and valuable discussions of the poem may be found in C. M. Bowra's *The Romantic Imagination*, Ch. iii, and Prof. R. C. Bald's 'Coleridge and the Ancient Mariner' (in *Nineteenth-Century Studies in Honor of C. S. Northup*, U.S.A., 1940). Humphry House's *Coleridge* (The Clark Lectures 1951-52), 1953, examines these and other previous accounts of the poem. He would go some way with Warren's theory but believes the poem to be 'part of the experience which led Coleridge into his later theoretic statements (as of the theory of the Imagination) rather than a symbolic adumbration of the theoretic statements themselves'. J. B. Beer's *Coleridge the Visionary*, 1959, contains an excellent critique of the poem in which emphasis is put upon Coleridge's debt to neoplatonic and Egyptian mythology. R. L. Brett's *Reason and Imagination*, 1960, looks at the poem through the statements about poetry made by Coleridge in *Biographia Literaria* and elsewhere and argues that the poet's conscious control of his material never falters.

Wordsworth's 'Note to the Ancient Mariner' from the 1800 edition of *Lyrical Ballads*

I cannot refuse myself the gratification of informing such Readers as may have been pleased with this Poem, or with any part of it, that they owe their pleasure in some sort to me; as the Author was himself very desirous that it should be suppressed. This wish had arisen from a consciousness of the defects of the Poem, and from a knowledge that many persons had been much displeased with it. The Poem of my Friend has indeed great defects; first, that the principal person has no distinct character, either in his profession of Mariner, or as a human being who having been long under the controul of supernatural impressions might be supposed himself to partake of something supernatural: secondly, that he does not act, but is continually acted upon: thirdly, that the events having no necessary connection do not produce each other; and lastly, that the imagery is somewhat too laboriously accumulated. Yet the Poem contains many delicate touches of passion, and indeed the passion is every where true to nature; a great number of the stanzas present beautiful images, and are expressed with unusual felicity of language; and the versification, though the metre is itself unfit for long poems, is harmonious and artfully varied, exhibiting the utmost powers of that metre, and every variety of which it is capable. It therefore appeared to me that these several merits (the first of which, namely that of the passion, is of the highest kind,) gave to the Poem a value which is not often possessed by better Poems. On this account I requested of my Friend to permit me to republish it.

Extract from a letter of Charles Lamb, dated January 1801, in which he thanks Wordsworth for the gift of the 1800 edition of *Lyrical Ballads*

I am sorry that Coleridge has christened his *Ancient Marinere*, a *Poet's Reverie*; it is as bad as Bottom the Weaver's declaration that he is not a lion, but only the scenical representation of a lion. What new idea is gained by this title but one subversive of all credit – which the tale should force upon us – of its truth.

For me, I was never so affected with any human tale. After first reading it, I was totally possessed with it for many days. I dislike all the miraculous part of it; but the feelings of the man under the operation of such scenery, dragged me along like Tom Piper's magic whistle. I totally differ from your idea that the Marinere should have had a character and profession. This is a beauty in *Gulliver's Travels*, where the mind is kept in a placid state of little wonderments; but the Ancient Marinere undergoes such trials as overwhelm and bury all individuality or memory of what he was – like the state of a man in a bad dream, one terrible peculiarity of which is, that all consciousness of personality is gone. Your other observation is, I think as well, a little unfounded: the Marinere, from being conversant in supernatural events, *has* acquired a supernatural and strange cast of phrase, eye, appearance, etc., which frighten the wedding guest. You will excuse my remarks, because I am hurt and vexed that you should think it necessary, with a prose apology, to open the eyes of dead men that cannot see.

To sum up a general opinion of the second volume, I do not feel any one poem in it so forcibly as the *Ancient Marinere*, and the *Mad Mother*, and the *Lines at Tintern Abbey*, in the first.

The Foster-Mother's Tale, A Dramatic Fragment (p. 35)

This poem together with *The Dungeon* was taken from Coleridge's play *Osorio*, a tragedy which he completed in October 1797. He had written the play at the request of Richard Sheridan with a view to its production at Drury Lane, but it was rejected. In its final form and with the new title *Remorse* it was produced in January 1813 and ran for twenty performances.

The Foster-Mother's Tale was first published in 1798 and reprinted 1800, 1802 and 1805. It was omitted from the acting version of *Remorse* but was printed in the form of an Appendix to the second edition of the play in 1813. It is included in *Sibylline Leaves*, 1817 and 1852.

Lines left upon a Seat in a Yew-Tree which stands near the Lake of Esthwaite (p. 38)

Wordsworth modified this poem considerably between 1798 and 1820. 'Composed in part at school at Hawkshead. The tree has disappeared, and the slip of Common on which it stood, that ran parallel to the lake, and lay open to it, has long been enclosed; so that the road has lost much of its attraction. This spot was my favourite walk in the evenings during the latter part of my school-time. The individual whose habits and character are here given, was a gentleman of the neighbourhood, a man of talent and learning, who had been educated at one of our Universities, and returned to pass his time in seclusion on his own estate. He died a bachelor in middle age. . . .' [*I.F.*]

'Wordsworth's statement that the poem was "composed in part at Hawkshead" does not necessarily imply that he wrote it while still at school, for he visited Hawkshead in both 1788 and 1789. But very little can have been written as early as that; for the poem as a whole represents his revulsion from the intellectual arrogance and self-sufficiency of Godwinism, from which he recovered during his years at Racedown, and the warning that man should "still suspect and still revere himself" implies renunciation of the Godwinian view that man's vices are due to society rather than to the innate imperfection of human nature. In 1815 Wordsworth dated the poem 1795, and drafts of it are found in a rough notebook in use at Racedown (1795-7); but some lines of it, not in their final form, and written in the hand of Mary Hutchinson, who was at Racedown in the early months of 1797, prove that the poem did not reach its published form before that date.' [*P.W.*, i. 329.]

The 'gentleman of the neighbourhood' referred to by Wordsworth was a Rev. Mr. Braithwaite of Satterhow who shortly before his death in 1800 bought some of the unenclosed land on the shore of Esthwaite thus ruining Wordsworth's favourite walk. The yew-tree itself was cut down in 1820 because of the belief that it was poisoning cattle.

Harper points out that in this poem 'there is heard a note which is quite rare in Wordsworth's poetry, a note of personal resentment for the world's neglect, its failure to appreciate him and his ideals.' [*G.M.H.*, p. 180.]

In 1815 Wordsworth changed the line:

> The stone-chat, or the glancing sand-piper [l. 24]

to

> the sand-lark, restless Bird,
> Piping along the margin of the lake

but restored the original 'glancing sand-piper' in 1820 after Lamb had protested about the suppression of that 'line all alive'.

The Nightingale; A Conversational Poem (p. 40)

Coleridge wrote this poem in April 1798. It was first published in 1798 and reprinted in 1800, 1802 and 1805. It was included in *Sibylline Leaves*, 1817. *The Nightingale* replaced *Lewti*, a love poem which had been printed for the 1798 volume but [*v*. Appendix A] which was withdrawn to preserve anonymity, since it had already appeared in the *Morning Post*. A few copies of the 1798 edition containing the cancelled sheets of *Lewti* were actually issued.

l. 69. The 'most gentle maid' was Miss Ellen Cruikshank, the sister of Coleridge's friend, John Cruikshank, whose 'dream' of a skeleton ship had inspired this image in the *Ancient Mariner* [*v*. Note to the *Ancient Mariner*].

l. 71. The castle in the poem is Enmore Castle, the seat of Lord Egmont, near Stowey.

Coleridge sent the MS. of the poem by post on the 10th May 1798 to Wordsworth at Alfoxden with the following lines:

> In stale blank verse a subject stale
> I send *per post* my *Nightingale*;
> And like an honest bard, dear Wordsworth,
> You'll tell me what you think, my Bird's worth.

My opinion's briefly this –
His *bill* he opens not amiss;
And when he has sung a stave or so,
His breast, & some small space below,
So throbs & swells, that you might swear
No vulgar music's working there.
So far, so good; but then, 'od rot him !
There's something falls off at his bottom.
Yet, sure, no wonder it should breed,
That my Bird's Tail's a tail indeed
And makes it's own inglorious harmony
Æolio crepitû, non carmine.

                              [*C. Letters*, i. 406]

The Female Vagrant (p. 44)

This poem was reprinted in 1800, 1802 and 1805 and in the *Poems*, 1820-1836, but underwent constant and thorough revision. In 1815 an extract from it was printed prefaced by the words: *Having described her own Situation with her Husband, serving in America during the War, she proceeds,* followed by a version which begins at line 131. The poem was finally incorporated into a longer and quite early poem originally called *Salisbury Plain* but printed under the title *Guilt and Sorrow* which after considerable and protracted revisions was first published in its final form in 1842. The textual history of the poem is long and complex and is outlined by de Selincourt. [*P.W.*, i. 330-334. See also *P.W.*, i. xvi. 292-5.] The version printed in 1798 must be regarded as that part of an early version of *Salisbury Plain* which concerns the vagrant woman. Wordsworth was clearly very dissatisfied with the poem. He was conscious of breaking his own rule of 'looking steadily at his object' and considered that the 'diction of that Poem is often vicious, and the descriptions are often false, giving proofs of a mind inattentive to the true nature of the subject on which it was employed'. [*E.L.*, p. 270.] Coleridge, however, compared the style and diction of the poem favourably with that of the *Descriptive Sketches* [*v. Biog. Lit.*, ch. iv].

In 1802 he made a number of additions and corrections to the text and again in 1805 the effect of which was to blunt the sharp edge of his attack on wealthy landowners, on soldiering and war, and social oppression. Indeed, as the poem stands in 1798 it is clearly a product of the revolutionary Wordsworth, whose passionate humanitarianism leads him to write about the injustices of a social system which oppresses the poor and turns them into outcasts. As early as 1802, ll. 118-126, describing the British soldiers, were omitted.

'Political disaffection shows itself in the fifth and sixth stanzas of *The Female Vagrant* as originally printed, where the legalized oppression of a poor man by his neighbour, a rich land-owner, is feelingly described. The passage was afterwards completely altered, being represented finally by the vague statement:

> But through severe mischance and cruel wrong,
> My father's substance fell into decay.

It is significant that another passage in the thirty stanzas originally printed as *The Female Vagrant* was also softened later into a far less bitter indictment of society. One of the main sources of evil represented in the Woman's Story as well as in the Man's [*v. Salisbury Plain*] is war. In the fragment printed in 1798, the soldiery after whom the poor creature has dragged herself through America are called

> the brood

That lap (their very nourishment) their brother's blood.

This was omitted in all editions after 1800. . . . As *Guilt and Sorrow* was finally published, it contained not a word against capital punishment, but ends with the poor Sailor's voluntary submission to the law, which avenges in his person a crime for which he has atoned, and the guilt of which has left no stain upon his soul.' [*G.M.H.*, pp. 198-199.] By 1842, when *Guilt and Sorrow* was first published, Wordsworth had written fourteen sonnets in favour of capital punishment. This is a long way from his original intention which was partly to 'expose the vices of the penal law and the calamities of war as they affect individuals'. [*E.L.*, p. 145.]

De Selincourt maintains that a comparison of the various texts throw interesting light on the development of Wordsworth's thought, and in his discussion of the MSS. of *Guilt and Sorrow* [see above] he demonstrates the progressive 'softening' of Wordsworth's attitude towards society which transformed *Salisbury Plain* into *Guilt and Sorrow* [*P.W.*, i. viii. 94-127]; compare *Prelude*, x. 236-330, for his state of mind at this period and his attitude towards the soldiery and the oppressed. A version of *The Female Vagrant* appears as stanzas xxiii-l of *Guilt and Sorrow*. The poem was probably begun in 1791-2 and is, therefore, the earliest poem in the 1798 edn. The metre is Spenserian. In the text we have noted only the important variants in the 1800, 1802, 1805 edns.

Goody Blake, and Harry Gill, A True Story (p. 54)

Based on a story from Erasmus Darwin's *Zoönomia, or the laws of Organic Life*, 2 vols., 1794-6, which Wordsworth persuaded Joseph Cottle to borrow for him in June 1797. [*E.L.*, p. 169.] 'A young farmer in Warwickshire, finding his hedges broke, and the sticks carried away during a frosty season, determined to watch for the thief. He lay many cold hours under a haystack, and at length an old woman, like a witch in a play, approached, and began to pull up the hedge; he waited till she had tied up her bottle of sticks, and was carrying them off, that he might convict her of the theft, and then springing from his concealment, he seized his prey with violent threats. After some altercation, in which her load was left upon the ground, she kneeled upon her bundle of sticks, and, raising her arms to Heaven beneath the bright moon then at the full, spoke to the farmer already shivering with cold, "Heaven grant, that thou mayest never know again the blessing to be warm." He complained of cold all the next day, and wore an uppercoat, and in a few days another, and in a fortnight took to his bed, always saying nothing made him warm; he covered himself with many blankets, and had a sieve over his face as he lay; and from this one insane idea he kept his bed above twenty years for fear of the cold air, till at length he died.' The name Gill was probably borrowed from Joseph Gill, a poor relative of the Pinneys who was employed as caretaker of the house and grounds at Racedown. He kept a diary which is preserved at Racedown among the Pinney Papers. The poem shows Wordsworth's concern for the conditions of the Dorsetshire peasantry [*v. M.M.*, p. 284]. 'The peasants are miserably poor; their cottages are shapeless structures (I may almost say) of wood and clay – indeed they are not at all beyond what might be expected in savage life.' [*E.L.*, p. 148.]

The poem was probably composed just before *Peter Bell*, early in April 1798 [Wordsworth returned the Erasmus Darwin to Cottle May 9th, 1798 – *L.Y.*, iii. 1339]. It belongs together with the *Ancient Mariner, The Three Graves* and *Peter Bell* to the 'curse-cycle' of poems and "shows Wordsworth's growing interest in the psychology of fear" [*M.M.*, p. 383].

Wordsworth's attitude in this poem is characteristically Godwinian but the psychology involved may derive from Hartley. On 24th October 1795 he wrote of the Dorsetshire peasantry that 'the country people here are wretchedly poor; ignorant and overwhelmed with every vice that usually attends ignorance in that class, viz. lying and picking and stealing, etc.' [*L.Y.*,

iii. 1334.] The association of ignorance with vice is typical Godwinianism. The poem is directed against the farmer and landowner who at that time were enjoying unusual prosperity while the peasants were suffering severe hardships. Although Goody Blake is caught stealing sticks for fuel, Wordsworth stresses the worth of her character in the long devotion to her work and shows how the moral law supports her in inflicting Harry Gill with perpetual cold. The idea of warmth and cold is clearly not only related to the search for firewood but is metaphorically linked with Wordsworth's appeal to humanitarian principles. The poem is written in short ballad metre, which occupied Wordsworth during March, April, May 1798. Up to that period he had been engaged, almost entirely, in writing in blank verse.

When Wordsworth in the *Advertisement* says that the poem 'is founded on a well-authenticated fact which happened in Warwickshire' he has, of course, the original story of Darwin in mind. Darwin, in fact, prefaces his version of the story by asserting that he 'received good information of the truth of the following case, which was published a few years ago in the newspapers'.

Lines written at a small distance from my House, and sent by my
*   little Boy to the Person to whom they are addressed.* (Later given the
*   short title of To My Sister) (p. 58)*

'Composed in front of Alfoxden House. My little boy-messenger on this occasion was the son of Basil Montagu. The larch mentioned in the first stanza was standing when I revisited the place in May, 1841, more than forty years after . . .' [*I.F.*]

'This lyric is probably the "singular but fine little poem of Wordsworth's" which, says James Losh, Southey repeated to him in Bath on April 3rd. Southey may have obtained it through Cottle, to whom perhaps Coleridge sent a copy.' [*M.M.*, p. 379.] Probably written at the end of May 1798, together with *Expostulation and Reply* and *The Tables Turned* which it resembles and with which Wordsworth grouped it under *Poems of Sentiment and Reflection*. However, this poem is a contribution to the poets' traditional celebration of spring and the delight taken in the renewal of life and the heart of man and should not be accepted as embodying any profound philosophical attitudes.

Simon Lee, the Old Huntsman (p. 60)

Written in the spring of 1798, the text of this poem underwent considerable changes between 1798 and 1845, the object of which seems to have been to heighten the contrast between Simon's youth and age. A full discussion of these changes is given in *P.W.*, i. 413. In Preface of 1800 he says his intention in this poem was to place the reader 'in the way of receiving from ordinary moral sensations another and more salutary impression than we are accustomed to receive from them'.

'This old man had been huntsman to the Squires of Alfoxden, which, at the time we occupied it, belonged to a minor. The old man's cottage stood upon the common, a little way from the entrance to Alfoxden Park. But it had disappeared. Many other changes had taken place in the adjoining village, which I could not but notice with a regret more natural than well-considered. Improvements but rarely appear such to those who, after long intervals of time, revisit places they have had much pleasure in. It is unnecessary to add, the fact was as mentioned in the poem; and I have, after an interval of 45 years, the image of the old man as fresh before my eyes as if I had seen him yesterday. The expression when the hounds were out, "I dearly love their voices" was word for word from his own lips.' [*I.F.*] This poem, written in the short ballad metre, is another of Wordsworth's poems based on an incident taken from life, although he removes the setting from Alfoxden to Cardigan, Wales.

Legouis has drawn attention to the fact that this poem is written in opposition to Godwin's opinion, as put forward in *Political Justice* and in *Caleb Williams*, that 'if by gratitude we understand a sentiment of preference which I entertain towards another, upon the ground of my having been subject of his benefits, it is no part of justice or virtue.' [*La Jeunesse de Wordsworth*, E. Legouis, 1896 (Eng. trans. 1897), pp. 309-15; *M.M.*, pp. 382-3.] In this respect it should be read together with *Anecdote for Fathers* and *The Last of the Flock*.

The poem makes an interesting social comment regarding the enclosure of common land. Simon in old age is still able to live on and to cultivate a small piece of land to which he laid claim in his youth. Between 1700 and 1844, 1,765,711 acres of common land were enclosed by Act of Parliament and it is interesting to notice that Wordsworth, later in his life, succeeded in preventing the enclosure of Grasmere's commons. [*K.M.*, pp. 20-21.]

Anecdote for Fathers (p. 64)

The child referred to in this poem, and in *Lines written at a small distance from my house, and sent by my little boy to the person to whom they are addressed*, is Edward, son of Basil Montagu, but is always referred to as Basil by William and Dorothy in their letters. His father was at Cambridge with Wordsworth, and his first wife with whom he lived in Cambridge while Wordsworth was still in residence there, died in childbirth. The Wordsworths took the boy into their home first at Racedown and then at Alfoxden, and he served as a continual reminder to Wordsworth of childhood and, of course, particularly of his own childhood. 'He is my perpetual pleasure', Dorothy wrote [*E.L.*, p. 151], but Wordsworth complained that although 'Basil is quite well, *quant au physique, mais pour le moral il-y-a bien à craindre*. Among other things he lies like a little devil.' [*E.L.*, p. 154.] Wordsworth's intention in writing a poem on the conversation between Basil and himself was 'to point out the injurious effects of putting inconsiderate questions to Children, and urging them to give answers upon matters either uninteresting to them, or upon which they have no decided opinion'. [*L.Y.*, i. 253.] In 1845 Wordsworth suppressed the poem's sub-title and substituted a quotation from Eusebius which made the poem's intention clearer; '*Retine vim istam, falsa enim dicam, si coges*'.

The poem consciously refutes Godwin's belief that lying is unnatural to children and is only the product of an evil social system. Curiously, Edward's father was an enthusiastic believer in Godwinianism who, at one time, seriously considered giving up his practice in law because he considered the law a social evil.

'This was suggested in front of Alfoxden. The Boy was a son of my friend Basil Montagu, who had been two or three years under our care. The name of Kilve is from a village on the Bristol Channel, about a mile from Alfoxden; and the name of Liswyn Farm was taken from a beautiful spot on the Wye . . .' [*I.F.*]

We are Seven (p. 66)

'Written at Alfoxden in the spring of 1798, under circumstances somewhat remarkable. The little girl who is the heroine I met within the area of Goodrich Castle in the year 1793. Having left the Isle of Wight and crossed Salisbury Plain. . . . I proceeded by Bristol up the Wye, and so on to N. Wales, to the Vale of Clwydd, where I spent my summer under the roof of the father of my friend, Robert Jones. . . . I composed it while walking in the grove at Alfoxden. My friends will not deem it too trifling to relate that while walking to and fro I composed the last stanza first, having begun with the last line. When it was all but finished, I came in and recited it to Mr. Coleridge and my Sister, and said, "A prefatory stanza must be added, and I should sit down to our little tea-meal with greater pleasure if my task were finished." I mentioned in substance what I wished to be expressed, and Coleridge immediately threw off the stanza thus:

> A little child, dear brother Jem, –

I objected to the rhyme, "dear brother Jem", as being ludicrous, but we all enjoyed the joke of hitching-in our friend, James Tobin's name, who was familiarly called Jem. . . . I have only to add that in the spring of 1841 I revisited Goodrich Castle, not having seen that part of the Wye since I met the little Girl there in 1793. It would have given me greater pleasure to have found in the neighbouring hamlet traces of one who had interested me so much; but that was impossible, as, unfortunately, I did not even know her name. . . .' [I.F.]

The visit which Wordsworth here describes was extremely productive – not only this poem but also *Guilt and Sorrow* (see *Female Vagrant*), *Peter Bell* and *Tintern Abbey* have their origin in the incidents and impressions of this journey from the Isle of Wight into N. Wales. It is of this period that he talks of having an 'appetite' for Nature (*v. Tintern Abbey* and *Prel.* xi (1805), ll. 99-100). Wordsworth retained Coleridge's first stanza in publishing the poem – changing 'little child' to 'simple child' – though later in 1815 he dropped out 'dear brother Jem' entirely and left the first line incomplete as 'A simple child . . .'

Wordsworth stated that his intention in this poem was to illustrate the perplexity and obscurity which in childhood attend our notion of death, or rather our utter inability to admit that notion, in which case Coleridge's contribution does not help to introduce this idea. Wordsworth himself recalled that, 'Nothing was more difficult for me in childhood than to admit the notion of death as a state applicable to my own being. I have said elsewhere

> A simple child,
> That lightly draws its breath,
> And feels its life in every limb,
> What should it know of death! –

. . . I was often unable to think of external things as having external existence, and I communed with all that I saw as something not apart from, but inherent in, my own immaterial nature. Many times while going to school have I grasped at a wall or tree to recall myself from this abyss of idealism to the reality. At that time I was afraid of such processes.' [I.F. Note on *Ode. Intimations of Immortality from Recollections of Early Childhood*. Lines 117-123

of the address to the child in that Ode (1807) are particularly
relevant:

> Thou, over whom thy Immortality
> Broods like the Day, a Master o'er a Slave,
> A Presence which is not to be put by;
>   To whom the grave
> Is but a lonely bed without the sense or sight
>   Of day or the warm light,
> A place of thought where we in waiting lie;]

Lines written in early spring (p. 69)

Written in the spring, 1798. 'Actually composed while I was
sitting by the side of the brook that runs down the Comb, in
which stands the village of Alford, through the grounds of
Alfoxden. It was a chosen resort of mine. The brook fell down a
sloping rock so as to make a waterfall considerable for that
country, and across the pool below had fallen a tree, an ash, if I
rightly remember, from which rose perpendicularly boughs in
search of the light intercepted by the deep shade above. The
boughs bore leaves of green that for want of sunshine had faded
into almost lily-white; and from the underside of this natural
sylvan bridge depended long and beautiful tresses of ivy which
waved gently in the breeze that might poetically speaking be
called the breath of the waterfall. The motion varied of course in
proportion to the power of water in the brook.' [*I.F.*]

The theme of this lyric is similar to that of the other lyrics –
*Lines Written at a Small Distance from my House, Expostulation and
Reply* and *The Tables Turned* – which convey a feeling of
spontaneous love and joy at the approach of spring and the
renewal of nature. Yet in this lyric a note of sadness is introduced,
'while the same faith is testified with even greater vehemence in
the joy and "pleasure" of living Nature, a shadow lies over the
spring landscape'. [*M.M.*, p. 381.]

The Thorn (p. 70)

No significant changes were made in the text of this poem until
1820, that is, until *after* Coleridge had singled the poem out for
criticism. [*Biog. Lit.*, ii. 36ff.]

The *Advertisement* of 1798 points out that the poem, 'as the reader will soon discover, is not supposed to be spoken in the author's own person: the character of the loquacious narrator will sufficiently shew itself in the course of the story'. In 1800 this note is considerably expanded: 'This Poem ought to have been preceded by an introductory Poem, which I have been prevented from writing by never having felt myself in a mood when it was probable that I should write it well. – The character which I have here introduced speaking is sufficiently common. The Reader will perhaps have a general notion of it, if he has ever known a man, a Captain of a small trading vessel for example, who being past the middle age of life, had retired upon an annuity or small independent income to some village or country town of which he was not a native, or in which he had not been accustomed to live. Such men having little to do become credulous and talkative from indolence; and from the same cause, and other predisposing causes by which it is probable that such men may have been affected, they are prone to superstition. On which account it appeared to me proper to select a character like this to exhibit some of the general laws by which superstition acts upon the mind. Superstitious men are almost always men of slow faculties and deep feelings; their minds are not loose, but adhesive; they have a reasonable share of imagination, by which word I mean the faculty which produces impressive effects out of simple elements; but they are utterly destitute of fancy, the power by which pleasure and surprize are exited by sudden varieties of situation and by accumulated imagery.

'It was my wish in this poem to show the manner in which such men cleave to the same ideas; and to follow the turns of passion, always different, yet not palpably different, by which their conversation is swayed. I had two objects to attain; first, to represent a picture which should not be unimpressive yet consistent with the character that should describe it, secondly, while I adhered to the style in which such persons describe, to take care that words, which in their minds are impregnated with passion, should likewise convey passion to Readers who are not accustomed to sympathize with men feeling in that manner or using such language. It seemed to me that this might be done by calling in the assistance of Lyrical and rapid Metre. It was necessary that the Poem, to be natural, should in reality move slowly; yet I hoped, that, by the aid of the metre, to those who should at all enter into the spirit of the Poem, it would appear to move quickly. The Reader will have the kindness to excuse this note as I am sensible that an introductory Poem is necessary to give this Poem its full effect.

'Upon this occasion I will request permission to add a few words closely connected with "The Thorn" and many other Poems in these volumes. There is a numerous class of readers who imagine that the same words cannot be repeated without tautology: this is a great error: virtual tautology is much oftener produced by using different words when the meaning is exactly the same. Words, a Poet's words more particularly, ought to be weighed in the balance of feeling and not measured by the space which they occupy upon paper. For the Reader cannot be too often reminded that Poetry is passion: it is the history or science of feelings; now every man must know that an attempt is rarely made to communicate impassioned feelings without something of an accompanying consciousness of the inadequateness of our own powers, or the deficiencies of language. During such efforts there will be a craving in the mind, and as long as it is unsatisfied the Speaker will cling to the same words, or words of the same character. There are also various other reasons why repetitition and apparent tautology are frequent beauties of the highest kind. Among the chief of these reasons is the interest which the mind attaches to words, not only as symbols of the passion, but as *things*, active and efficient, which are of themselves part of the passion. And further, from a spirit of fondness, exultation, and gratitude, the mind luxuriates in the repetition of words which appear successfully to communicate its feelings. The truth of these remarks might be shown by innumerable passages from the Bible and from the impassioned poetry of every nation. "Awake, awake Deborah" [Relevant passages quoted] Judges, chap. 5th Verses 12th, 27th, and part of 28th.— See also the whole of that tumultuous and wonderful Poem.'

Coleridge objected that, 'it is not possible to imitate truly a dull and garrulous discourser, without repeating the effects of dullness and garrulity. However this may be, I dare assert, that the parts (and these form the far larger portion of the whole) which might as well or still better have proceeded from the poet's own imagination, and have been spoken in his own character, are those which have given, and which will continue to give, universal delight; and that the passages exclusively appropriate to the supposed narrator . . . are felt by many unprejudiced and unsophisticated hearts, as sudden and unpleasant sinkings from the height to which the poet had previously lifted them, and to which he again re-elevates both himself and his reader.' [*Biog. Lit.*, ii. 36-38; see also subsequent discussion, pp. 38-43, of Wordsworth's theory of language as expressed in his note to *The Thorn* and in his *Preface*.]

Helen Darbishire, commenting on the poem, concludes that it

'is a great and remarkable poem. It is easy to see the elements out of which it was made: the "elementary feelings" or "essential passions of the heart", love of maid for man, agony at the lover's desertion, love of mother for child, misery of the distraught mind which seeks relief in the wild or calm companionship of Nature. But the kind and quality, the deeper implications of the poetry composed from these elements, are not so easy to see. *The Thorn* has its weak places, its crudenesses, its tiresome redundancies – the old sea-captain's rambling style stumbles at times on the edge of bathos, perhaps tips over in "I've measured it from side to side, 'Tis three feet long and two feet wide" – but the poem remains alive, powerful, able to capture the imagination. Its triumph is in its fusion of the elements, the human passion and the natural scene, so that each expresses itself in and through the other: the misery and love of the woman, and the bleakness yet beauty of the tree, pond and mound. We see the wild desolate scene *through* the human passion, whilst the stark human passions are lifted into permanence, even beauty, by the setting of earth, air, and sky.' [*H.D.*, pp. 43-44.]

This poem 'is the only poem in the *Lyrical Ballads* which owes its origin to a "natural object" seen in a moment of excitement'. [*M.M.*, p. 386.] Wordsworth recalls its composition thus; '1798. Arose out of my observing, on the ridge of Quantock Hill, on a Stormy day, a thorn which I had often passed in calm and bright weather without noticing it. I said to myself, "Cannot I by some invention do as much to make this Thorn permanently an impressive object as the storm has made it to my eyes at this moment?" I began the poem accordingly, and composed it with great rapidity. . . .' [*I.F.*, see also *D.W.*, i. 13, March 19, 1798.]

The poem has also a literary source. 'William Taylor's version of Bürger's ballad *Das Pfarrer's Tochter von Taubenheim* printed under the title of *The Lass of Fair Wone* in the *Monthly Magazine*, 1796, has been suggested by Barron Field and others as a source of *The Thorn*. Hutchinson points to a more probable source in a Scots ballad printed in Johnson's *Musical Museum*, 1787-1803.' [*P.W.*, ii. 514.] Helen Darbishire says, 'In an early notebook of Wordsworth's I find the following lines copied out from a ballad in Hurd's *Ancient and Modern Scottish Songs*:

> Ah there she's lean'd her back to a thorn
> O and alas-a-day, O and alas-a-day
> And there she has her baby born.
> Ten thousand times good-night and be wi' thee.

> She has houked a grave ayont the sun,
>
> O and alas-a-day, O and alas-a-day
>
> And there she has buried the sweet babe in.
>
> Ten thousand times good-night and be wi' thee.'
>
> [*H.D.*, pp. 37-8]

l. 116 [Martha Ray]. Martha Ray, Basil Montagu's mother, was the mistress of Lord Sandwich who in 1779 was murdered by a jealous lover. The murder trial received considerable publicity at the time. It is completely inexplicable why Wordsworth should have chosen the name of his friend's unfortunate mother to be the heroine of the poem.

The Last of the Flock (p. 78)

Underwent little revision although in 1800 the shepherd's family was reduced from ten children (l. 41) to six.

Written in the spring of 1798, 'The incident occurred in the village of Holford, close by Alfoxden' [*I.F.*]. The poem illustrates Wordsworth's disagreement with the fundamental doctrine of Godwinian belief that property is the root of all evil. 'The man who holds with Godwin that property is the cause of every vice and the source of all the misery of the poor is naturally astonished to find that this so-called evil, the offspring of human institutions, is a vigorous instinct closely interwoven with the noblest feelings. It represents familiar and dearly-loved fields, a hereditary cottage, and flocks every animal of which has its own name.' [Legouis, *Early Life of Wordsworth*, tr. Matthews, p. 310; quoted *P.W.*, ii. 476.] Wordsworth is also pointing out the weakness of a system of parish relief which prevented a man from receiving any benefits while he still owned property, however little.

The Dungeon (p. 82)

This poem, together with *The Foster-Mother's Tale*, was taken from Coleridge's tragedy *Osorio* [*v.* Note to *The Foster-Mother's Tale*]. It was first published in 1798 and reprinted in 1800. It was omitted in 1802 and 1805 and was first collected (as a separate poem) in the 1893 edition of Coleridge's *Poems*.

The Mad Mother (p. 83)

In 1815 this poem was given the title *Her Eyes Are Wild*. Written in the spring of 1798. 'Alfoxden, 1798. The subject was reported to me by a lady of Bristol who had seen the poor creature.' [*I.F.*]

Mary Moorman notices 'a similarity between the language of some of the stanzas . . . and that of Annette's letters'. She quotes, as an example, 'Behold your wife . . . sorrow has altered her much. Do you know her? If her features are altered . . . her heart is unchanged, &c.' She further points out that although Wordsworth never received this particular letter, 'there were others doubtless much the same in tone'. [Cf. *William Wordsworth and Annette Vallon*, E. Legouis, 1922 p. 128; *M.M.*, p. 385.]

In 1815 Wordsworth acknowledged a general debt to Percy's *Reliques* in his essay supplementary to the Preface to the *Lyrical Ballads*, 'I do not think there is an able writer of the present day who would not be proud to acknowledge his debt to the *Reliques*. I am happy to make a public avowal of my own.' [Cf. Scottish ballad *Lady Anne Bothwell's Lament*.]

The Idiot Boy (p. 86)

'Alfoxden, 1798. The last stanza – "The Cocks did crow to-whoo, to-whoo, And the sun did shine so cold" – was the foundation of the whole. The words were reported to me by my dear friend, Thomas Poole; but I have since heard the same repeated of other Idiots. Let me add that this long poem was composed in the groves of Alfoxden, almost extempore; not a word, I believe, being corrected, though one stanza was omitted. I mention this in gratitude to those happy moments, for, in truth, I never wrote anything with so much glee.' [*I.F.*] This poem remained one of Wordsworth's favourites. He was particularly hurt by Robert Southey's attack on it in the *Critical Review*, October 1798, in which Southey says, 'Of these experimental poems [he is reviewing the 1798] the most important is the *Idiot Boy*. . . . No tale less deserved the labour that appears to have been bestowed upon this. It resembles a Flemish picture in the worthlessness of its design and the excellence of its execution. From Flemish artists we are satisfied with such pieces: who would not have lamented, if Corregio or Rafaelle had wasted their talents in painting Dutch boors or the humours of a Flemish wake?' [*v.* Appendix C.] Wordsworth objected that Southey knew full well 'that I published those poems for money and money alone. He knew that money was of importance to me. If he could not conscientiously have spoken differently of the volume, he ought to have declined the task of reviewing it . . . I care little for the praise of any other professional critic, but as it may help me to pudding. . . .' [*E.L.*, pp. 229-30].

Later, Coleridge also attacked *The Idiot Boy*; 'In the *Idiot Boy*, indeed, the mother's character is not so much a real and native product of a "situation where the essential passions of the heart find a better soil, in which they can attain their maturity and speak a plainer and more emphatic language", as it is an impersonation of an instinct abandoned by judgment. Hence the two following charges seem to me not wholly groundless: at least, they are the only plausible objections, which I have heard to that fine poem. The one is, that the author has not, in the poem itself, taken sufficient care to preclude from the reader's fancy the disgusting images of *ordinary morbid idiocy*, which yet it was by no means his intention to represent. He has even by the "burr, burr, burr", uncounteracted by any preceding description of the boy's beauty, assisted in recalling them. The other is, that the idiocy of the *boy* is so evenly balanced by the folly of the *mother*, as to present to the general reader rather a laughable burlesque on the blindness of anile dotage, than an analytic display of maternal affection in its ordinary workings.' [*Biog. Lit.*, ii. 35-6.]

As de Selincourt points out, the 'importance that Wordsworth attached to the *Idiot Boy* is shown by the fact that in the *L.B.* 1800 it and the *Ancient Mariner* are the only poems which are given a separate title-page, and that in *The Prelude*, where he recounts the companionship with Coleridge "on Quantock's grassy hills" he only mentions it and *The Thorn* of his own and *The Ancient Mariner* and *Christabel* of Coleridge.' [*P.W.*, ii. 478.] In 1802, in reply to a letter from the seventeen-year-old John Wilson [*v.* Appendix C] Wordsworth undertook a long and extremely valuable defence of his poem [*v. Introduction*, p. xxviii].

Lines Written Near Richmond, Upon the Thames, At Evening (p. 102)

'The title [*Lines written when sailing in a boat at evening*] is scarcely correct. It was during a solitary walk on the Banks of the Cam that I was first struck with this appearance, and applied it to my own feelings in the manner here expressed, changing the scene to the Thames, near Windsor. This, and the three stanzas of the following poem, *Remembrance of Collins*, formed one piece; but, upon the recommendation of Coleridge, the three last stanzas were separated from the other.' [*I.F.*]

The poem was originally composed in 1798.

l. 30. The lines from Collins' *Ode on the Death of Thomson* are:

> Remembrance oft shall haunt the shore
>   When Thames in summer wreaths is drest,
> And oft suspend the dashing oar
>   To bid his gentle spirit rest.

Expostulation and Reply (p. 104)

'This poem is a favourite among the Quakers, as I have learnt on many occasions. It was composed in front of the house at Alfoxden in the spring of 1798.' [*I.F.*]

The *Advertisement* gives the poem's setting as arising 'out of conversation with a friend who was somewhat unreasonably attached to modern books of moral philosophy'.

The friend was William Hazlitt who visited Wordsworth at Alfoxden in May-June 1798. Hazlitt was engaged, at that time, in writing his *Essay on the Principles of Human Action*. In the essay, *On my First Acquaintance with Poets* he tells how he 'got into a metaphysical argument with Wordsworth while Coleridge was explaining the different notes of the nightingale to his sister, in which we neither of us succeeded in making ourselves perfectly clear and intelligible'.

'No candid student of Wordsworth can suppose that he is here declaring himself an enemy to literature', but he did consider that some philosophers, particularly in this instance, Godwin, 'ignored or even disapproved of what he called the 'primary passions' of men – affection, pity, gratitude, kindness'. [*M.M.*, p. 381.]

See *Lines written in Early Spring and* Note.

Matthew – although the poem arose out of a conversation with Hazlitt, the person addressed is a composite figure who also owes something to William Taylor, his Hawkshead schoolmaster. 'This [*Matthew*] and other poems connected with Matthew', Wordsworth said, would not gain by a literal detail of facts. Like the Wanderer in *The Excursion*, this Schoolmaster was made up of several both of his class and men of other occupations.' [*I.F.*]

The Tables Turned; An Evening Scene, On the Šame Subject (p. 105)

See Note to previous poem to which this must be regarded as a companion piece.

l. 10. 'woodland linnet' – 'Wordsworth knew little about the names and species of birds. Linnets are not "woodland" birds at all, and they are here merely symbols of all the smaller singers who inhabit trees and bushes.' [*M.M.*, p. 380.]

Old Man Travelling; Animal Tranquillity and Decay, A Sketch (p. 106)

'If I recollect right these verses were an overflowing from *The Old Cumberland Beggar*'. [*I.F.*] 'The present poem was split off [from *The Old Cumberland Beggar*] as a study of the inward state of the

Old Man expressed in his outward form: "resigned to quietness"
in the margin of ll. 7-8 [in the MS.] expresses the spiritual core of
it'. [*P.W.*, iv. 448.] The poem was probably begun as early as 1795.

After, 1805, ll. 15-20 were suppressed and in 1800 the sub-title
became the heading and the words *Old Man Travelling* were
discarded.

'Thinking as always in terms of association and memory,
Wordsworth saw the regular appearances of the beggar on his
rounds as a reminder of acts of kindness, of all kinds, not just of
those to the beggar himself. His round thus served to keep all the
human sympathies alive. The beggar indeed performed somewhat
the same associative function as nature, being, however, just
reminder and not, as nature, symbol and reminder both.' [*K.M.*,
p. 61.]

The Complaint of a Forsaken Indian Woman (p. 108)

'Written in Alfoxden in 1798, where I read Hearne's Journey with
deep interest. It was composed for the volume of *Lyrical Ballads*.'
[*I.F.*] Wordsworth refers to this poem in the Preface of 1800 as
an example of the attempt 'to follow the fluxes and refluxes of the
mind when agitated by the great and simple affections of our
nature' and to picture the mind in extremity, 'the last struggles of
a human being, at the approach of death, cleaving in solitude to
life and society'.

Hearne's Journey to which Wordsworth refers is *A Journey from
Prince of Wales's Fort in Hudson's Bay to Northern Ocean 1769-
1772, by order of the Hudson's Bay Company* by Samuel Hearne
1795. Chapter vii of the book describes a woman left behind by her
Indian companions who three times succeeded in coming up to
them. 'At length, poor creature! she dropt behind, and no one
attempted to go back in search of her.' [*P.W.*, ii. 474-5.] In 1802
this poem was printed in Vol. II.

The Convict (p. 111)

Possibly written as early as 1793, this poem is clearly an expression
of Wordsworth's Godwinian beliefs. It was first published in the
Morning Post, 14th December 1797, where it is signed 'Mortimer.'
' "Mortimer" was the name given to Marmaduke in the more
recent manuscripts of *The Borderers*, and no doubt, with this play
much in mind, Wordsworth affixed it to this poem, because he also
was, or had been, a "Mortimer" in his self-deception and absorp-
tion in false doctrines.' [*M.M.*, p. 351.] 'Mortimer' was a pseudonym
sometimes used by Coleridge, and it has been suggested that
Coleridge 'sent it to the paper in his own name to appease the

editorial craving for "copy" '. [v. Athenaeum, 27th August 1904, and Littledale, p. 221.]

Legouis notes that in this 'thoroughly Godwinian poem', Wordsworth dramatized 'the philosopher's favourite idea for the reformation of the penal laws' – i.e. transportation as a substitute for capital punishment [v. G.M.H., p. 225].

The poem was not reprinted after 1798, Coleridge's Love being given its place in the 1800 edition.

Lines written a few miles above Tintern Abbey, on Revisiting the Banks of the Wye during a Tour, July 13, 1798 (p. 113)

'July 1798. No poem of mine was composed under circumstances more pleasant for me to remember than this. I began it upon leaving Tintern, after crossing the Wye, and concluded it just as I was entering Bristol in the evening, after a ramble of 4 or 5 days, with my sister. Not a line of it was altered, and not any part of it written down till I reached Bristol. It was published almost immediately after. . . .' [I.F.]

De Selincourt quotes from a letter to the Rev. T. S. Howson from the Duke of Argyle written in September 1848: 'He told us he had written Tintern Abbey in 1798, taking four days to compose it, the last 20 lines or so being composed as he walked down the hill from Clifton to Bristol.' [P.W., ii. 517.]

In 1800 Wordsworth added the following note; 'I have not ventured to call this Poem an Ode; but it was written with a hope that in the transitions, and the impassioned music of the versification, would be found the principal requisites of that species of composition.'

Wordsworth's first visit to Tintern Abbey was in 1793, but see Note to The Female Vagrant.

Mary Moorman points out several interesting matters connected with Wordsworth's visit to Tintern Abbey. 'In the first place, the tour was one of the most energetic undertaken by William and Dorothy together. In three days they walked over fifty miles – a feat which for Dorothy must have required some endurance. Further, they seem to have taken with them Gilpin's Tour of the Wye, which had first appeared in 1771 and had often been reprinted. The opening lines of the poem, describing the Wye scenery, owe a distinct though unobtrusive debt to Gilpin. And, for all the "impassioned music of the versification", which in Wordsworth's view made it comparable to an Ode, Tintern Abbey is, at least in its beginning, a "landscape-poem" in the eighteenth-century tradition. Finally, the title of the poem is not quite accurate. If it was composed, as Wordsworth says, "upon leaving Tintern Abbey" on July 13th, the scene of its composition must have been not "above" Tintern Abbey, but below it. In fact, it must have been composed largely on board the "small vessel" which took them back to Bristol. Much more probably, however, it was begun on the first day at Tintern when they were walking up the river towards Monmouth, and simply completed on the 13th.

'It is a curious fact that nowhere in the poem does Wordsworth mention Tintern Abbey itself, though we know that he must have admired it, for they returned from Chepstow to spend a second night there. Gilpin describes its condition; the grass in the ruins was kept mown, but it was a dwelling-place of beggars and the wretchedly poor. The river was then full of shipping, carrying coal and timber from the Forest of Dean. This also Wordsworth does not mention, though he does notice, in a footnote to the phrase "a soft, inland murmur", the change from tidal to non-tidal waters not far above Tintern.' [*M.M.*, pp. 402-3.]

The following passage in Gilpin should be compared with *Tintern Abbey*, ll. 8-18. 'Many of the furnaces, on the banks of the river, consume charcoal, which is manufactured on the spot; and the smoke, which is frequently seen issuing from the sides of the hills; and spreading its thin veil over a part of them, beautifully breaks their lines, and unites them with the sky.' Gilpin also mentions the absence of arable land and the predominance of wood and pasture.

Helen Darbishire considers that 'This is the first poem in which Wordsworth's genius finds full expression: the blank verse, low-toned and familiar, yet impassioned, moves with a sureness and inevitable ease from phase to phase of his mood. It has the quiet pulse, suggesting "central peace", which is felt under all his great poetry.' [*H.D.*, pp. 59-60.]

l. 107. Cf. Young's *Night Thoughts*, vi. 424:

> And half-create the wondrous world they see.

Love (p. 119)

This poem first appeared (with four preliminary and three concluding stanzas) in the *Morning Post* for the 21st December 1799, under the title *Introduction to the Tale of the Dark Ladie*, and was then published in a shorter form with the title *Love* in the *Lyrical Ballads* of 1800, 1802 and 1805. It was included in *Sibylline Leaves* in 1828. The four opening and three concluding stanzas were republished in *Literary Remains*, 1836. The *Dark Ladie* itself is a fragment of ballad which Coleridge never finished but which he tells us in *Biographia Literaria* [ii. 6] he was preparing at about the time he wrote the *Ancient Mariner*. This ballad fragment belongs to the Stowey period, though Coleridge may have revised it during or after his stay in Germany [*v. C. Notebooks*, i. 343n.]. But *Love*, though a companion piece, probably belongs to the time when Coleridge visited Sockburn at the end of 1799 [*v.* Introduction] and is inspired by his love for Sara Hutchinson. In the first draft of *Love* [*v.* British Museum Add. MSS. 27,902] lines 13-16 are as follows:

> She lean'd against a grey stone rudely carv'd,
> The statue of an arméd Knight:
> She lean'd in melancholy mood
> Amid the lingering light.

In Sockburn church, now in ruins, there is a recumbent statue of a knight and in a field close to the nearby house where the Hutchinsons lived there is a 'Grey-Stone' which commemorates the slaying by this knight of a monstrous wyvern, 'the Sockburn worme'. It may be that the lines above were suggested by the statue and the stone [*v. P. of C.*].

Charles James Fox, to whom Wordsworth had sent a copy of the 1800 edition of *Lyrical Ballads*, declared that *Love*, whose authorship he did not know, was 'the most beautiful poem in the language'.

The letter with which Coleridge sent his poem to the *Morning Post* is reprinted in *C. Letters*, i. 550-1.

Hart-Leap Well (p. 127)

Composed January or February 1800.

'Town-End. 1800. *Grasmere*. The first eight stanzas were composed extempore one winter evening in the cottage; when, after having tired myself with labouring at an awkward passage in "The Brothers", I started with a sudden impulse to this to get rid of the other, and finished it in a day or two. My sister and I had past the place a few weeks before in our wild winter journey from Sockburn on the banks of the Tees to Grasmere. A peasant whom we met near the spot told us the story so far as concerned the name of the well, and the hart, and pointed out the stones. Both the stones and the well are objects that may easily be missed; the tradition by this time may be extinct in the neighbourhood: the man who related it to us was very old.' [*I.F.*]

The three-day journey from Sockburn to Grasmere referred to in this Note was begun on 17th December 1799 and is described in a letter from Wordsworth to Coleridge. [*E.L.*, p. 234.] The visionary experience described in this poem also finds its way into lines which Wordsworth intended to incorporate in *The Recluse* but never did. [*v. P.W.*, ii. 514-5.]

There was a Boy, ye knew him well, ye Cliffs (p. 134)

Written in Germany October-December 1798. First published in 1800 and later in *Poems in Two Volumes* [1815] where it is the first poem under the heading 'Poems of the Imagination' and where it is referred to in the Preface: 'I have begun with one of the earliest processes of Nature in the development of this faculty. Guided by one of my own primary consciousnesses, I have represented a commutation and transfer of internal feelings, co-operating with external accidents to plant, for immortality, images of sound and sight, in the celestial soil of the Imagination. The Boy, there introduced, is listening, with something of a feverish and restless anxiety, for the recurrence of the riotous sounds which he had previously excited; and, at the moment when the intenseness of his mind is beginning to remit, he is surprised into a perception of the solemn and tranquillizing images which the Poem describes.'

The poem was later incorporated in *The Prelude*, v. 389-422 [1805].

ll. 9-10 'This practice of making an instrument of their own fingers is known to most boys, though some are more skilful at it than others.' [*I.F.*]

The Brothers (p. 135)

This poem was begun in December 1799.

'1800. This poem was composed in a grove at the north-eastern end of Grasmere Lake, which grove was in a great measure destroyed by turning the high-road along the side of the water. The few trees that are left were spared at my intercession. The poem arose out of the fact, mentioned to me at Ennerdale, that a shepherd had fallen asleep upon the top of the rock called The Pillar, and perished as here described, his staff being left midway on the rock.' [*I.F.*]

Coleridge described *The Brothers* as 'that model of English pastoral, which I have never yet read with unclouded eye'. [*Biog. Lit.*, ii. 62n.]

Mary Moorman describes the poem as 'a simple tale, told in very restrained language, yet it possesses dramatic pathos of a high order'. She suggests that Wordsworth was thinking of his own brother John who arrived while the poem was being written. 'There is in *The Brothers* no concern with the derangement produced by grief as in *The Thorn* and the *Mad Mother*: we have moved away from the moonlight world of *The Idiot Boy* and *Peter Bell* into the light of common day.' 'The same normality', she adds, 'character-izes all the poetry of this year.' [*M.M.*, pp. 479-480.]

l. 141. "There were two Springs which bubbled side by side," The impressive circumstance here described, actually took place some years ago in this country, upon an eminence called Kidstow Pike, one of the highest of the mountains that surround Hawes-water. The summit of the pike was stricken by lightning; and every trace of one of the fountains disappeared, while the other continued to flow as before. [Wordsworth's Note 1800.]

l. 183. "The thought of death sits easy on the man," &c. There is not any thing more worthy of remark in the manners of the inhabitants of these mountains, than the tranquillity, I might say indifference, with which they think and talk upon the subject of death. Some of the country church-yards, as here described, do not contain a single tombstone, and most of them have a very small number.' [Wordsworth's Note 1800.]

Ellen Irwin, or the Braes of Kirtle (p. 151)
Written 1799-1800 probably in Germany.

'It may be worth while to observe that as there are Scotch Poems on the subject in the simple ballad strain, I thought it would be both presumptuous and superfluous to attempt treating it in the same way; and, accordingly, I chose a construction of stanza quite new in our language; in fact the same as that of Bürger's *Leonora*, except that the first and third line do not, in my stanzas, rhyme. At the outset I threw out a classical image to prepare the reader for the style in which I meant to treat the story, and so to preclude all comparison.' [*I.F.*]

Strange Fits of passion I have known (p. 153)
Written in Germany 1799. Interesting versions of this poem and the poem below are to be found in *E.L.* pp. 204-206.

Song, She dwelt among th' untrodden ways (p. 154)
Written in Germany 1799. There is a river Dove in Derbyshire, in Yorkshire and in Westmorland and it is not clear which river Wordsworth had in mind.

A Slumber did my spirit seal (p. 154)
Written in Germany 1799.

'Some months ago Wordsworth transmitted to me a most

sublime Epitaph. Whether it had any reality, I cannot say. Most probably, in some gloomier moment he had fancied the moment in which his Sister might die.' S. T. Coleridge to T. Poole, 6th April [*C. Letters*, i. 479].

The identity of Lucy has been the subject of extensive critical discussion [*e.g.* H. W. Margoliouth, *Wordsworth and Coleridge 1795-1834*, p. 52 *et seq.*, and F. W. Bateson, *Wordsworth, A Reinterpretation*].

These last three poems, together with *I travelled among unknown Men* [published 1807], form the group known as the Lucy poems.

The Waterfall and the Eglantine (p. 155)
Written 1800.

'Suggested nearer to Grasmere [nearer than *The Oak and the Broom*] on the same mountain track. The eglantine remained many years afterwards, but is now gone.' [*I.F.*]

The Oak and the Broom, A Pastoral (p. 157)
Written 1800.

'Suggested upon the mountain path that leads from Upper Rydal to Grasmere. The ponderous block of stone, which is mentioned in the poem, remains, I believe, to this day, a good way up Nab-Scar. Broom grows under it and in many places on the side of the precipice.' [*I.F.*]

Lucy Gray (p. 161)

'Written at Goslar in Germany in 1799. It was founded on a circumstance told me by my Sister, of a little girl who, not far from Halifax in Yorkshire, was bewildered in a snow-storm. Her footsteps were traced by her parents to the middle of the lock of a canal, and no other vestige of her, backward or forward, could be traced. The body however was found in the canal. The way in which the incident was treated and the spiritualizing of the character might furnish hints for contrasting the imaginative influences which I have endeavoured to throw over common life with Crabbe's matter of fact style of treating subjects of the same kind.' [*I.F.*] Crabb Robinson records that Wordsworth said that his object in *Lucy Gray* 'was to exhibit poetically entire *solitude*, and he represents the child as observing the day-moon, which no town or village girl would ever notice'. [*Diary*, September 11th 1816.]

The poem was later given the title *Lucy Gray, or Solitude*.

The Idle Shepherd-Boys, or Dungeon-Gill Force, A Pastoral (p. 164)

'Grasmere Town-End, 1800. I will only add a little monitory anecdote concerning this subject. When Coleridge and Southey were walking together upon the Fells, Southey observed that, if I wished to be considered a faithful painter of rural manners, I ought not to have said that my Shepherd-boys trimmed their rustic hats as described in the poem. Just as the words had passed his lips two boys appeared with the very plant entwined round their hats.' [*I.F.*]

'Tis said, that some have died for love (p. 168)

Written 1800. In the poem, Wordsworth tries to reassure and to comfort Emma – i.e. Dorothy, his sister, – in the event of his dying; cf. *Tintern Abbey* in this respect.

Poor Susan (p. 170)

'This arose out of my observation of the affecting music of these birds hanging in this way in the London streets during the freshness and stillness of the Spring morning.' [*I.F.*] Probably written in 1797. The title was later changed to *The Reverie of Poor Susan*, which is a translation of the title of Bürger's poem *Des Armen Süschens Traum*.

The fifth stanza appeared only in 1800 and was cancelled probably because of Lamb's objection; 'The last verse of Susan was to be got rid of at all events. It threw a kind of dubiety upon Susan's moral conduct. Susan is a maid servant. I see her trundling her mop, and contemplating the whirling phenomenon through blurred optics; to term her a poor outcast seems as much as to say that poor Susan is no better than she should be, which I trust was not what you meant to express.' [*Lamb*, ii. 158.]

Inscription, For the Spot where the Hermitage stood on St. Herbert's Island, Derwent-Water (p. 171)

Written 1800.

Inscription, For the House (an Outhouse) on the Island at Grasmere (p. 172)

Written in 1800. Title changed in 1802 to *Lines, Written with a pencil upon a stone in the wall of the house (an Outhouse) on the Island at Grasmere*.

To a Sexton (p. 173)

Written in Germany 1799.

Andrew Jones (p. 174)

Written in 1798 but not reprinted after 1815.

The Two Thieves, or the last Stage of Avarice (p. 175)

Written 1800.

'This is described from the life as I was in the habit of observing when a boy at Hawkshead School. Daniel was more than 80 years older than myself when he was daily thus occupied, under my notice. No book could have so early taught me to think of the changes to which human life is subject, and while looking at him, I could not but say to myself – we may, any of us, I, or the happiest of my playmates, live to become still more the object of pity than this old man, this half-doating pilferer.' [*I.F.*]

   l. 1. 'the genius of Bewick', Thomas Bewick (1753-1828) artist and wood-engraver.

A whirl-blast from behind the hill (p. 177)

Written in 1798, not 1799 as stated below.

'Observed in the holly grove at Alfoxden, where these verses were written in the spring of 1799. I had the pleasure of again seeing, with dear friends, this grove in unimpaired beauty, 41 years after.' [*I.F.*]

Song, for the Wandering Jew (p. 178)

Written in 1800. Mary Moorman observes that this poem 'deserves to be better known than it is, if only for the last two lines'. [*M.M.*, p. 480.]

Ruth (p. 179)

'Written in Germany 1799. Suggested by an account I had of a wanderer in Somersetshire.' [*I.F.*]

The poem was revised in 1802 [*v. D.W.*, 7th March 1802] and again in 1805.

Mary Moorman suggests that there is perhaps a memory of Wordsworth's own childhood in the picture of the young Ruth and points out that the last verse, visualizing a Christian funeral for the poor vagrant, strikes a new note in Wordsworth's poetry – the dead Lucy having been consigned to the earth without apparent concern for her 'immortal part'. [*M.M.*, pp. 427-8.]

Lines, Written with a Slate-pencil upon a Stone (p. 189)
Written 1800.
    l. 8. Sir William refers to Sir William Fleming of Rydal Hall,
    the first Baronet, who died 1736.

In the School of ——— is a tablet on which are inscribed, etc. (p. 190)
Written 1799. This poem was re-titled *Matthew* in 1837.
    'Such a Tablet as is here spoken of continued to be preserved in
Hawkshead School, though the inscriptions were not brought down
to our time. This and other poems connected with Matthew would
not gain by a literal detail of facts. Like the Wanderer in "The
Excursion", this Schoolmaster was made up of several both of his
class and men of other occupations. I do not ask pardon for what
there is of untruth in such verses, considered strictly as matters of
fact. It is enough if, being true and consistent in spirit, they move
and teach in a manner not unworthy of a Poet's calling.' [*I.F.*]

The Two April Mornings (p. 191)
Written 1799.

The Fountain, A Conversation (p. 194)
Written 1799.

Nutting (p. 196)
Written in 1798.

    'Written in Germany; intended as part of a poem on my own
life [*v. P.W.*, ii. 504-506], but struck out as not being wanted there.
Like most of my school-fellows I was an impassioned nutter. For
this pleasure, the Vale of Esthwaite, abounding in coppice-wood,
furnished a very wide range. These verses arose out of the remem-
brance of feelings I had often had when a boy, and particularly in
the extensive woods that still stretch from the side of Esthwaite
Lake towards Graythwaite, the seat of the ancient family of
Sandys.' [*I.F.*]
    Wordsworth believed that *Joanna* and *Nutting* 'show the
greatest genius of any poems in the second volume' [1800]
although he said that *Michael* contained his most important views.
[*M.M.*, p. 506.]

Three years she grew in sun and shower (p. 198)
'1799. Composed in the Hartz Forest.' [*I.F.*]
    This poem has been grouped with the other Lucy poems. Mary

Moorman points out that it cannot be taken as descriptive of Dorothy for, to mention only one detail, Lucy is described as having a form 'of stately height' and Dorothy was neither tall nor stately [*M.M.*, p. 424 and n.]

The Pet-Lamb, A Pastoral (p. 200)

'Town-End, 1800. Barbara Lewthwaite, now [1843] living at Ambleside, though much changed as to beauty, was one of two most lovely sisters. Almost the first words my poor Brother John said, when he visited us for the first time at Grasmere, were, "Were those two angels that I have just seen?" and from his description I have no doubt they were those two sisters. The mother died in childbed; and one of our neighbours at Grasmere told me that the loveliest sight she had ever seen was that mother as she lay in her coffin with her babe in her arm. I mention this to notice what I cannot but think a salutary custom once universal in these vales. Every attendant on a funeral made it a duty to look at the corpse in the coffin before the lid was closed, which was never done (nor I believe is now) till a minute or two before the corpse was removed. Barbara Lewthwaite was not in fact the child whom I had seen and overheard as engaged [*sic*] in the poem. I chose the name for reasons implied in the above; and will here add a caution against the use of names of living persons. Within a few months after the publication of this poem, I was much surprised, and more hurt, to find it in a child's school-book which, having been compiled by Lindley Murray, had come into use at Grasmere School where Barbara was a pupil. And, alas, I had the mortification of hearing that she was very vain of being thus distinguished; and, in after-life, she used to say that she remembered the incident and what I said to her upon the occasion.' [*I.F.*]

Written in Germany, On one of the coldest days of the Century (p. 2031)

'1798 and 1799. A bitter winter it was when these verses were composed by the side of my Sister, in our lodging at a draper's house in the romantic imperial town of Goslar, on the edge of the Hartz Forest.' [*I.F.*]

The Childless Father (p. 204)

'Town-End, 1800. When I was a child at Cockermouth, no funera took place without a basin filled with sprigs of boxwood being placed upon a table covered with a white cloth in front of the house. The huntings on foot, in which the Old Man is supposed to join as here described, were of common, almost habitual, occurrence in our vales when I was a boy; and the people took much delight in them. They are now less frequent.' [*I.F.*]

The Old Cumberland Beggar, A Description (p. 205)
Written 1797.

'Observed, and with great benefit to my own heart, when I was a child: written at Racedown and Alfoxden in my 28th year. The political economists were about that time beginning their war upon mendicity in all its forms, and by implication, if not directly, on Almsgiving also. This heartless process has been carried as far as it can go by the AMENDED poor-law bill, though the inhumanity that prevails in this measure is somewhat disguised by the profession that one of its objects is to throw the poor upon the voluntary donations of their neighbours; that is, if rightly interpreted, to force them into a condition between relief in the Union poor-house, and Alms robbed of their Christian grace and spirit, as being *forced* rather than given by them; while the avaricious and selfish, and all in fact but the humane and charitable, are at liberty to keep all they possess from their distressed brethren.' [*I.F.*; *v.* Note to *Old Man Travelling.*]

Rural Architecture (p. 211)
'These structures, as every one knows, are common among our hills, being built by shepherds as conspicuous marks, occasionally by boys in sport. It was written at Town-End, in 1801.' [*I.F.*] Obviously the date given cannot be correct as the poem was printed in 1800. It was probably written in 1800.

A Poet's Epitaph (p. 212)
Written in Goslar, 1799.

Cf. Theocritus, *Epigram* xix [*Times Literary Supplement*, 11th September 1937, article by T. E. Casson].

Lamb criticized the poem as an unsuccessful attempt at satire on parsons and lawyers which, together with the 'coarse epithet "pin-point" in the sixth stanza', disfigured the poem. [*Lamb*, i. 239.]

A Character, in the antithetical Manner (p. 214)
'The principal features are taken from that of my friend, Robert Jones.' [*I.F.*] It was with Robert Jones that Wordsworth under-

took the Continental tour described in *Descriptive Sketches*, and the tour in Wales referred to in *The Prelude*, xiv.

This poem was omitted from the 1802 and 1805 editions.

A Fragment (p. 215)

'Written in Germany 1799. It was entirely a fancy, but intended as a prelude to a ballad poem never written.' [*I.F.*] 'These stanzas were designed to introduce a Ballad upon the Story of a Danish Prince who had fled from Battle, and, for the sake of the valuables about him, was murdered by the Inhabitant of a Cottage in which he had taken refuge. The House fell under a curse, and the Spirit of the Youth, it was believed, haunted the Valley where the crime had been committed.' [Wordsworth's Note, 1827]

The similarity of rhythm and metre in this and *The Thorn* has been pointed out. The poem was re-entitled *The Danish Boy* in 1836. 'It is interesting as being one of the few poems of Wordsworth which refer to the folk-tales of his own country of West Cumberland. These tales of ghostly Danish harpers still lingered among the fells.' [*M.M.*, p. 429.]

Poems on the Naming of Places (p. 217)

This group of poems has a half-title, and the Advertisement a separate leaf, in all editions of *Lyrical Ballads*. As a group these poems celebrate actual walks, places and incidents familiar to the Wordsworths.

It was an April Morning (p. 218)

'Grasmere, 1800. This poem was suggested on the banks of the brook that runs through Easedale, which is, in some parts of its course, as wild and beautiful as brook can be. I have composed thousands of verses by the side of it.' [*I.F.*]

To Joanna (p. 219)

Joanna Hutchinson (1780-1843), younger sister to Mary Wordsworth. (Cf. *P.W.*, ii. 486; also comment in *P.W.* on *To Joanna* in MS. 2.]

'Grasmere, 1800. The effect of her laugh is an extravagance; though the effect of the reverberation of voices in some parts of the mountains is very striking. There is, in the *Excursion*, an allusion to the bleat of a lamb thus re-echoed, and described without any exaggeration, as I heard it, on the side of Stickle Tarn, from the precipice that stretches on to Langdale Pikes.' [*I.F.*] See Note to *Nutting*.

There is an Eminence (p. 222)

'1800. It is not accurate that the Eminence here alluded to could be seen from our orchard-seat. It rises above the road by the side of Grasmere lake, towards Keswick, and its name is Stone-Arthur.' [*I.F.*]

A narrow girdle of rough stones and crags (p. 223)

'1800. The character of the eastern shore of Grasmere Lake is quite changed, since these verses were written, by the public road being carried along its side. The friends spoken of were Coleridge and my Sister, and the fact occurred strictly as recorded.' [*I.F.*]

To M.H. (p. 225)

Written in 1799.

'To Mary Hutchinson, two years before our marriage. The pool alluded to is in Rydal Upper Park.' [*I.F.*]

Michael, A Pastoral Poem (p. 226)

Written Oct.-Dec. 1800.

'Town-End, 1801. Written about the same time as *The Brothers*. The Sheepfold, on which so much of the poem turns, remains, or rather the ruins of it. The character and circumstances of Luke were taken from a family to whom had belonged, many years before, the house we lived in at Town-End, along with some fields and woodlands on the eastern shore of Grasmere. The name of the Evening Star was not in fact given to this house but to another on the same side of the valley more to the north.' [*I.F.*]

'I have attempted to give a picture of a man, of strong mind and lively sensibility, agitated by two of the most powerful affections of the human heart; the parental affection, and the love of property, *landed* property, including the feelings of inheritance, home, and personal and family independence.' [*E.L.*, p. 266.]

'The poem itself has always been one of the best loved of all Wordsworth's writings, not only because of the pathos of the story, but because of the profound yet extraordinarily simple statements of thought and feeling, arising from the power of Wordsworth's ethical discovery that suffering, when illuminated by love, creates its own nobility of heart.' [*M.M.*, p. 500.]

In a letter to Thomas Poole of 9th April 1801 [*v. E.L.*, pp. 266-268] Wordsworth gives the following information about the text of the poem:

'The 2nd Vol: is throughout miserably printed, and after [the following] line,

"Receiving from his father hire of praise,"

by a shameful negligence of the printer there is an omission of fifteen lines absolutely necessary to the connection of the poem. If in the copy sent to you this omission has not been supplied you may be furnished with half a sheet which has been reprinted, if you have any acquaintance who will call at Longman's for it and send it down to you. In the meanwhile my Sister will transcribe for you the omitted passage. I should be vexed if your copy is an imperfect one, as it must have then been impossible for you to give the poem a fair trial.'

As it was clearly the author's intention to include these lines in the 1800 edn. we have restored them although they were not in fact printed until 1802. They appear in the present text as lines 202-216.

The same letter contains a note in Dorothy Wordsworth's hand given below. The lines she quotes never appeared in any of the texts.

'My Brother has written the following lines to be inserted Page 206 after the 9th line – Murmur as with the sound of summer flies.

Though in these occupations they would pass
Whole hours with but small interchange of speech,
Yet were there times in which they did not want
Discourse both wise and prudent, shrewd remarks
Of daily providence, clothed in images
Lovely and beautiful, in rural forms
That made their conversation fresh and fair
As is a landscape: – And the shepherd oft
Would draw out of his heart the obscurities
And admirations that were there, of God
And of His works, or yielding to the bent
Of his peculiar humour, would let loose
The tongue and give it the wind's freedom – then
Discoursing on remote imaginations, story,
Conceits, devices, day-dreams, thoughts and schemes,
The fancies of a solitary man.'

The composition of the poem and its relation to *The Prelude* are discussed in *P.W.* ii. 479-484.

l. 268. 'The story alluded to here is well known in the country. The chapel is called Ings Chapel; and is on the right hand side of the road leading from Kendal to Ambleside.' [Wordsworth's Note 1800.]

ll. 333-4. 'It may be proper to inform some readers, that a sheep-
fold in these mountains is an unroofed building of stone
walls, with different divisions. It is generally placed by
the side of a brook, for the convenience of washing the
sheep; but it is also useful as a shelter for them, and as a
place to drive them into, to enable the shepherds con-
veniently to single out one or more for any particular
purpose.' [Wordsworth's Note 1800.]

Appendix A

The following is the text of Coleridge's *Lewti; or, the Circassian Love-Chant*, which first appeared in the *Morning Post*, 13th April 1798, under the signature of 'Nicias Erythraeus'. It was to have been included in the 1798 edition, but was withdrawn while the book was in the press and Coleridge's *The Nightingale* substituted (*v. Foreword*). It was included in a shortened form in the *Annual Anthology* of 1800 and in *Sibylline Leaves*, 1817. The present text is the cancelled 1798 version.

> At midnight, by the stream I rov'd
>   To forget the form I lov'd.
> Image of LEWTI ! from my mind
> Depart; for LEWTI is not kind.
> The moon was high, the moonlight gleam
>   And the shadow of a star
> Heav'd upon Tamaha's stream;
>   But the rock shone brighter far.
> The rock half-sheltered from my view,
> By pendent boughs of tressy yew. –   10
> So shines my LEWTI's forehead fair,
> Gleaming thro' her sable hair.
> Image of LEWTI ! from my mind
> Depart; for LEWTI is not kind.
> I saw a cloud of palest hue,
>   Onward to the moon it pass'd.
> Still brighter and more bright it grew,
> With floating colours not a few,
>   Till it reach'd the moon at last.
> Then the cloud was wholly bright,   20
> With a rich and amber light;
> And so with many a hope I seek,
>   And with such joy I find my LEWTI;
> And even so my pale wan cheek
>   Drinks in as deep a flush of beauty !
> Nay, treach'rous image ! leave my mind,
> If LEWTI never will be kind.

The little cloud – it floats away,
  Away it goes – away so soon!
Alas! it has no pow'r to stay: 30
Its hues are dim, its hues are grey –
  Away it passes from the moon.
How mournfully it seems to fly,
  Ever fading more and more,
To joyless regions of the sky –
  And now 'tis whiter than before,
As white as my poor cheek will be,
  When, LEWTI! on my couch I lie,
A dying man, for love of thee.
Nay, treach'rous image! leave my mind –   40
And yet thou didst not look unkind!
  I saw a vapour in the sky,
  Thin and white and very high.
I ne'er beheld so thin a cloud –
  Perhaps the breezes that can fly
  Now below, and now above,
Have snatch'd aloft the lawny shroud
  Of lady fair, that died for love:
  For Maids, as well as Youths, have perish'd
  From fruitless love, too fondly cherish'd!   50
  Nay, treach'rous image! leave my mind –
  For LEWTI never will be kind.
Hush! my heedless feet from under
  Slip the crumbling banks for ever;
Like echoes to a distant thunder,
  They plunge into the gentle river:
The river-swans have heard my tread,
And startle from their reedy bed.
O beauteous birds! methinks ye measure
  Your movements to some heav'nly tune!   60
O beauteous birds! 'tis such a pleasure
  To see you move beneath the moon;
I would, it were your true delight
To sleep by day and wake all night.
I know the place where LEWTI lies,
When silent night has clos'd her eyes –
It is a breezy jasmin bow'r,
  The Nightingale sings o'er her head;
Had I the enviable pow'r
  To creep unseen with noiseless tread,   70

Then should I view her bosom white,
Heaving lovely to my sight,
As those two swans together heave
On the gently swelling wave.
O that she saw me in a dream,
    And dreamt that I had died for care!
All pale and wasted I would seem,
    Yet fair withal, as spirits are.
I'd die indeed, if I might see
Her bosom heave, and heave for me!   80
Soothe, gentle image! soothe my mind!
To-morrow LEWTI may be kind.

Appendix B

Appendix on Poetic Diction

This was added by Wordsworth in the 1802 edition of *Lyrical Ballads*. There was no further change in the 1805 text.

See Preface, page 262, – "by what is usually called Poetic Diction."

As perhaps I have no right to expect from a Reader of an Introduction to a volume of Poems that attentive perusal without which it is impossible, imperfectly as I have been compelled to express my meaning, that what I have said in the Preface should throughout be fully understood, I am the more anxious to give an exact notion of the sense in which I use the phrase *poetic diction*; and for this purpose I will here add a few words concerning the origin of the phraseology which I have condemned under that name.— The earliest Poets of all nations generally wrote from passion excited by real events; they wrote naturally, and as men: feeling powerfully as they did, their language was daring, and figurative. In succeeding times, Poets, and men ambitious of the fame of Poets, perceiving the influence of such language, and desirous of producing the same effect, without having the same animating passion, set themselves to a mechanical adoption of those figures of speech, and made use of them, sometimes with propriety, but much more frequently applied them to feelings and thoughts with which they had no natural connection whatsoever. A language was thus insensibly produced, differing materially from the real language of men in *any situation*. The Reader or Hearer of this distorted language found himself in a perturbed and unusual state of mind: when affected by the genuine language of passion he had been in a perturbed and unusual state of mind also: in both cases he was willing that his common judgment and understanding should be laid asleep, and he had no instinctive and infallible perception of the true to make him reject the false; the one served as a passport for the other. The agitation and confusion of mind were in both cases delightful, and no wonder if he confounded the one with the other, and believed them both to be produced by the same, or similar causes. Besides, the Poet spake to him in the character of a man to be looked up to, a man of genius and authority. Thus, and from a variety of other causes, this distorted language was received with admiration; and Poets, it is probable, who had before contented themselves for the most part with misapplying only expressions which at first had been dictated by real passion, carried the abuse still further, and introduced phrases composed apparently in the spirit of the original figurative language of passion, yet altogether of their own ivnention, and distinguished by various degrees of wanton deviation from good sense and nature.

It is indeed true that the language of the earliest Poets was felt to differ materially from ordinary language, because it was the language of extraordinary occasions; but it was really spoken by men, language which the Poet himself had uttered when he had been affected by the events which he described, or which he had heard uttered by those around him. To this language it is probable that metre of some sort or other was early superadded. This separated the genuine language of Poetry still further from common life, so that whoever read or heard the poems of these earliest Poets felt himself moved in a way in which he had not been accustomed to be moved in real life, and by causes manifestly different from those which acted upon him in real life. This was the great temptation to all the corruptions which have followed: under the protection of this feeling succeeding Poets constructed a phraseology which had one thing, it is true, in common with the genuine language of poetry, namely, that it was not heard in ordinary conversation; that it was unusual. But the first Poets, as I have said, spake a language which, though unusual, was still the language of men. This circumstance, however, was disregarded by their successors; they found that they could please by easier means: they became proud of a language which they themselves had invented, and which was uttered only by themselves; and, with the spirit of a fraternity, they arrogated it to themselves as their own. In process of time metre became a symbol or promise of this unusual language, and whoever took upon him to write in metre, according as he possessed more or less of true poetic genius, introduced less or more of this adulterated phraseology into his compositions, and the true and the false became so inseparably interwoven that the taste of men was gradually perverted and this language was received as a natural language: and at length, by the influence of books upon men, did to a certain degree really become so. Abuses of this kind were imported from one nation to another, and with the progress of refinement this diction became daily more and more corrupt, thrusting out of sight the plain humanities of nature by a motley masquerade of tricks, quaintnesses, hieroglyphics, and enigmas.

It would be highly interesting to point out the causes of the pleasure given by this extravagant and absurd language; but this is not the place; it depends upon a great variety of causes, but upon none perhaps more than its influence in impressing anotion of the peculiarity and exaltation of the Poet's character, and in flattering the Reader's self-love by bringing him nearer to a sympathy with that character; an effect which is accomplished by unsettling ordinary habits of thinking, and thus assisting the Reader to approach to that perturbed and dizzy state of mind in which if he does not find himself, he imagines that he is *balked* of a peculiar enjoyment which poetry can and ought to bestow.

The sonnet which I have quoted from Gray, in the Preface, except the lines printed in Italics, consists of little else but thi diction, though not of the worst kind; and indeed, if one may be permitted to say so, it is far too common in the best writers both antient and modern. Perhaps I can in no way, by positive example, more easily give my Reader a notion of what I mean by the phrase *poetic diction* than by referring him to a comparison between the metrical paraphrases which we have of passages in the old and new Testament, and those passages as they exist in our common Translation. See Pope's "Messiah" throughout, Prior's "Did sweeter sounds adorn my flowing tongue," &c. &c. "Though I speak with the tongues of men and of angels," &c. &c. See 1st Corinthians, chapter xiii. By way of immediate example, take the following of Dr. Johnson:

> 'Turn on the prudent Ant thy heedless eyes,
> Observe her labours, Sluggard, and be wise;
> No stern command, no monitory voice,
> Prescribes her duties, or directs her choice;
> Yet, timely provident, she hastes away
> To snatch the blessings of a plenteous day;
> When fruitful Summer loads the teeming plain,
> She crops the harvest and she stores the grain.
> How long shall sloth usurp thy useless hours,
> Unnerve thy vigour, and enchain thy powers?
> While artful shades thy downy couch enclose,
> And soft solicitation courts repose,
> Amidst the drowsy charms of dull delight,

Year chases year with unremitted flight,
Till want now following, fraudulent and slow,
Shall spring to seize thee, like an ambushed foe.'[1]

From this hubbub of words pass to the original. "Go to the Ant, thou Sluggard, consider her ways, and be wise: which having no guide, overseer, or ruler, provideth her meat in the summer, and gathereth her food in the harvest. How long wilt thou sleep, O Sluggard? when wilt thou arise out of thy sleep? Yet a little sleep, a little slumber, a little folding of the hands to sleep. So shall thy poverty come as one that travaileth, and thy want as an armed man." Proverbs, chap. vith.

One more quotation and I have done. It is from Cowper's verses supposed to be written by Alexander Selkirk:

"Religion! what treasure untold
Resides in that heavenly word!
More precious than silver and gold,
Or all that this earth can afford.
But the sound of the church-going bell
These valleys and rocks never heard,
Ne'er sighed at the sound of a knell,
Or smiled when a sabbath appeared.

Ye winds, that have made me your sport
Convey to this desolate shore
Some cordial endearing report
Of a land I must visit no more.
My friends, do they now and then send
A wish or a thought after me?
O tell me I yet have a friend,
Though a friend I am never to see."

I have quoted this passage as an instance of three different styles of composition. The first four lines are poorly expressed; some Critics would call the language prosaic; the fact is, it would be bad prose, so bad that it is scarcely worse in metre. The epithet "church-going" applied to a bell, and that by so chaste a writer as Cowper, is an instance of the strange abuses which Poets have introduced into their language till they and their Readers take them as matters of course, if they do not single them out expressly as objects of admiration. The two lines "Ne'er sighed at the sound,"

---

[1] "The Ant," *Poems of Johnson*, ed. Nichol Smith and McAdam, Oxford, 1941, pp. 151-2.

&c., are, in my opinion, an instance of the language of passion wrested from its proper use, and, from the mere circumstance of the composition being in metre, applied upon an occasion that does not justify such violent expressions; and I should condemn the passage, though perhaps few Readers will agree with me, as vicious poetic diction. The last stanza is throughout admirably expressed: it would be equally good whether in prose or verse, except that the Reader has an exquisite pleasure in seeing such natural language so naturally connected with metre. The beauty of this stanza tempts me here to add a sentiment which ought to be the pervading spirit of a system, detached parts of which have been imperfectly explained in the Preface – namely, that in proportion as ideas and feelings are valuable, whether the composition be in prose or in verse, they require and exact one and the same language.

Appendix C

Some Contemporary Criticisms of *Lyrical Ballads*

From 'The Critical Review', Vol. XXIV, October 1798
A review by Southey.

The majority of these poems, we are informed in the Advertisement, are to be considered as experiments.

'They were written chiefly with a view to ascertain how far the language of conversation in the middle and lower classes of society is adapted to the purpose of poetic pleasure.'

Of these experimental poems, the most important is the *Idiot Boy*. . . . Upon this subject the author has written nearly 500 lines. . . . No tale less deserved the labour that appears to have been bestowed upon this. It resembles a Flemish picture in the worthlessness of its design and the excellence of its execution. From Flemish artists we are satisfied with such pieces: who would not have lamented, if Corregio or Rafaelle had wasted their talents in painting Dutch boors or the humours of a Flemish wake?

The other ballads of this kind are as bald in story, and are not so highly embellished in narration. With that which is entitled *The Thorn*, we were altogether displeased. The advertisement says, it is not told in the person of the author, but in that of some loquacious narrator. The author should have recollected that he who personates tiresome loquacity, becomes tiresome himself. The story of a man who suffers the perpetual pain of cold, because an old woman prayed that he might never be warm, is perhaps a good story for a ballad, because it is a well-known tale: but is the author certain that it is 'well authenticated'? And does not such an assertion promote the popular superstitition of witchcraft?

In a very different style of poetry is the *Rime of the Ancient Mariner*; a ballad (says the advertisement) 'professedly written in imitation of the *style*, as well as the spirit of the elder poets.' We are tolerably conversant with the early English poets; and can discover no resemblance whatever, except in antiquated spelling and a few obsolete words. This piece appears to us perfectly original in style as well as in story. Many of the stanzas are laboriously beautiful; but in connection they are absurd or unintelligible. Our readers may exercise their ingenuity in attempting to unriddle what follows:

'The roaring wind, it roar'd far off.
It did not come anear.' etc., etc.

We do not sufficiently understand the story to analyse it. It is a Dutch attempt at German sublimity. Genius has here been employed in producing a poem of little merit.

With pleasure we turn to the serious pieces, the better part of the volume. *The Foster Mother's Tale* is in the best style of dramatic narrative. *The Dungeon*, and the *Lines upon the Yew Tree Seat*, are beautiful. *The Tale of the Female Vagrant* is written in the stanza, not the style, of Spenser. . . . Admirable as this poem is, the author seems to discover still superior powers in the *Lines written near Tintern Abbey*. On reading this production, it is possible not to lament that he should have condescended to write such pieces as the *Last of the Flock*, the *Convict*, and most of the ballads. In the whole range of English poetry, we scarcely recollect anything superior to a part of the following passage:

'And so I dare to hope,
Though changed, no doubt, from what I was when first
I came among these hills.' etc.

The 'experiment,' we think, has failed, not because the language of conversation is little adapted to 'the purposes of poetic pleasure,' but because it has been tried upon uninteresting subjects. Yet every piece discovers genius; and, ill as the author has frequently employed his talents, they certainly rank him with the best of living poets.

From 'The Analytical Review', Vol. XXVIII, December, 1798

After quoting the *Advertisement* to *Lyrical Ballads*, the writer proceeds:

There is something sensible in these remarks, and they certainly serve as a very pertinent introduction to the studied simplicity which pervades many of the poems. *The Rime of the Ancyent Marinere*, a ballad in seven parts, is written professedly in imitation of the style as well as of the spirit of the ancient poets. We are not pleased with it; in our opinion it has more of the extravagance of a mad German poet, than of the simplicity of our ancient ballad writers. . . .

Among the poems which particularly pleased us from their

character either of simplicity or tenderness, or both, are, that from which we have made the preceding extract (*The Nightingale*), *The Thorn*, *The Mad Mother*, *The Idiot Boy*, and the tale of *Goody Blake and Harry Gill*: a tale founded on a well-authenticated fact, which happened in Warwickshire. Dr. Darwin relates it among other curious instances of maniacal hallucination in the second volume of his *Zoönomia*.

From 'The Monthly Review', Vol. XXIX, June 1799

A review by Dr. Burney:

The author of these ingenious compositions presents the major part of them as *experiments*; since they were written, as he informs us in the *advertisement* prefixed, 'chiefly with a view to ascertain how far the language of conversation in the middle and lower classes of society is adapted to the purposes of poetic pleasure.' Though we have been extremely entertained with the fancy, the facility, and (in general) the sentiments, of these pieces, we cannot regard them as *poetry*, of a class to be cultivated at the expense of a higher species of versification, unknown in our language at the time when our elder writers, whom this author condescends to imitate wrote their ballads.

The author shall style his rustic delineations of low-life, poetry if he pleases, on the same principle on which Butler is called a poet, and Teniers a painter: but are the doggerel verses of the one equal to the sublime numbers of a Milton, or are the Dutch boors of the other to be compared with the angels of Raphael or Guido? – When we confess that our author has had the art of pleasing and interesting in no common way by his natural delineations of human passions, human characters, and human incidents, we must add that these effects were not produced by the *poetry*; – we have been as much affected by pictures of misery and unmerited distress, in prose. The elevation of soul, when it is lifted into the higher regions of imagination, affords us a delight of a different kind from the sensation which is produced by the detail of common incidents.

The author's first piece, the *Rime of the Ancyent Marinere*, in imitation of the *Style* as well as the spirit of the elder poets, is the strangest story of a cock and a bull that we ever saw on paper: yet, though it seems a rhapsody of unintelligible wildness and incoherence, there are in it poetical touches of an exquisite kind.

The Dramatic Fragment, if it means anything, seems to throw disgrace on the savage liberty preached by some modern philosophers.

The Yew Tree seems a seat for Jean Jacques; while the reflections on the subject appear from a more pious pen.

The Nightingale sings a strain of true and beautiful poetry; – Miltonic, yet original; reflective, and interesting, in an uncommon degree.

The Female Vagrant is an agonizing tale of individual wretchedness, highly coloured, though, alas, but too probable. Yet, as it seems to stamp a general stigma on all military transactions, it will perhaps be asked whether the hardships described never happen during revolution, or in a nation subdued.

Distress from poverty and want is admirably described in the true story of *Goody Blake and Harry Gill*: but are we to imagine that Harry was bewitched by Goody Blake? The hardest heart must be softened into pity for the poor old woman; and yet, if all the poor are to help, and supply their wants from the possessions of their neighbours, what imaginary wants and real anarchy would it not create? Goody Blake should have been relieved of the two millions annually allowed by the state to the poor of this country not by the plunder of an individual.

Lines on the first mild day of March abound with beautiful sentiments from a polished mind.

Simon Lee, the old Huntsman, is the portrait, admirably painted, of every huntsman who, by toil, age, and infirmities, is rendered unable to guide and govern his canine family.

Anecdote for Fathers. Of this, the dialogue is ingenious and natural: but the object of the child's choice, and the inferences, are not quite obvious.

We are Seven. – innocent and pretty infantine prattle.

On An Early Spring. – The first stanza of this poem seems unworthy of the rest, which contain reflections truly pious and philosophical.

The Thorn. – All our author's pictures, in colouring, are dark as those of Rembrandt . . .

The Last of the Flock is more gloomy than the rest. . . . No oppression is pointed out; nor are any means suggested for his relief. If the author be a wealthy man, he ought not to have suffered this poor peasant to part with the last of the flock.

The Dungeon. – Here candour and tenderness for criminals seem pushed to excess.

The Mad Mother. – Admirable painting in Michael Angelo's bold and masterly manner.

The Idiot Boy leads the reader on from anxiety to distress, and from distress to terror, by incidents and alarms which, though of the most mean and ignoble kind, interest, frighten, and terrify, almost to torture, during the perusal of more than a hundred stanzas.

Lines written near Richmond. – Literally 'most musical, most melancholy.'

Expostulation and Reply. – These two pieces will afford our readers an opportunity of judging of the author's poetical talents, in a more modern and less gloomy style than his Ballads.

The Old Man Travelling, A Sketch. – Finely drawn, but the termination seems pointed against the war, from which, however, we are now no more able to separate ourselves, than Hercules was to free himself from the shirt of Nessus. The old traveller's son might have died by disease.

Each ballad is a tale of woe. The style and versification are those of our ancient ditties but much polished, and more constantly excellent. In old songs, we have only a fine line or stanza now and then; here we meet with few that are feeble; but it is *poesie larmoiante*. The author is more plaintive than Gray himself.

The Complaint of the Forsaken Indian Woman: another tale of woe of the most affecting and harrowing kind.

The Convict. – What a description! What misplaced commiseration! . . . We do not comprehend the drift of lavishing that tenderness and compassion on a criminal, which should be reserved for virtue in unmerited misery and distress, suffering untimely death from accident, injustice, or disease.

Lines written near Tintern Abbey. – The reflections of no common mind; poetical, beautiful, and philosophical: but somewhat tinctured with gloomy, narrow, and unsociable ideas of seclusion from the commerce of the world: as if men were born to live in woods and wilds, unconnected with each other. . . . So much genius and originality are discovered in this publication, that we wish to see another from the same hand, written on more elevated subjects and in a more cheerful disposition.

From the 'British Critic', Vol. XIV, October 1799

The following was probably written by a friend of Wordsworth and Coleridge, the Reverend Francis Wrangham, himself a poet.

The attempt made in this little volume is one that needs our cordial approbation; and it is an attempt by no means unsuccessful. The endeavour of the author is to recall our poetry from the fantastical excess of refinement, to simplicity and nature. The account of this design, and its probable effects upon modern readers, is very sensibly given in the Introduction. . . .

We fully agree with the author, that the true notion of poetry must be sought among the poets, rather than the critics; and we will add, that, unless a critic is a poet also, he will generally make but indifferent work in judging of the effusions of Genius. In the collection of poems subjoined to this introduction, we do not often find expressions that we esteem too familiar, or deficient in dignity; on the contrary, we think that in general the author has succeeded in attaining that judicious degree of simplicity, which accommodates itself with ease even to the sublime. It is not pomp of words, but by energy of thought, that sublimity is most success-fully achieved; and we infinitely prefer the simplicity even of the most unadorned tale in this volume, to all the meretricious frippery of the *Darwinian* taste.

The Poem of the Ancyent Marinere with which the collection opens, has many excellencies, and many faults; the beginning and the end are striking and well-conducted; but the intermediate part is too long, and has, in some places, a kind of confusion of images, which loses all effect, from not being quite intelligible. The author, who is confidently said to be Mr. Coleridge, is not correctly versed in the old language, which he undertakes to employ. 'Noises of a swound' and 'broad as a weft,' are both nonsensical; but the ancient style is well imitated, while the antiquated words are so very few, that the latter might with advantage be entirely removed without any detriment to the effect of the Poem. The opening of the Poem is admirably calculated to arrest the reader's attention, by the well-imagined idea of the Wedding Guest, who is held to hear the tale, in spite of his efforts to escape. The beginning of the second canto has much merit, if we except the very unwarrantable comparison of the Sun to which no man can conceive: 'like God's own head,' a simile which makes a reader shudder, not with poetic feeling, but with religious disapprobation. The following passage is eminently good.

> 'The breezes blew, the white foam flew
> The furrow followed free;
> We were the first that ever burst
> Into that silent sea.
>
> Down dropt the breeze, the sails dropt down,
> 'Twas sad as sad could be;
> And we did speak only to break
> The silence of the sea.

All in a hot and copper sky,
The bloody Sun, at noon,
Right up above the mast did stand,
No bigger than the Moon,

Day after day, day after day,
We struck, nor breath nor motion;
As idle as a painted ship
Upon a painted ocean.

Water, water, everywhere,
And all the boards did shrink;
Water, water, every where,
Nor any drop to drink.

The conclusion is very good, particularly the idea that the
Marinere has periodical fits of agony, which oblige him to relate his
marvellous adventure; and this,

I pass, like night, from land to land;
I have strange power of speech;
That moment that his face I see,
I know the man that must hear me;
To him my tale I teach.

Whether the remaining poems of the volume are by Mr. Cole-
ridge, we have not been informed; but they seem to proceed from
the same mind; and in the Advertisement, the Writer speaks of
himself as a single person accountable for the whole. They all have
merit, and many among them a very high rank of merit, which our
feelings respecting some parts of the supposed author's character
do not authorize or incline us to deny. *The Poem on the Nightingale*,
which is there styled *a conversational Poem*, is very good, but we
do not perceive it to be more conversational than Cowper's *Task*,
which is the best poem in that style that our language possesses.
The *Female Vagrant* is a composition of exquisite beauty, nor is
the combination of events, related to it, out of the compass of
possibility; yet, we perceive, with regret, the drift of the author in
composing it; which is to show the worst side of civilized society,
and thus to form a satire against it. But let fanciful men rail as
they will at the evils which no care can always prevent, they can
have no dream more wild than the supposition, that any human

wisdom can possibly exclude from a state which divine Providence has decreed, for reasons the most wise, to be a state of suffering and trial. The sufferers may be changed, by infinite revolutions, but sufferers there will be, till Heaven shall interfere to change the nature of our tenure upon earth. From this beautiful Poem, partly on account of its apparent design and partly because the loss of the connection would destroy much of its effect, we shall make no extract.

The story of *Goody Blake and Harry Gill* is founded on a well-authenticated fact which happened in Warwickshire. Yet it is a miracle; and modern miracles can seldom be admitted, without some degree of credulity, or a very uncommon weight of evidence. One of the simplest stories in the book is that entitled *We are Seven*; yet he must be a very fastidious reader who will deny that it has great beauty and feeling.

The tale of *The Thorn* has many beauties; nor can we pass without notice the *Mad Mother*, or the long and familiar tale of the *Idiot Boy*, which, though it descends quite to common life, is animated by much interest, and told with singular felicity. One more Poem we shall particularly notice for its pathos, and shall indeed insert the whole. The imagery of it is in many instances new, and is introduced with admirable effect.

[He then quotes *The Complaint of a Forsaken Indian Woman*.]

The purchaser of this little volume will find that, after all we have said, there are poems, and passages of poems, which we have been obliged to pass over, that will deserve attention and commendation; nor does there appear any offensive mixture of enmity to present institutions, except in one or two instances, which are so unobtrusive as hardly to deserve notice.

From the 'British Critic', Vol. XVII, February 1801

This long review appeared after the publication of the 1800 edition of *Lyrical Ballads* and was probably written by Wrangham again.

In our Review for October, 1799, we noticed, with considerable satisfaction, the first edition of this work, then comprised in one anonymous volume. It is now extended by the addition of another volume; and the author has given his name to it, with the exception of the *Ancient Mariner*, the *Foster Mother's Tale*, the *Nightingale*, the *Dungeon*, and the poem entitled *Love*; all of which, as he informs us, are furnished by a friend, whose opinions on the subject of poetry agree most entirely with his own. From this similarity of mind, and from some expressions in the *Advertisement* prefixed to the first edition, we were led to attribute the whole to Mr. Coleridge, the supposed author of the *Ancient Marinere*; we now, therefore, add to the list of our Poets another name, no less likely to do it honour. Mr. Wordsworth has, indeed, appeared before the public some years ago, as author of *Descriptive Sketches in Verse*, and of *An Evening Walk*; compositions in which were discoverable the fire and fancy of a true poet, though obscured by diction, often and intentionally inflated. His style is now wholly changed, and he has adopted a purity of expression, which, to the fastidious ear, may sometimes perhaps sound poor and low, but which is infinitely more correspondent with true feeling than what, by the courtesy of the day, is usually called poetical language.

Whatever may be thought of these poems, it is evident that they are not to be confounded with the flood of poetry which is poured forth in such profusion by the modern Bards of Science, or their Brethren, the Bards of Insipidity. The author has thought for himself; he has deeply studied human nature, in the book of human action; and he has adopted his language from the same sources as his feelings. Aware that his Poems are so materially different from those upon which general approbation is at present bestowed, he has now defended them in a Preface of some length; not with the foolish hope of reasoning his readers into the approbation of these particular Poems, but as a necessary justification of the species of poetry to which they belong. This Preface, though written in some parts with a degree of metaphysical obscurity, conveys much penetrating judicious observation, important at all times, but especially when, as it is well observed, 'the invaluable works of our elder writers are driven into neglect by frantic novels, sickly and stupid German tragedies, and deluges of idle and extravagant stories in verse.' Perhaps it would be expecting too much from any one but Shakespeare, were we to demand that he should be the Poet of human nature. It would be no mean, it would indeed be a very lofty praise, to assert of a writer, that he is able to pour into other bosoms powerful feelings of a particular class, or belonging to a particular order of men. To this praise, Mr. Wordsworth lays a well-supported claim. He declares himself the poet chiefly of low and rustic life (some specimens of ability he has given in other lines, but this is evidently his excellence) and he pourtrays it, not under its disgusting forms, but in situations affording, as he thinks, the best soil for the essential passions of the heart, incorporated with an elementary and durable state of manners, and with the beautiful and permanent forms of nature.[1]

Each separate Poem has, as its distinct *purpose*, the development of a feeling, which gives importance to the action and situation, and not the action or situation to the feeling. Whether the particular purpose is, in every case, *worthy* of a Poet, will perhaps admit of some doubt. We have no hesitation in saying, that it is generally interesting, often invaluable. . . .

Of the judicious degree of simplicity in language which the author attained in his first volume, we formerly expressed our approbation. The second is written with equal felicity, being alike grounded upon an accurate and attentive observation of those modes of speech, which are prompted by the natural flow of passion. Where the subjects are supplied by rustic life, the language of rustics, purified only from accidental associations of disgust, is also adopted. . . .

The author has argued with great ingenuity, and at some length, on the absurdity of diction frequently made between the appropriate language of prose, and that of metrical composition. He has shown that the two species of writing may be wholly similar in every thing but metre; and that neither of them can be dignified by any other means than energy and loftiness of thought. A great part of this argument would appear useless, had we not unhappily witnessed, in some striking instances, how much the public taste may be misled by affected pomp and false glitter of language. We cannot too often repeat that the frippery and fustian of the Darwinian phraseology, is no more compatible with a just Classical taste, than the heterogeneous mixture of science and fancy is allowable in a poetical subject. The faults of this kind, in the second volume, are so very few, as to deserve no notice, in comparison with the general purity of the style. As to the subjects, it must be owned that their worth does not always appear at first sight; but, judging from our own feelings, we must assert, that it generally grows upon the reader by subsequent perusal. The follow-

---

[1] Mr. Wordsworth seems to be peculiarly well situated for the subjects of such a study. The vicinity of the Lakes in Cumberland and Westmoreland (the scene of most of his Poems) is chiefly inhabited by an order of men nearly extinct in other parts of England. These are small farmers, called in that part of the country 'Statesmen', who, cultivating their own little property, are raised above the immediate pressure of want, with very few opportunities of acquiring wealth. They are a mild, hospitable people, with some turn for reading; and their personal appearance is, for the most part, interesting.

ing remarks may, perhaps, illustrate the cause of this improving interest.

1. It is not requisite that the poetic feeling should be strictly referable to any of those known and powerful classes, called the sublime, the terrible, the pathetic, etc. It may sometimes consist in a gentle agitation of the contending emotions, from which a preponderance of pleasure is ultimately produced, as from the melancholy recollections of a cheerful old man, in the *Two April Mornings*, and the *Fountain*; sometimes it may arise from the mixture of lively imagery with various feelings, as with exultation and pity, in the two parts of *Hartleap Well*; sometimes it may be sounded on the soft and almost insensible affections which we receive from natural scenery, aided, perhaps, by some accidental association in our minds. Of this kind are the different *Poems on the Naming of Places, Lines Written with a Slate Pencil*, etc. *Rural Architecture* and some others.

2. Even where the feeling intended to be called forth is of a rich and noble character, such as we may recur to, and feed upon, it may yet be wrought up so gradually, including so many preparatory circumstances of appropriate manners of local description, of actual events, etc. that the subtle uniting thread will be lost, without a persevering effort towards attention on the part of the reader. Who that has studied Shakespeare, must not be conscious how often the connection of minute and trifling incidents with the main story has eluded his observation, until after repeated perusals? Something of this kind will probably occur to the readers of the *Brothers*, the *Cumberland Beggar*, and more particularly of the Poem, entitled *Michael*; yet these three are of the highest order of Poems in the volume. The interest, especially of the first, is so dramatically wrought up, the minute touches are so accurately studied, the general effect is so insensibly produced, and appeals so forcibly to the heart, as to rank its author far beyond the reach of common-place praise or censure.

3. There is a third class of Poems possessing a strong effect, which results equally from the power of imagination and of feeling; in these, the prominent features of the story are all along attended with a concurring splendour of poetic ornament, and the combined influence of these agents pervades every part of the composition. This is greatly the case in the *Poem of Ruth*, and in that of *Ellen Irwin*, of which the latter is merely narrative; the former intermixes much of deep and interesting speculation: to this class also may be referred *Lucy Gray* and *Poor Susan*, with several beautiful specimens in the second volume.

4. Other small pieces have different characteristics. *The Fragment of the Danish Boy* is a mere creation of fancy; *the Pet Lamb* presents a portraiture of infantine simplicity; and the lines in pages [152-4], are masterly sketches of those '*strange fits of passion*,' which sometimes unaccountably flash across a poetical mind.

From the longer Poems it is almost impossible to select any passage without injury to the effect, owing to a want of that interest which the context supplies. We shall, however, venture to cite the following tender touches from the *Brothers*.

> 'though their Parents
> Lay buried side by side', etc.

In the *Poet's Epitaph*, an effusion of good-humoured satire, is succeeded by this picture of animated and engaging sensibility.

> 'But who is He with modest looks,' etc.

Perhaps the English Language can boast few instances of descriptive poetry, enlivened with a happier variety of imagery, than the fanciful echo in the *Poem inscribed to Joanna*. The lady's laugh, to be sure, is loud, but it is not unpleasing.

> 'When I had gaz'd perhaps two minutes' space,' etc.

But the most singular specimens of unpretending yet irresistible pathos, are the two Songs, pages [152-3]. In artlessness, they strongly remind us of Burns; but perhaps go beyond him in delicacy. As they have a secret connection we shall insert both

> '*Strange fits of passion I have known*' etc.
> '*She dwelt among th' untrodden ways*,' etc.

When the art of poetry has long been cultivated among a polished people, and brought to a state of great refinement, the natural operation of an ill-judged ambition, to excel even those who have most successfully adorned the language, leads writers either to employ an affected and over-laboured style, or, at least, to keep always upon the high stilts of elegance, to the exclusion of Nature and Simplicity. In such a state of poetic art, that man may be considered as a public benefactor, who, with talents equal to the task, which is arduous, recalls attention to the more natural style, and shows what may be effected by simple language, expressive of human passions, and genuine, not artificial feelings. In this character, Mr. Wordsworth appears, and appears with success, to which we could by no means refuse our approbation.

We will not deny that sometimes he goes so far in his pursuit of simplicity, as to become flat or weak; but, in general, he sets an example which the full dressed poet of affectation might wish, but wish in vain, to follow.[1] He would correct Mr. Wordsworth as the dancing master of Hogarth would correct the attitude of Antinous.

A Letter from John Wilson [Christopher North] addressed to Words-worth in May, 1802, when the writer was only seventeen years old. In later years Wilson was to become Professor of Moral Philosophy at Edinburgh. He was also closely associated with 'Blackwood's Magazine'.

My dear Sir,

You may perhaps be surprised to see yourself addressed in this manner by one who never had the happiness of being in company with you, and whose knowledge of your character is drawn solely from the perusal of your poems. But, sir, though I am not person-ally acquainted with you, I may almost venture to affirm that the qualities of your soul are not unknown to me. In your poems I discovered such marks of delicate feeling, such benevolence of disposition, and such knowledge of human nature, as made an impression on my mind that nothing will ever efface; and while I felt my soul refined by the sentiments contained in them, and filled with those delightful emotions which it would be almost impossible to describe, I entertained for you an attachment made up of love and admiration. Reflection upon that delight which I enjoyed from reading your poems, will ever make me regard you with gratitude; and the consciousness of feeling those emotions you delineate makes me proud to regard your character with esteem and admiration. . . . To receive a letter from you would afford me more happiness than any occurrence in this world, save the happiness of my friends, and greatly enhance the pleasure I receive from reading the *Lyrical Ballads*. . . . To you, sir, mankind are indebted for a species of poetry, which will continue to afford pleasure while respect is paid to virtuous feelings, and while sensibility continues to pour forth tears of rapture. The flimsy ornaments of language, used to conceal meanness of thought and want of feeling, may for a short time captivate the ignorant and unwary; but true taste will discover the imposture, and expose the authors of it to merited contempt. The real feelings of human

[1] The title of the *Poems* is, in some degree, objectionable; for what *Ballads* are not *lyrical*? Besides, there are many compositions in blank verse, not at all lyrical.

nature, expressed in simple and forcible language, will, on the
contrary, please those only who are capable of entertaining them,
and in proportion of the attention which we pay to the faithful
delineation of such feelings, will be the enjoyment derived from
them. The poetry, therefore, which is the language of Nature, is
certain of immortality, provided circumstances do not occur to
pervert the feelings of humanity, and occasion a complete revolu-
tion in the government of the mind.

That your poetry is the language of Nature, in my opinion,
admits of no doubt. Both the thoughts and expressions may be
tried by that standard. You have seized upon those feelings that
most deeply interest the heart, and that also come within the
sphere of common observation. You do not write merely for the
pleasure of philosophers and men of improved taste, but for all who
think, for all who feel. If we have ever known the happiness
arising from parental or fraternal love; if we have ever known that
delightful sympathy of soul connecting persons of different sex;
if we have ever dropped a tear at the death of friends, or grieved
for the misfortunes of others; if, in short, we have ever felt the
more amiable emotions of human nature, it is impossible to read
your poems without being greatly interested, and frequently in
raptures. Your sentiments, feelings, and thoughts are therefore
exactly such as ought to constitute the subject of poetry, and
cannot fail of exciting interest in every heart. But, sir, your merit
does not solely consist in delineating the real features of the human
mind under those different aspects it assumes when under the
influence of various passions and feelings; you have, in a manner
truly admirable, explained a circumstance, very important in its
effect upon the soul when agitated, that has indeed been frequently
alluded to, but never generally adopted by any author in tracing
the progress of emotions – I mean that wonderful effect which the
appearances of external Nature have upon the mind when in a
state of strong feeling. We must have all have been sensible that,
when under the influence of *grief*, Nature, when arrayed in her
gayest attire, appears to us dull and gloomy, and that, when our
hearts abound with joy, her most deformed prospects seldom fail of
pleasing. This disposition of the mind to assimilate the appearances
of external Nature to its own situation, is a fine subject for poetical
allusion, and in several poems you have employed it with a most
electrifying effect. But you have not stopped here, you have shown
the effect which the qualities of external Nature have in forming
the human mind, and have presented us with several characters
whose particular bias arose from that situation in which they were

planted with respect to the scenery of Nature. The idea is inexpressibly beautiful, and though, I confess, that to me it appeared to border upon fiction when I first considered it, yet at this moment I am convinced of its foundation in Nature, and its great importance in accounting for various phenomena in the human mind. It serves to explain those diversities in the structure of the mind, which have baffled all the ingenuity of philosophers to account for it. It serves to overturn the theories of men who have attempted to write on human nature without a knowledge of the causes that affect it, and who have discovered greater eagerness to show their own subtlety than arrive at the acquisition of truth. May not the face of external nature through different quarters of the globe account for the dispositions of different notions? May not mountains, forests, plains, groves, and lakes, as much as the temperature of the atmosphere, or the form of government, produce important effects upon the human soul; and may not the difference subsisting between the former of these in different countries produce as much diversity among the inhabitants as any varieties among the latter? The effect you have shown to take place in particular cases so much to my satisfaction, most certainly may be extended so far as to authorize general inferences. This idea has no doubt struck you; and I trust that, if it be founded on Nature, your mind, so long accustomed to philosophical investigation, will perceive how far it may be carried, and what consequences are likely to result from it.

Your poems, sir, are of very great advantage to the world, from containing in them a system of philosophy that regards one of the most curious subjects of investigation, and, at the same time, one of the most important. But your poems may not be considered merely in a philosophical light, or even as containing refined and natural feelings; they present us with a body of morality of the purest kind. They represent the enjoyment resulting from the cultivation of the social affections or our nature; they inculcate a conscientious regard to the rights of our fellow-men; they show that every creature on the face of the earth is entitled in some measure to our kindness. They prove that in every mind, however depraved, there exist some qualities deserving our esteem. They point out the proper way to happiness. They show that such a thing as perfect misery does not exist. They flash on our souls convictions of immortality. Considered, therefore, in this view, the *Lyrical Ballads* is, to use your own words, the book which I value next to my Bible; and though I may, perhaps, never have the happiness of seeing you, yet I always consider you as a friend, who has, by his instructions, done me a service which it can never be in my power to repay. Your instructions have afforded me inexpressible pleasure; it will be my own fault if I do not reap from them much advantage.

I have said, sir, that in all your poems you have adhered strictly to natural feelings, and described what comes within the range of every person's observation. It is from following out this plan that, in my estimation, you have surpassed every poet both of ancient and modern times. But to me it appears that in the execution of this design you have inadvertently fallen into an error, the effects of which are, however, exceedingly trivial. No feeling, no state of mind ought, in my opinion, to become the subject of poetry, that does not please. Pleasure may, indeed, be produced in many ways, and by means that at first sight appear calculated to accomplish a very different end. Tragedy of the deepest kind produces pleasure of a high nature. To point out the causes of this would be foreign to the purpose.

But we may lay this down as a general rule, that no description can please where the sympathies of our soul are not excited, and no narration interest where we do not enter into the feelings of some of the parties concerned. On this principle, many feelings which are undoubtedly natural, are improper subjects of poetry, and many situations, no less natural, incapable of being described so as to produce the grand effect of poetical composition. This, sir, I would apprehend, is reasonable, and founded on the constitution of the human mind. There are a thousand occurrences happening every day which do not in the least interest an unconcerned spectator, though they no doubt occasion various emotions in the breast of those to whom they immediately relate. To describe these in poetry would be improper.

Now, sir, I think that in several cases you have fallen into this error. You have described feelings with which I cannot sympathize, and situations in which I take no interest. I know that I can relish your beauties, and that makes me think that I can also perceive your faults. But in this matter, I have not wholly trusted to my own judgment, but heard the sentiments of men whose feelings I admired, and whose understanding I respected. In a few cases, I think that even you have failed to excite interest. In the poem entitled the *Idiot Boy*, your intention, as you inform us in your preface, was to trace the maternal passion through its more subtle windings. This design is no doubt accompanied with much difficulty, but, if properly executed, cannot fail of interesting the heart. But, sir, in my opinion, the manner in which you have executed this plan has frustrated the end you intended to produce by it; the affection of *Betty Foy* has nothing in it to excite interest. It exhibits merely the effects of that instinctive feeling inherent in the constitution of every animal. The excessive fondness of the mother disgusts us, and prevents us from sympathizing with her. We are unable to enter into her feelings; we cannot conceive ourselves actuated by the same feelings, and consequently take little or no interest in her situation. The object of her affection is indeed her son, and in that relation much consists, but then he is represented as totally destitute of any attachment towards her; the state of his mind is represented as perfectly deplorable, and, in short, to me it appears almost unnatural, that a person in a state of complete idiotism should excite the warmest feelings of attachment in the breast even of his mother. This much I know, that among all the people I ever knew to have read this poem, I never met one who did not rise rather displeased from the perusal of it, and the only cause I could assign for it was the one now mentioned. This inability to receive pleasure from descriptions such as that of *The Idiot Boy*, is I am convinced, founded upon established feelings of human nature, and the principle of it constitutes, as I daresay you recollect, the leading feature of Smith's theory of moral sentiments.[1] I therefore think that in the choice of this subject you have committed an error.

You never deviate from Nature; in you that would be impossible; but in this case you have delineated feelings which, though natural, do not please, but which create a certain degree of disgust and contempt. With regard to the manner in which you have executed your plan, I think too great praise cannot be bestowed upon your talents. You have most admirably delineated the idiotism of the boy's mind, and the situations in which you place him are perfectly calculated to display it. The various thoughts that pass through the mother's mind are highly descriptive of her foolish fondness, her extravagant fears, and her ardent hopes. The manner in which you show how bodily sufferings are frequently removed by mental anxieties or pleasures, in the description of the cure of Betty Foy's female friend, is excessively well managed, and serves to establish a very curious and important truth. In short, everything you proposed to execute has been executed in a masterly manner. The fault if there be one, lies in the plan, not in the execution. This poem we heard recommended as one in your best manner, and accordingly it is frequently read in this belief. The judgment

---

[1] Adam Smith's *Theory of Moral Sentiments*, first pubd. 1759.

formed of it is, consequently, erroneous. Many people are displeased with the performance; but they are not careful to distinguish faults in the execution, and the consequence is that they form an improper opinion of your genius. In reading any composition, most certainly the pleasure we receive arises almost wholly from the sentiment, thoughts, and descriptions contained in it. A secondary pleasure arises from admiration of those talents requisite to the production of it. In reading the *Idiot Boy*, all persons who allow themselves to think, must admire your talents, but they regret that they have been so employed, and while they esteem the author, they cannot help being displeased with his performance. I have seen a most excellent painting of an idiot, but it created in me inexpressible disgust. I admired the talents of the artist, but I had no other source of pleasure. The poem of *The Idiot Boy* produced upon me an effect in every respect similar. I find that my remarks upon several of your other poems must be reserved for another letter. If you think that this one deserves an answer, a letter from Wordsworth would be to me a treasure. . . .

JOHN WILSON.

Extracts from a letter written by Henry Crabb Robinson to his brother, Thomas, on June 6th 1802, from Frankfurt

A few days since I received Wordsworth's *Lyrical Ballads*. . . . I am at present in danger of becoming unjust to English Literature being absorbed in the beauties of the German. These exquisite Volumes were enough to bring me back to justice. There are a few ballads – *The Thorn, The Idiot Boy, Goody Blake and Harry Gill*, which will rank with the first rate compositions in the Language. I have already quoted eight lines

> ['Nor less I deem that there are powers
> Which of themselves our minds impress,
> That we can feed this mind of ours,
> In a wise passiveness.
>
> Think you, mid all this mighty sum
> Of things for ever speaking,
> That nothing of itself will come,
> But we must still be seeking?']

which have a profundity of thought and a felicity of Expression truly admirable quite in Schiller's style. Wordsworth has the Art – the characteristick Art of Genius – of doing much with simple means. His repetition of simple phrases, and his dwelling on simple but touching Incidents, his Skill in drawing the deepest moral, and tenderest interest out of trifles evince a great Master, a Talent truly Shakespearean, for instance in *Goody Blake*:

> 'And fiercely by the arm he took her,
> And by the arm he held her fast,
> And fiercely by the arm he shook her,
> And cried, "I've caught you then at last!" '

How cunning this delay! this dwelling on so slight a Circumstance. . . . How prosaic all vulgar every day Expressions – true and therefore doubly powerful – doubly poetic in their effect. The following Stanza, 'Oh joy for her' is exquisite as well as the whole a most pathetically poetical display of poverty. Wordsworth is equally happy in his expression of moral Sentiments:

> 'Oh reader! had you in your mind
> Such stores as silent thought can bring,
> Oh gentle reader! you would find
> A tale in every thing.' etc.

There is in my mind more Genius and Merit in such Reflections and such Descriptions unostentatious and simple as they are; than in many an admired Ode. I would rather have written *The Thorn* than all the tinsel gaudy Lines of Darwin's *Botanic Garden*. The one is an artificial Versifier, the other is a feeler and a painter of feelings. But all the pieces have not this superior Merit. *The Female Vagrant*, etc. are cold and trite. – Wordsworth's excellence appears greatest when he is most original.

Index of Titles

*(The numbers given in italics refer the reader to the Notes to the Poems. The titles marked * are those of the poems written by Coleridge.)*

═══════

Index of First Lines